GOVERNING CALIFORNIA

Second Edition

Lawrence L. Giventer
California State University, Stanislaus

Boston Burr Ridge, IL Dubuque, IA New York
San Francisco St. Louis Bangkok Bogotá Caracas Kuala Lumpur
Lisbon London Madrid Mexico City Milan Montreal New Delhi
Santiago Seoul Singapore Sydney Taipei Toronto

The McGraw·Hill Companies

Higher Education

GOVERNING CALIFORNIA

Published by McGraw-Hill, an imprint of The McGraw-Hill Companies, Inc., 1221 Avenue of the Americas, New York, NY 10020. Copyright © 2008 by The McGraw-Hill Companies, Inc. All rights reserved. No part of this publication may be reproduced or distributed in any form or by any means, or stored in a database or retrieval system, without the prior written consent of The McGraw-Hill Companies, Inc., including, but not limited to, in any network or other electronic storage or transmission, or broadcast for distance learning.

2 3 4 5 6 7 8 9 0 CCW/CCW 10 9 8 7 6 5 4 3 2 1

ISBN: 978-0-07-352633-1
MHID: 0-07-352633-9

Editor-in-chief: *Emily Barrosse*
Publisher: *Frank Mortimer*
Sponsoring editor: *Monica Eckman*
Developmental editor: *Larry Goldberg*
Marketing manager: *Jennifer Reed*
Production editor: *David Blatty*
Production supervisor: *Tandra Jorgensen*
Designer: *Violota Diaz*
Art editor: *Ayelet Arbel*
Illustrators: *Dartmouth Publishing, Inc. and Mapping Specialists*
Photo researcher: *Nova Agbayani*
Compositor: *Laserwords Private Limited, Chennai, India*
Typeface: *10/12 Sabon*
Paper: *45# New Era Matte*
Printer and binder: *Courier Inc.*

Cover photo: © *J. Emilio Flores/Getty Images*

Library of Congress Cataloging-in-Publication Data

Giventer, Lawrence, L.
    Governing California / Lawrence L. Giventer—2nd ed.
        p. cm
    Includes bibliographical references and index.
    ISBN-13: 978-0-07-352633-1 (pbk : alk. paper)
    ISBN-10: 0-07-352633-9 (pbk : alk. paper)
    1. California—Politics and government—1951–I. Title.

    JK8716.G58 2007
    320.9794—dc22   2006048083

The Internet addresses listed in the text were accurate at the time of publication. The inclusion of a website does not indicate an endorsement by the authors or McGraw-Hill Higher Education, and McGraw-Hill does not guarantee the accuracy of the information presented at these sites.

www.mhhe.com

In memory of my father, Max Giventer,
and my friend William E. Neeley

ABOUT THE AUTHOR

LAWRENCE L. GIVENTER is a professor in the Department of Politics and Public Administration at California State University, Stanislaus. He teaches post-baccalaureate-level courses in public policy analysis, public sector quantitative methods, and computer applications, and undergraduate courses in American government. Professor Giventer is also the author of *Statistical Analysis for Public Administration*, 2nd ed. (Jones & Bartlett, 2008). He joined CSU Stanislaus in 1975 and soon afterward founded the university's nationally accredited Master of Public Administration (MPA) program, which he directed for twenty years. He has served as department chair, Speaker of the Faculty, consultant and advisory committee chair for state and local government agencies, book reviewer, and accreditation site-visitor. He has a Ph.D. in public administration from the University of Pittsburgh and engineering degrees from the New Jersey Institute of Technology and Massachusetts Institute of Technology. He is often called upon as a political analyst by radio, television, print, and Internet media.

CONTENTS

PREFACE

The second edition provides a well-designed, updated, and relatively afford-able text that addresses the important processes of California government. The objective remains the same. This book is for Californians. It is about your government—how it works, how it affects you, and what some of its successes and failures are. The fundamental question that I address is this: What do you and I, as ordinary residents, citizens, and taxpayers of California, need to know about our government? That's not an easy question. In searching for the answer, I solicited the insights of many who observe, deal with, or comment on government every day—nonprofit policy institutes and centers, newspaper reporters and columnists, interest groups, and government agencies themselves—about the essentials of the California government experience: what information they regard as important and how they convey it.

Many politics and government texts describe what government *is*. They tend to be organized around the executive, legislative, and judicial branches of government. While this structural/functional descriptive approach does convey essential information, I prefer to focus on what government *does*—more of a process and public policy approach centering on how government affects nearly every aspect of our lives—hence the book title *Governing California* rather than *The Government of California*. The result, I think, is a useful *ground-level* guide to how government works and how it affects us all. You be the judge. I invite your reactions: LGiventer@csustan.edu

While the overall chapter outline of *Governing California* remains the same as the first edition, there are important updates throughout the text. Chapter 1, California Contrasts, is more clearly organized in terms of political demography, political parties, political economy, and political geography, with new original figures emphasizing the growth of California's Latino population and the concentration of Democratic voter registration along the coast and in major urban areas. Chapter 2, The Structure of Government, has been reorganized to acknowledge the executive-legislative-judicial preference for some users rather than the previous national-state-local description. The unique full-color maps of California's congressional and legislative districts now show the entire state, rather than just the northern and southern urban areas. Chapter 3, Elections, has new details about the role of money in political campaigns. Chapter 4, Lawmaking, is also updated, particularly with respect to lobbyist and interest group activity. Many students, faculty, and reviewers have said that Chapter 5, It's Your Money, and Chapter 6, Pursuit of Justice, are interesting, informative, yet concise, presentations of complex subjects. So these chapters are improved mostly in terms of data and formatting for the second edition. Chapter 7, Employment, Education, and Social Services, and Chapter 8, Energy and the Environment, have been revised as well with respect to data and policy issues.

PEDAGOGICAL FEATURES

You will also notice that this text is designed differently from others in the California politics and government market. A key feature of *Governing California* is the extensive use of exhibits—informative tables and figures, including an 8-page full-color insert. The exhibits provide essential information and enhance the narrative explanation. Each of the eighty or so exhibits *tells a story*. All have been updated and several are new to this edition. Most exhibits are accompanied by questions that prompt readers to examine and interpret them, leading to better comprehension of concepts and principles discussed in the text.

Chapter-ending features include a list of online resources and publications, a glossary defining the boldface key terms in the text, and suggested answers to exhibit questions. At the back of the book, Appendixes A, B, and C present up-to-date lists of state and national government representatives. Appendix D includes Article 1 of the California Constitution—the Declaration of Rights—which, to Californians, is just as important as the U.S. Constitution's Bill of Rights.

THE SUPPLEMENTS

Visit our *Governing California*'s Website at **www.mhhe.com/giventer2**. Resources for *instructors* include a password-protected instructor's manual, an extensive test bank, and chapter-by-chapter PowerPoint® presentations. Resources for *students* include an Image Library of exhibits from the text, Web links, and self-quizzes.

ACKNOWLEDGMENTS

I wish to thank the many students in politics and public administration I have met over the years whose excitement and optimism, and even boredom and cynicism, inspired and from time-to-time reinvigorated the text. My friends and colleagues in the California State University, especially the Department of Politics and Public Administration at CSU, Stanislaus, provided invaluable encouragement. Sarah and Doug, Dominion, Cindy, and Jasmine, and my wife Mary, were constantly supportive. I wish to acknowledge the excellent staff at McGraw-Hill Higher Education. Monica Eckman, Larry Goldberg, and David Blatty worked hard to fulfill my vision of the text while keeping the final cost to students as low as possible.

Finally, I appreciate the comments and helpful suggestions from the following reviewers:

Ed Costantini, University of California, Davis

Eugene R. Goss, Long Beach City College

Nooshan Rafii, Santiago Canyon College

Donald Ranish, Antelope Valley College

Nancy Speckmann, San Diego State University and Grossmont College

Lawrence L. Giventer

California State University, Stanislaus
LGiventer@csustan.edu

CHAPTER ONE

CALIFORNIA CONTRASTS

California is a land of dynamic growth and dramatic change, a land of opportunities and disappointments, a land of paradoxes and contrasts. This book is about the government and politics of California and how, as a Californian, this government affects you.

A **government** is the set of organizations, processes, and rules that control a land and its people. **Politics** is the process by which governmental decisions are made between competing and conflicting interests. Is government important? Pick up one of California's major daily newspapers and read the headlines in the front sections—until you reach the sports pages. Every day, nearly every story is related to government. Sometimes the story is about the effect of a public policy, regulation, or law. Sometimes it quotes the president, governor, or some other official. Sometimes it's about the action of a governmental agency—the school district, police, fire, or planning departments. Think about it: Government affects everyone, every day, all the time; it is pervasive. Everything, without exception, that affects our lives, livelihood, and well-being—and the lives, livelihoods and well-being of our loved ones and fellow community members—involves government. Government is involved in health care, education, environmental protection, workplace safety, recreational facilities, financial security, transportation, housing, drinking water, land use, civil rights, fire and police services, and much more.

We expect government to function with fairness, competence, and integrity—to help us realize our birthright to life, liberty, and happiness. And, usually, it does. But sometimes governmental action is wasteful or misguided, or fails to provide the services, solve the problems, and address the issues or to function honestly and efficiently. We have learned to be cynical and dismissive of government, but government is necessary. We need to be supportive but skeptical. We rely on government, but it requires our attention and vigilance.

How does government work in a huge, and hugely diverse, state like California? As residents of California, what do we need to know about government? These are the basic questions addressed in this text. We begin in this chapter with an orientation to the land and its people.

Political Demography

The people and their society, economy, politics, and government, along with some unique geographic features, make California important. Once a northern province of Mexico, California was conquered and annexed to the United States in the Mexican–American War (1846–1848). The war was fought both as an expression of the U.S. concept of Manifest Destiny, calling for the expansion of the United States across the continent from the Atlantic to the Pacific, and because of unresolved border disputes following the earlier Texas War of Independence at a cost of over 13,000 U.S. and 25,000 Mexican lives. In 1848, the Treaty of Guadalupe Hidalgo added the northern half of Mexico to the United States (what eventually became the states of California, Nevada, Arizona, New Mexico, and Utah). California became a state in 1850, shortly after the Gold Rush. The population has grown steadily since then, drawn over the years by the wealth of the state's natural resources in minerals, forests, farmland, and petroleum, and by the expansion of industries in such fields as manufacturing, transportation, defense, aerospace, agribusiness, electronics, tourism, and entertainment.

Exhibit 1-1 is called a **cartogram**. By distorting each state's dimensions so that its size is proportional to its population, the map shows that California is the most populous state. About 5 percent of the people in the world live in the United States—and of these, one of every eight (12 percent) live in California. The 2000 **census** counted nearly 34 million residents.[1] Exhibit 1-2 is a time-series graph showing California's

---

[1]The next-largest states are Texas, with nearly 21 million people, and New York, with about 19 million.

EXHIBIT 1-1   The Shape of America

This cartogram depicts the relative size of each state in proportion to its population. Each square represents 100,000 people. Which is the most populous state? Which are the fastest-growing states?

Source: The New York Times, December 29, 2000. Copyright © 2000 The New York Times Co. Reprinted by permission.

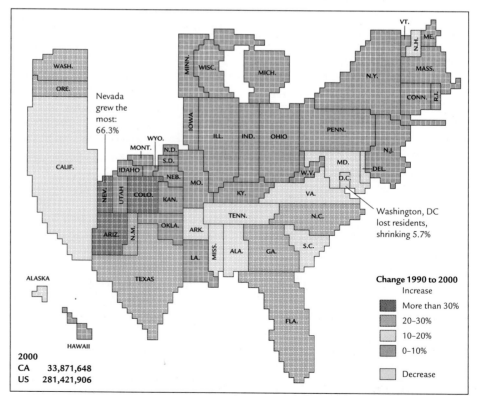

Nevada grew the most: 66.3%

Washington, DC lost residents, shrinking 5.7%

Change 1990 to 2000
Increase
- More than 30%
- 20–30%
- 10–20%
- 0–10%

Decrease

2000
CA   33,871,648
US   281,421,906

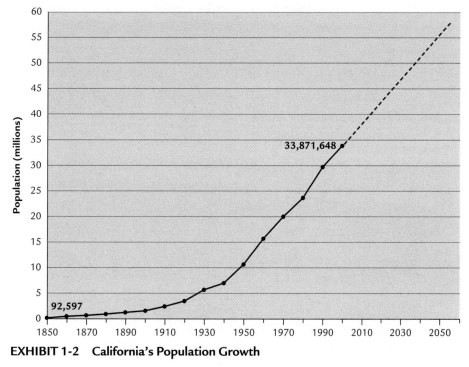

EXHIBIT 1-2   California's Population Growth

How fast is California's population growing?

Source: U.S. Bureau of the Census and California Department of Finance.

population growth. Increasing by more than 1,000 every day, California's population now exceeds 37 million. Population growth and demographic change have significant effects on California government. Every day California needs to open 70 new elementary school classrooms, and the housing market needs to expand by 250 or so additional apartments or houses.

California is the most racially diverse state in the nation. No single racial or ethnic group makes up a majority of the population. Along with population growth, dramatic demographic change has taken place. Within only thirty years the **Anglo** (white non-Hispanic) proportion of California's population has decreased from 77 percent in 1970, to 69 percent in 1990, to 47 percent in 2000. Exhibit 1-3 is a **choropleth map** showing the **Latino** population in the United States as a percentage of the total population in each county. The Latino population is increasing, particularly in the West and Southwest. Latinos now make up nearly one-third of all Californians (32.4 percent), up from 12 percent in 1970 and 25.8 percent in 1990. Overall, Latinos account for about three-fourths of California's population increase since 1990. Currently, one of every four Californians is foreign born, a higher rate than in any other state. One of every nine is a native of Mexico.

California's population increased by 4.1 million (14 percent) between the census counts of 1990 and 2000. Exhibit 1-4 shows California's population change during the 1990s. The largest components of population change are natural increase (births minus deaths) and immigration. California has a high birthrate (fourth highest among the fifty states in 1996). More than 500,000 people are born in California each year—about one per minute—and deaths are half that number. Natural increase accounts for more than 3.3 million people since 1990. International immigration, mostly from Mexico and Asia but also from every other country and culture, added about 2.5 million people

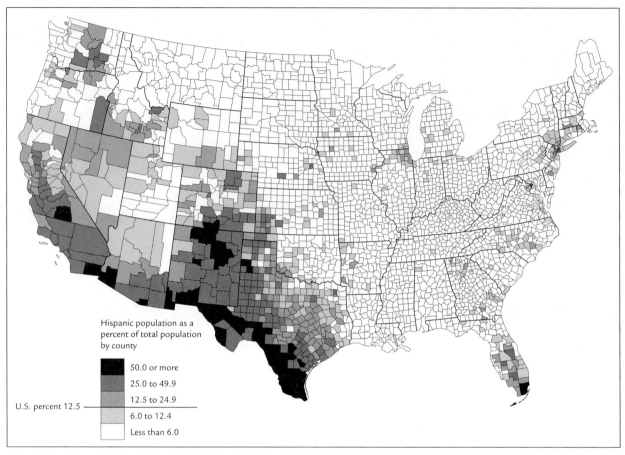

Hispanic population as a
percent of total population
by county

50.0 or more
25.0 to 49.9
12.5 to 24.9
6.0 to 12.4
Less than 6.0

U.S. percent 12.5

EXHIBIT 1-3   Latino (Hispanic) Population

Which states have the highest proportions of Hispanic residents? Why do Florida and New York
have large Hispanic populations?

Source: U.S. Census Bureau, Census 2000.

during the 1990s (250,000 per year, including estimated illegal entries). One-fourth of
all immigrants to the United States come to California. About 1.7 million more people
moved out of California to elsewhere in the United States during the 1990s than came
here from other states. Exhibit 1-5 tells a story of demographic change. Eighty percent
of California's population growth is Latino and Asian. The state's Anglo population actually *decreased* to what it was in 1980 due to domestic out-migration. The Anglo proportion of the population is now less than 50 percent. Latinos will make up the
majority of Californians within a few years, and some writers even foresee the recon-
quest of California by Mexican immigrants.[2] Despite the decrease, the Anglo population continues to dominate the electorate (citizens over the age of 18) and thereby
strongly influences political representation and public policy. Anglos make up about 67
percent of California voters while Latinos account for only 19 percent.

Three Latinos register as Democrats for every one that registers as a Republican.
About one-fourth of registered Democrats, but only about 12 percent of Republicans,
are Latino.[3] As Latinos gain political influence, there may be a greater acceptance of

[2]See, for example, Victor Hanson, *Mexifornia: A State of Becoming* (San Francisco: Encounter Books, 2003).
[3]*2006 Primary Election Profiles: California*, National Association of Latino Elected and Appointed Officials, www.naleo.org/downloads/CAPrimaryProfile2006.pdf

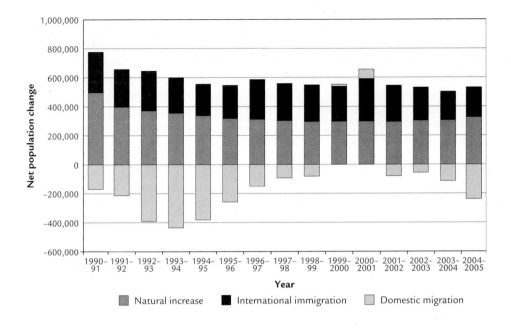

EXHIBIT 1-4
Components of
Population Growth
in California

Which components of
population change
increased California's
population since 1990?
Which decreased it?

Source: U.S. Bureau of the
Census and California
Department of Finance.

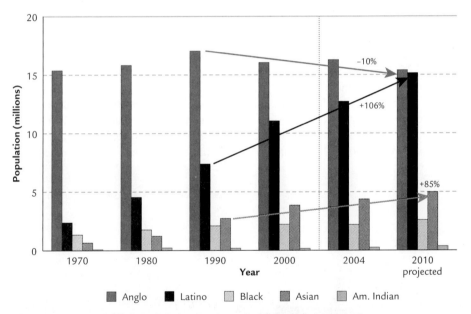

EXHIBIT 1-5   Racial/Ethnic Distribution of California's Population

How did the size and share of each population group change since 1990? What is the projected
racial/ethnic makeup of California's population by 2010?

Source: State of California, Department of Finance, *Population Projections by Race/Ethnicity, Gender and Age for
California and Its Counties 2000–2050*, Sacramento, May 2004.

government public service programs. But it should also be noted that 60 percent of
Latinos are Catholic. As the population grows, the proportion of Catholics will increase from 30 percent in 2005 to more than 36 percent by 2025. This may indicate
a greater acceptance of conservative social policies such as limits on access to abortion for women and continued opposition to proposals recognizing gay marriage.

Political Parties

On the national scene, California is generally regarded as a "blue state" favoring the Democratic Party (see Exhibit 1-6). Currently, both U.S. senators are Democrats and Democrats hold the majority of the seats among California's congressional representatives and both houses of the state legislature. In 2000, the state voted for Democratic presidential candidate Al Gore (by a margin of 53.5 percent for Gore to 41.7 percent for George W. Bush). California's fifty-five electoral votes offset the Republican wins in much of the Midwest and South, leaving the election to be decided by only a few hundred votes in Florida. In the 2004 presidential election, California voted for Democrat John Kerry over Republican George W. Bush by 54.4 to 44.4 percent.

Political Economy

It may seem that California is rich—and it is. California has the fifth- or sixth-largest economy in the world, with a **gross state product** greater than the **gross domestic product** of France, Italy, or China (but less than that of Japan, Germany, and the United Kingdom, and, of course, the United States). One-half of California households have incomes over $53,629 (ninth highest among the fifty states plus the District of Columbia). Twenty-nine percent of Californians over the age of 25 have attained at least a bachelor's degree (thirteen in national ranking). However, other measures indicate a **two-tier** economic stratification between have and have-not Californians—described by a keen California observer, Peter Schrag—that is, between the affluent, older, and predominantly Anglo upper tier, and the younger, browner, lower tier more dependent on public schools and other governmental social services.[4] Middle-class families, earning from $35,000 to $75,000 a year, make up only 32 percent of California families—second lowest among the fifty states. And California has more people at the economic extremes than the national average. Over the last thirty years, the rich have gotten richer and the poor have gotten poorer. During this period, **median** family income increased about 20 percent in California versus 40 percent in the rest of the United States. Incomes among the top 10 percent of richest families increased about 60 percent, in

---

[4]Peter Schrag, *California: America's High-Stakes Experiment* (Berkeley: University of California Press, 2006).

EXHIBIT 1-6   Political Party Registration in California

This graph indicates the relative concentrations of Democratic (gray) and Republican (red) voters.

Why is California called a "blue state"?

Source: Patrick Brooke, Geographic Information Systems Analyst.

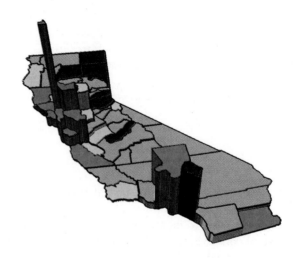

both California and the United States. However, whereas incomes of the poorest 10 percent of families rose about 20 percent nationally, particularly since 1995, they actually dropped about 20 percent in California. In the year 2003, 13.4 percent of Californians were poor (defined as equivalent to a family of four making $17,000 or less annually) compared with 12.7 percent nationally (including 18.6 percent of children under 18 years old, compared with 17.3 percent nationally). California is a relatively expensive place to live and work. San Francisco, Los Angeles, and San Diego are among the ten most expensive metropolitan areas in the United States, especially with regard to the cost of housing.[5]

There is a *yin-and-yang* aspect to life in California. On the one hand, California is seen as a trend-starting and trend-setting state, whether in fashion, entertainment, culture, economics, or politics—a place for opportunity, innovation, growth, and development. For thirty years after World War II, California exhibited activist government—particularly evident in public works, education, and social programs. The massive California Aqueduct delivers water from the north to the south. The state's 15,000-mile freeway system was the exemplar of interstate highways. The California Community Colleges, California State University, and University of California, until relatively recently, offered virtually free higher education. Regarded as ideologically and culturally to the liberal left, California is stereotyped as a safe haven for pro-abortion, gay-tolerant environmentalists. Bordering Mexico and home to Hollywood, it seems to be a breeding ground for *identity* politics—evidenced by immigrants, whether legal or illegal, waving the Mexican flag as a symbol of cultural heritage rather than national loyalty—and *celebrity* politics—evidenced most recently by Governor Arnold Schwarzenegger, but preceded by Governor and later President Ronald Reagan, Senator George Murphy, and Congressman Sonny Bono— winning political office after Hollywood fame.

On the other hand, facing ongoing growth and change—social, technological, economic, and environmental challenges on every front—Californians yearn for a slower, more orderly pace to life. California has transitioned from can-do optimism and confidence in government to a general attitude of withdrawal of public investment and commitment. In hindsight, 1978 was the watershed year. The key event was Proposition 13, a voter-approved ballot measure to limit one of the key revenue sources of government—property taxes.[6] Since then, there has been a steady succession of voter actions to further restrict and circumscribe governmental action. Important issues involving societal goals and values and policy development are the focus of ballot **propositions** submitted for a statewide vote, rather than acts of the legislature or governor. Voters have outlawed gay marriage, passed and then refused to loosen "Three Strikes" and other laws mandating stiff prison sentences for felony crimes, passed and then refused to loosen term limits for legislative and other state political officers, and kept in place a constitutional requirement for a two-thirds legislative majority in order to adopt a state budget or to fund state programs.

Immigrant-dominated population growth has added to the stress. Twenty-six percent of Californians are foreign born, and one of four schoolchildren are from a household where English is not the primary language. Latino students often attend

---

[5]Cost of Living Index, Arlington, VA, ACCRA.

[6]Property taxes are one of the principal means of funding government. The amount of the tax is based on the value of the property. Proposition 13 replaced the practice of annually reassessing property at full cash value with a system based on cost at acquisition. Under Proposition 13, property is assessed at market value for tax purposes only when it changes ownership. Increases in value are limited to an annual inflation factor of no more than 2 percent. In addition, Proposition 13 requires any measure enacted for the purpose of increasing state revenues to be approved by a two-thirds vote of each house of the legislature.

segregated, overcrowded schools, and less than 10 percent go on to attend four-year universities. Overall, only 23 percent of California high schoolers pursue a bachelor's degree, compared to 47 percent in Massachusetts. Although California ranks eleventh among the states in per capita income, for many years it ranked nearly last in K–12 educational spending. Recent Latino and Asian immigrants are following the assimilation patterns of previous immigrants. By the second generation, most are bilingual and increasingly participating in education, work, and political opportunities. And by the third generation, English and middle-class values dominate. It will be interesting to see whether and how public investments change as Latinos assimilate and gain political awareness and influence.

Political Geography

See
color insert,
Exhibit 1-7

Many aspects of life in California and many policy issues are directly related to California's terrain and climate. California's distinctive Central Valley, with irrigated farmlands and a long, hot, dry summer, is the dominant feature on the landform map (see Exhibit 1-7). Most of California's population, however, is concentrated in metropolitan areas (Los Angeles, San Francisco, and San Diego) hugging the Pacific Coast. Mountain ranges surround the Central Valley—the Cascade Range to the north and the Sierra Nevada Range to the east accumulate a vital winter snow pack. The Coastal Range, covered with oak, grasses, and chaparral, separates the Central Valley from the Pacific Coast. The only gap is the Delta, where waters from the Sierra Nevada join the Sacramento and San Joaquin rivers and eventually flow into San Francisco Bay. At the southern end, the Tehachapi Mountains separate the Central Valley from arid deserts to the south. Political subdivisions are superimposed on this landform. The most important of these are California's fifty-eight **counties**—in effect, administrative units of state government and the basic reference for all social and economic measures.

See
color insert,
Exhibit 1-8

There are actually many Californias. First described by Dan Walters as more than convenient tourism references, the **regions** of California have distinct political, demographic, and economic identities.[7] Following Walters's work, Exhibit 1-8 shows the names of California's fifty-eight counties and ten regional groupings. The most significant regions by population and economic influence are the five-county Metropolitan Los Angeles, with one-half of the state's population[8]; the nine-county San Francisco Bay Area; San Diego County; the eight-county San Joaquin Valley; and the six-county Sacramento region.

The regions are linked by, and the economy is dependent on, the state's public works **infrastructure**. These are projects on a grand scale. California has been **terra-formed**. Terra-forming is a popular science fiction theme whereby a desolate, dry, inhospitable planet is transformed by immense projects into a place that can sustain a large population of colonists. The stories typically describe massive public works projects that overcome the terrain and climate, food produced on enormous hydroponic farms, whole rivers diverted hundreds of miles, and people transported both short and long distances in the most modern individual conveyances. In California, terra-forming is not fiction; it's reality. Although the prevailing climate in central and southern California is arid, water is captured from the Sierra Nevada Range by a series of dams and irrigation projects and carried hundreds of miles from the Sierra to the coast and from north to south for farms and cities. In addition, complex energy networks link California's public utility companies to the western states' electrical power grid and

---

[7]Dan Walters, *The New California: Facing the 21st Century*, 2nd ed. (Sacramento: California Journal Press, 1992).

[8]The eastern parts of San Bernardino and Riverside counties are actually part of the desert region.

import natural gas from Canada and Texas for distribution throughout the state. People and commodities are moved by transportation systems—roads and bridges (especially **freeways**), railroads for freight and commuting, airports, and harbors. This entire infrastructure is subject to governmental planning and regulation. Most of the systems were built and are owned, funded, and operated by California governments.

METROPOLITAN LOS ANGELES

Los Angeles, Orange, and Ventura Counties and the Inland Empire
(western halves of San Bernardino and Riverside counties)

The five-county Los Angeles region is the second largest metropolitan area in the United States. (The largest is the New York/northern New Jersey area.) One-half of all Californians live here—more than one-fourth in Los Angeles County alone. The urban region is a jigsaw pattern of cities and neighborhoods roughly the size of the state of Connecticut. The character of the neighborhoods runs the gamut of urban conditions. Some are affluent (such as Larchmont Heights and Brentwood); on the other extreme, places such as East Los Angeles exhibit poverty, despair, and gang violence. Many neighborhoods have a distinct ethnic identity (such as Latino in Huntington Park and Montebello, **black** in Watts and Compton, **Asian** in Torrance and Monterey Park, and Jewish in the Fairfax district and the southwestern part of the San Fernando Valley).

It is, at the same time, both congested and sprawling. The neighborhoods, linked by a network of freeways, tend to be densely settled. Los Angeles County has one-fourth of the state's cars and trucks. Average freeway speeds are about thirty mph and slowing each year.

Politics tends to be associated with ethnic group and urban/suburban living. Traditionally Democratic African American and Jewish voters (although they are somewhat split into urban versus suburban) are joined by increasing numbers of Latino and Asian who perceive the Democratic Party as more sensitive to immigration issues and the needs of immigrants. The ethnic alignment can be seen in the June 2001 election for mayor of Los Angeles, won by *moderate* Democrat James K. Hahn against *liberal* Democrat Antonio Villaraigosa. Anglos, with a large Jewish turnout, and making up over half the voters, voted 59 percent for Hahn, along with blacks (80 percent, or 17 percent of total voters) and Asians (65 percent, or 8 percent of total voters). Eighty-two percent of Latinos (22 percent of total voters) voted for Villaraigosa. He won a seat on the Los Angeles City Council in March 2003 and then in May 2005 defeated Hahn for mayor in a close run-off race.

Politically, Metropolitan Los Angeles is the proverbial "800-pound gorilla." Its interests are a dominant influence in the state. The conservative Republican grip on Orange County is weakening as Metropolitan Los Angeles sprawls southward with a largely young Latino (average age is 25) and Asian makeup. Anglos are now a majority only among older residents. Despite Orange County's population growth, housing development has stagnated, housing prices have skyrocketed, and many new residents find themselves among the working poor.

An attempt by the San Fernando Valley to secede from the city of Los Angeles and form its own city government failed in the November 2002 election but indicated stark divisions in wealth, lifestyle, and expectations of government between the northern suburbs and the city sprawl to the south.

Western San Bernardino and Riverside Counties (the Inland Empire) seem to be extensions of their immediate neighbors as the Los Angeles sprawl spreads eastward, with San Bernardino reflecting Los Angeles County and Riverside looking like Orange County.

SAN DIEGO

San Diego County

Although San Diego is the country's fifth-largest city, San Diego County contains just over 8 percent of the state's population. It is a relatively prosperous region. The unemployment rate is consistently 1–2 percentage points below the state average. Most of the population and housing is near the coast where the climate is pleasant. Traveling east, one soon encounters the hot dry desert. The Anglo population constitutes a majority at 55 percent and tends to vote Republican.

SAN FRANCISCO BAY AREA

San Francisco City and County, East Bay
(Alameda, Contra Costa, and Solano counties)

North Bay
(Marin, Sonoma, and Napa counties)

South Bay
(San Mateo and Santa Clara counties)

The nine-county San Francisco Bay Area accounts for 20 percent of California's population. San Francisco itself seems to be a big theme park. Tourism is the number-one industry, and one-fourth of all visitors are foreign tourists. Tourism, however, is subject to the vagaries of the economy and international currency exchange rates.

Asians are the largest nonwhite group in the Bay Area. Blacks have been leaving the city and environs due to exploding housing costs. Ten percent of San Francisco's population is gay. However, this is not an isolated enclave, and gays are proportionately present as the Bay Area urban growth spreads south through San Jose and east toward the San Joaquin Valley.

Until recently, the economy of the Bay Area has been strong, with the South Bay home to the heralded Silicon Valley. Unemployment rates were among the lowest in the country (2.5–3 percent in 2000). Since the bubble burst on the dot-com industry in 2001, however, unemployment rates have increased.

SAN JOAQUIN VALLEY

San Joaquin, Stanislaus, Merced, Madera, Fresno, Kings, Tulare, and Kern Counties

The San Joaquin Valley, with only 9.8 percent of California's population, is the most productive agricultural region in the world.[9] In terms of the market value of agricultural products sold, Fresno, Kern, and Tulare counties are ranked first,

---

[9]The San Joaquin Valley is the southern half of the geographic feature called the Central Valley. The northern part, including Sacramento, Placer, Colusa, Sutter, Yuba, Glenn, and Butte counties, is called the Sacramento Valley. However, politically and economically, the San Joaquin Valley is a distinct region.

second, and third in the country, respectively; Merced, Stanislaus, and San Joaquin counties are sixth, seventh, and eighth.

Population growth and sprawl from the Bay Area has created linear urbanization along the north-south Highway 99 corridor with inevitable conflicts between residential and commercial development and agricultural preservation.

The San Joaquin Valley is a pocket of poverty. Double-digit unemployment rates (consistently exceeding 10 percent) are three to four times higher than the national average (around 4 percent). The seasonal nature of the economy is reflected in the region's unemployment rates, which regularly rise six percentage points within only a couple of months early each year and fall just as rapidly during the late summer and fall. Child poverty rates in most of the region exceed 30 percent, and the median household income throughout is substantially below the state average.

The summary census data show the population as principally Anglo and Latino (Anglos are a majority only in Stanislaus County). However, there are many unique ethnic communities throughout the San Joaquin Valley (including Assyrian, Portuguese, Sikh, and Hmong). The proportion of residents who identify themselves as multiracial is double the national average, making up over 5 percent of the population in the northern part of the San Joaquin Valley. The same counties in which the Latino population is growing also have the youngest population and the most families with children. For example, the population of Merced County, in the heart of the San Joaquin Valley, is 45 percent Latino, with a median age of 29 (34 percent of the population is under the age of 18), and one-third of the families have children. The general outlook is politically and culturally conservative.

SACRAMENTO

Sacramento, El Dorado, Sutter, Placer, Yolo, and Yuba Counties

The six-county Sacramento Region, with 4.1 percent of California's population, has transitioned from an agricultural to a service-based economy centered on the activities of state government in the capital, Sacramento. The unemployment rate, though variable, generally stays below the state average. Anglo majorities tend to favor Democrats.

CENTRAL COAST

Santa Cruz, Monterey, San Benito, San Luis Obispo, and Santa Barbara Counties

The Central Coast, with 4 percent of California's population, is known for its beautiful coastal scenery. It is an agricultural region famous for artichokes, garlic, fruits, and vegetables, as well as wine making, dairy and cattle ranching, and a fishing industry. Offshore oil platforms dot the horizon off of Santa Barbara County. Unemployment is close to the state average except during winter and spring months, when in some areas it rises to 12 percent or more.

RURAL CALIFORNIA

Gold Country and High Sierra
(Amador, Alpine, Calaveras, Tuolumne, Mariposa, and Mono counties)

Northern California
(Sierra, Nevada, Siskiyou, Modoc, Trinity, Shasta, Lassen, Tehama, Plumas, Glenn, Butte, and Colusa counties)

North Coast
(Del Norte, Humboldt, Mendocino, and Lake counties)

The Desert
(Inyo, Imperial, and eastern parts of San Bernardino and Riverside counties)

Altogether, only 5 percent of the state's population lives in the twenty-four counties that make up rural California. The fishing and timber industries have declined, and unemployment is high except in tourist areas. Apart from Imperial County, rural California has a predominantly Anglo population that has high voter turnout rates and that votes conservative. Imperial County is isolated in the far southeast corner of the state. Hot and dry, with an agricultural economy dependent on imported water, it resembles both Mexico and the San Joaquin Valley. Nearly three-fourths of Imperial County's population is Latino, and it has the highest unemployment (exceeding 20 percent) in California.

WEB LINKS

State of California **www.ca.gov**
U.S. Bureau of the Census **www.census.gov**

PUBLICATIONS

Baldassare, Mark. 2000. *California in the New Millennium: The Changing Social and Political Landscape.* Berkeley: University of California Press.

Bedolla, Lisa. 2005. *Fluid Borders: Latino Power, Identity, and Politics in Los Angeles.* Berkeley: University of California Press.

Erie, Steven P. 2006. *Beyond Chinatown: The Metropolitan Water District, Growth, and the Environment in Southern California.* Palo Alto, CA: Stanford University Press.

Fradkin, Philip L. 1995. *The Seven States of California: A Natural and Human History.* Berkeley: University of California Press.

Fulton, William. 1997. *The Reluctant Metropolis: The Politics of Urban Growth in Los Angeles.* Point Arena, CA: Solano Press.

Gentry, Curt. 1969. *Last Days of the Late, Great State of California.* New York: Ballantine.

Keene, Barry, ed. 2000. *Making Government Work: California Cases in Policy, Politics, and Public Management.* Berkeley: University of California, Institute for Governmental Studies.

McWilliams, Carey. 1973. *Southern California: An Island on the Land*, reprint ed. Santa Barbara, CA: Peregrine Smith.

McWilliams, Carey, and Lewis H. Lapman. 1999. *California: The Great Exception*, reprint ed. Berkeley: University of California Press.

Norris, Frank. 1994. *The Octopus: A Story of California*. New York: Penguin.

Pincetl, Stephanie Sabine. 1999. *Transforming California : A Political History of Land Use and Development*. Baltimore: Johns Hopkins University Press.

Reisner, Marc. 1993. *Cadillac Desert: The American West and Its Disappearing Water*. New York: Penguin.

Schrag, Peter. 1999. *Paradise Lost: California's Experience, America's Future*. Berkeley: University of California Press.

Schrag, Peter. 2006. *California: America's High-Stakes Experiment*. Berkeley: University of California Press.

Selz, Peter. 2006. *Art of Engagement: Visual Politics in California and Beyond*. Berkeley: University of California Press.

Starr, Kevin. 2005. *California: A History*. New York: Modern Library.

Walters, Dan. 1992. *The New California: Facing the 21st Century*, 2nd ed. Sacramento: California Journal Press.

GLOSSARY

Anglo   A reference to persons who identify themselves as white, non-Hispanic, generally implying a European ancestry, ethnicity, or heritage.

Asian (and Pacific Islander)   A reference to persons who identify themselves as having an ancestry, ethnicity, or heritage in the Pacific Rim, such as China, Japan, Korea, the Philippines, Southeast Asia, or Indonesia.

black (African American)   A reference to persons who identify themselves as having an African ancestry, ethnicity, or heritage.

cartogram   A one-variable geographic data presentation in which the sizes of political subdivisions on a map are distorted in proportion to data values.

census   A head count of the resident population within a political jurisdiction.

choropleth map   A one-variable geographic data presentation in which political subdivisions on a map are colored or patterned to correspond to data values.

county   A local government that is, in effect, an administrative subunit of state government. California is divided into fifty-eight counties.

freeway   A multilane highway without a toll.

government   The organizations, processes, and rules that control a land and its people.

gross domestic (state) product   The total value of output, income, or expenditure produced within the physical boundaries of a nation or state.

infrastructure   All of the buildings, highways, water mains, parks, sewage treatment plants, and other public works built and maintained by government.

Latino   A more specific reference than *Hispanic* to persons who identify themselves as having a Mexican or Central or South American ethnicity, heritage, or ancestry.

median   A statistical average. Half of the observations have values greater than the median, and the other half have values less than the median.

politics   The process by which governmental decisions are made between competing and conflicting interests.

proposition (initiative, ballot measure)   A measure—a proposed statute (law), constitutional amendment, or bond issue—placed on the ballot for a vote of the electorate.

regions   Multicounty areas of California defined by physical geography, demography, economy, and politics.

terra-forming   The act of building immense public works projects to transform a desolate, dry, inhospitable region into a place that can sustain a large population.

two-tier   A reference to an apparent have/have-not socioeconomic disparity.

SUGGESTED ANSWERS TO EXHIBIT QUESTIONS

Exhibit 1-1: This map is called a "cartogram." By distorting each state's dimensions so that its size is proportional to its population, it shows that California is the largest state in population; 12 percent of Americans live in California. The fastest-growing states are in the Southwest—Nevada, Arizona, and Colorado.

Exhibit 1-2: On average, California's population has grown by 4–5 million people every ten years since 1950.

Exhibit 1-3: The Hispanic population is increasing, particularly in the West and Southwest. About one-third of Californians are Latino. Many Hispanics in New York have a Puerto Rican, Caribbean, or Central or South American heritage while many Hispanics in Florida have a Cuban heritage.

Exhibit 1-4: California's population increased by 4.1 million people during the 1990s. Natural increase (births minus deaths) and international immigration (principally from Mexico and Asia) more than offset a significant out-migration from California to other states.

Exhibit 1-5: California's population growth is predominantly Latino and Asian. California's Anglo population actually has *decreased* since 1990, with the Anglo proportion of the population now less than 50 percent. Latinos will likely make up the majority of Californians within a few years.

Exhibit 1-6: Red and blue seem to have been adopted by the media as the symbolic colors of the Republican and Democratic parties, respectively. If we simply colored the counties, California would appear mostly red with blue confined to Los Angeles County, the San Francisco Bay Area, and most of the North Coast since most counties have a plurality in terms of Republican voter registration. (It's important to note that 18 percent of Californians do not express a party affiliation, registering as "Decline to State.") However, this geographic distribution is more than offset by the heavy concentration of Democratic registrants in the Los Angeles and San Francisco Bay areas. The height of the bars in this three-dimensional graph represents "Democratic concentration"—registered Democrats per square-mile. The shading of the bars indicates the difference between the proportion of Democrats and Republicans among the registered voters in the county with red shades indicating greater Republican registration and gray shades indicating greater Democratic registration.

Exhibit 1-7: Many aspects of life in California, and many policy issues, are directly related to California's terrain, climate, and land use. California's distinctive Central Valley surrounded by mountains is the dominant feature on the landform map. Most of California's population, however, is concentrated in confined metropolitan areas (Los Angeles, San Francisco, and San Diego) hugging the coast. The boundaries of California's fifty-eight counties are superimposed on the map. Sometimes political boundaries follow the physical terrain, such as the western boundary of Sacramento and Sutter counties along the Sacramento River. Other times political boundaries are longitudinal lines or compass headings, such as the northern boundary of San Luis Obispo, Kern, and San Bernardino counties.

CHAPTER TWO

THE STRUCTURE OF GOVERNMENT

The United States and California are **republics**, or *representative* **democracies**. Citizens choose representatives to act on their behalf. They are also *constitutional* democracies. They are governed in accordance with a constitution—a document that specifies the role and authority of these representatives (and of governmental institutions). The constitution is the supreme law. Its principles may even overrule the popular will. Citizens participate in government by periodically voting for representatives, communicating their opinions to representatives, and occasionally voting on measures submitted for a general vote.

Actually, there is not just one government for the United States and one government for the state of California. There are many governments forming a complicated, interacting, and overlapping mélange. In addition to the central government in Washington, DC, and fifty state governments, more than 80,000 other governmental units exist, including more than 3,000 counties, 19,000 cities of all sizes, 16,000 other towns, 13,000 school districts, and 36,000 special districts—all with their own elected officials, employees, and jurisdictions. As detailed in Exhibit 2-1, California has more than 6,800 governments, including 58 counties, 478 cities, 72 community college districts, more than 4,700 special districts, and nearly 1,000 elementary and high school districts.

This chapter reviews what these governments do and how they relate to one another: the structure of government, the levels of government, and the separation of powers.

DIVIDED GOVERNANCE

Americans harbor a distrust of government. Above all else, we fear a tyranny under which liberty is lost because the government is taken over by a faction—a group with a narrow political, ideological, or religious agenda—and the power of government is subverted to that faction's interests. James Madison addressed the concern in 1788. He wrote, "The accumulation of all powers, legislative, executive, and judiciary, in the same hands, whether of one, a few, or many, and whether hereditary,

		EXHIBIT 2-1
State	1	
Counties	58	**California**
Cities	478	**Governments**
Redevelopment agencies	418	*There are about*
Special districts	4,763	_____ *as many*
K–12 school districts	983	*K–12 school*
Community college districts	72	*districts as cities in*
		California.
Total	**6,773**	
American Indian tribes	95	

self-appointed, or elective, may justly be pronounced the very definition of tyranny."[1] To prevent the emergence of a dominant faction, government is divided. There is a tension between centralization and decentralization. Centralization is necessary in order to apply the power of government to the resolution of common problems, to provide national uniformity and consistency to public **policy,** and to keep the policy-making elite from being dominated by the transient will of the majority. Decentralization is necessary in order to respond to local problems and to check the emergence of a dominant faction.

Government is divided into levels, political districts, and branches. The United States has three levels of government: national, state, and local. The United States are united under one national government. The relationship between the national government and the state governments is called **federalism.** Authority is divided between a large central government at the national level and many smaller regional governments (the states). The national government (often called the federal government) and the state governments are separate and **sovereign.** They have different areas of responsibility, **authority,** and **jurisdiction.** In some **policy areas,** such as in national defense and the economy, the national government has primary authority. In other areas, such as consumer affairs, land use, and education, the state governments have primary authority. In those areas, a state government is more powerful than the national government. And in some policy areas, federal and state authority overlaps, and may even conflict.

At each level, representation—governance—is by geographic **district:** distinct political and administrative jurisdictions such as states, congressional districts, counties, cities, agencies, and departments, to name a few. Within a state, such as California, the structure of government is **unitary** (see Exhibit 2-2). The unitary structure is defined by the state constitution. Local units of government, such as counties and cities, are created by the state. They are subordinate rather than sovereign units and have only such authority and jurisdiction as is granted to them by the state government. Local governments must respond to the **mandates** imposed by state or national governments.

---

[1]James Madison, "Federalist No. 47: The Particular Structure of the New Government and the Distribution of Power Among Its Different Parts," *The Federalist Papers*, **memory.loc.gov/const/fed/fedpapers.html**

EXHIBIT 2-2
Federal and Unitary Governmental Relationships

List all the ways the federal, state, and local governments affect Californians.

Sources: Uncle Sam © Swim Ink 2, LLC/Corbis. California Flag © Spencer Grant/ PhotoEdit.

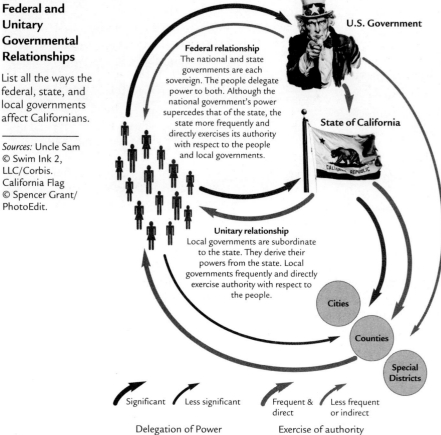

U.S. Government

Federal relationship
The national and state governments are each sovereign. The people delegate power to both. Although the national government's power supercedes that of the state, the state more frequently and directly exercises its authority with respect to the people and local governments.

State of California

Unitary relationship
Local governments are subordinate to the state. They derive their powers from the state. Local governments frequently and directly exercise authority with respect to the people.

Cities

Counties

Special Districts

Significant   Less significant   Frequent & direct   Less frequent or indirect

Delegation of Power   Exercise of authority

The powers of government—executive, legislative, and judicial—are divided among different institutions, the branches of government. At the national level, the president heads the executive branch, the administrative bureaucracy. The legislative institution is the Congress. The judicial institution is the U.S. Supreme Court (along with lower federal courts). A similar division occurs in California state government between the governor (and other elected executives), the state legislature, and the state supreme court (and lower state courts).

This federalist structure is defined by the U.S. Constitution. Authority among the levels, districts, and branches overlaps. Governance is a complicated system that requires intergovernmental coordination in order to minimize policy inconsistencies from state to state or between the national and state governments. There are so many veto points that governance becomes a complex process of cooperation and compromise (or sometimes conflict and competition).

THE EXECUTIVE BRANCH

At the national level, the executive functions are headed by the president of the United States. Americans indirectly vote for the president in fifty-one separate winner-takes-all elections (in each of the fifty states and in Washington, DC) every four years.[2] The vote of each state is weighted by the population of the state. Thus California, the most populous state, had the most presidential electoral votes in 2004 (fifty-five), and states with small populations, such as Alaska, Wyoming, and Delaware, had the least (three each). Whichever candidate wins the election in a state wins all of that state's electoral votes, no matter how close the margin of victory.

Most Californians have little direct interaction with the national government beyond obtaining a Social Security card and paying taxes to the U.S. Internal Revenue Service each year. But the national government's influence in California is pervasive, as we will see in the discussion of policy areas.

California has a **plural executive**. Eight executive officers—the governor, lieutenant governor, attorney general, secretary of state, controller, treasurer, insurance commissioner, and superintendent of public instruction—are directly elected by California voters to four-year terms in the same statewide general election. In 1990, Californians imposed a two-term limit on these statewide offices.

The governor is the chief executive officer and most prominent political figure in state government. California state government employs about 300,000 people (more than 100,000 work in the University of California and California State University systems).[3] The governor has the power to appoint the heads of ten large agencies and departments, as well as scores of other public sector managers and members of various boards and commissions (see Exhibit 2-3). The governor's political role includes defining the policy agenda for the state and being the center of attention for public policy debates, influencing voter initiatives and legislation, speaking for Californians on the national and international scene, and developing the revenue and spending priorities of state government.

In 2003, Californians replaced Governor Gray Davis, a Democrat, with Republican Arnold Schwarzenegger and sent a message to government (see Exhibit 2-4). They seemed to want a political leader who exhibited strength and optimism, who promised to tackle seemingly intractable problems, who was not a crony of entrenched political parties and structures, who would not complacently accept the status quo but would propose change and strike out in new directions. Schwarzenegger, a smart and charismatic Hollywood action hero, promised "Action! Action! Action!" on policy and fiscal reform while maintaining tolerance on social value issues such as gay rights and abortion.

Throughout 2004, Governor Schwarzenegger bided his time—negotiating with Democratic legislative leaders, avoiding policy disputes, and compromising with various interests, including prison guards, local governments, and educators. His principal fiscal reforms involved borrowing heavily to fund the state budget deficit and rescinding a scheduled restoration of vehicle license fee rates. Schwarzenegger promised government reform—not just by reorganization but also by "blowing up boxes" on the organization chart. Acting on recommendations of the 2004 California Performance Review, he proposed eliminating 88 of the state's 340 boards and commissions. The various panels evolved to regulate service delivery and performance in such areas as health care, accounting, and construction but were often viewed as $100 per diem political sinecures. Every board and commission, however, had a history, a purpose, and a political constituency. In the end, the proposal was quietly withdrawn.

In the November 2004 general election, Schwarzenegger endorsed several Republican legislative candidates. None of them won. Democrat John Kerry carried

---

[2]Except Maine and Nebraska, which allocate electoral votes.

[3]California has 110 state employees per 10,000 people and ranks forty-seventh among the states in state employees relative to population. The U.S. average is 143 state employees per 10,000 people.

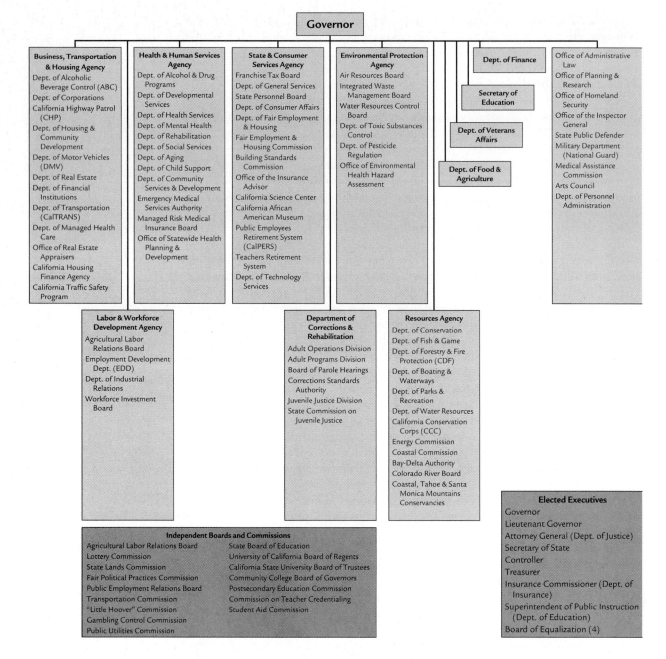

EXHIBIT 2-3   California State Government Bureaucracy (partial list of organizations)

How many agencies are listed in this chart? Find these agencies: California State University, Franchise Tax Board, Employment Development Department, Department of Motor Vehicles, California Highway Patrol, and Department of Parks and Recreation. What agencies deal with the environment? What agencies deal with public education?

California in the presidential election. But Schwarzenegger claimed "victories" on the deficit reduction bond measure and other ballot propositions he endorsed. Aware that the California Democratic Party was weakened by the exhausting 2004 campaigns, loss of key leaders due to term limits and retirements, and some recent

Governor (Party)	Served	EXHIBIT 2-4
Arnold Schwarzenegger (R)	2003–	**California Governors since 1943**
Gray Davis (D)	1999–2003	
Pete Wilson (R)	1991–1999	
George Deukmejian (R)	1983–1991	*The governor who had the shortest term in office was_____.*
Edmund G. "Jerry" Brown (D)	1975–1983	
Ronald Reagan (R)	1967–1975	
Edmund G. "Pat" Brown (D)	1959–1967	*The governor who had the longest term in office was_____.*
Goodwin Knight (R)	1953–1959	
Earl Warren (R)	1943–1953	

political scandals, and sensing that Californians are increasingly reform-minded and anti-establishment, Schwarzenegger in 2005 directly challenged the party's domination of California governance. Claiming a mandate from "the people," he launched a broad frontal offensive on the Democrats, threatening core interests in their political base—teachers and public employee unions—calling them "special interests." Miscalculating that his celebrity status and charismatic appeal translated into political power with respect to whatever policies he endorsed, he attempted to lead "the people" in a populist movement by calling a special election and endorsing a slate of propositions, his reform agenda, to amend state law and the state constitution. The propositions called for increasing K–12 teacher tenure requirements, restricting the use of public employee union dues for political campaign contributions, imposing state budgetary spending limits, and mandating mid-decade legislative redistricting. California voters rejected them all, and Schwarzenegger saw his approval rating among voters drop from 65 percent in 2004 to under 40 percent in 2005. In 2006, the Republican governor, anticipating the November 2006 gubernatorial election, changed course again—abandoning the confrontational ideology of the right wing in favor of striking deals with the Democratic majority in the legislature. Schwarzenegger signed bills to raise the minimum wage, force pharmaceutical companies to offer discounts to people without adequate insurance, cap greenhouse gas emissions, increase education funding, and install a "million solar roofs" on California homes and businesses. He struck a compromise with the legislative Democrats to place large board measures on the November 2006 ballot in support of school facilities and repairing California's infrastructure. In so doing, he blunted the criticism of Democratic gubernatorial candidate Phil Angelides and restored his popularity among voters. Schwarzenegger won reelection with 56 percent of the vote.

The plural executive of elected officers is shown in Exhibit 2-5. The lieutenant governor assumes the office of governor in the event of a governor's death or resignation but can also serve as acting governor any time the governor travels out of the state. Unlike the U.S. vice president, California's governor and lieutenant governor are separate elected offices. They are not a team, and the candidates run independent campaigns. The office of lieutenant governor is largely honorific, providing name recognition to a politician who may want to run for governor or other elected office.

The attorney general heads the Department of Justice. This department serves as legal counsel to state government officials and agencies, and assists county district

EXHIBIT 2-5

California's
Plural Executive*

*How many
California executive
officials are directly
elected?*

*How many federal
executive officials
are directly elected?*

Office	Duties and Salary	Incumbent (Party)
Governor	Chief executive officer of the state $206,500	Arnold Schwarzenegger (R)[2]
Lieutenant governor	Minor duties. Becomes chief executive if the governor's office is vacated. $154,875	John Garamendi (D)[1]
Attorney general	Chief law enforcement officer of the state $175,525	Jerry Brown (D)[1]
Secretary of state	Supervises state elections $154,875	Debra Bowen (D)[1]
Controller	Supervises receipts and disbursements of public funds $165,200	John Chiang (D)[1]
Treasurer	State's leading asset manager, banker, and financier $165,200	Bill Lockyer (D)[1]
Insurance commissioner	Supervises the regulation of the insurance industry $165,200	Steve Poizner (R)[1]
Superintendent of public instruction	General oversight of K-12 schools, teacher certification, and student testing. Heads Dept. of Education $175,525	Jack T. O'Connell[†2]
State Board of Equalization (four members by district)	Assures that county property tax assessment practices are equal and uniform throughout the state. Also responsible for collecting sales, cigarette, gasoline, alcohol beverage, and other taxes. $154,875	Betty y. Lee, 1st district (D)[1] Bill Leonard, 2nd district (R)[2] Michelle Steel, 3rd district (R)[1] Judy May Chu, 4th district (D)[1] (The state controller is the *ex officio* fifth member of the Board)

*The voters elect candidates to each of these twelve offices every four years. Officeholders are limited to two four-year terms.
†This is a nonpartisan office.
[1]First term
[2]Second term

attorneys, local law enforcement, and federal and international criminal justice agencies in the administration of justice. Important responsibilities include overseeing state forensic crime labs and central criminal identification services (including the Megan's Law sex offender registry).

The secretary of state is in charge of the state's elections and the chaptering of all new laws upon passage by the legislature and signature of the governor. In addition, the office administers the Safe-at-Home confidential mail program for victims of domestic violence, the California roster of public officials, and the Registry of Domestic Partners.

The controller is the state government's chief financial officer, responsible for all state disbursements (expenditures), conduct of state audits and reports on the state's financial condition, and administration of the payroll systems for state employees—in short, California's chief check-signer. The controller is also a member of the state Board of Equalization, along with four elected officers, elected by district for up to two four-year terms. The Board of Equalization is charged with ensuring the fair assessment, administration, and collection of property and sales taxes.

The treasurer is the state's asset manager, banker, and financier, responsible for all state investments and borrowing, including the financing of major infrastructure improvements such as buildings, highways, and environmental projects.

The insurance commissioner heads the Department of Insurance and regulates the rates and practices of the insurance industry, an important concern of California consumers.

The superintendent of public instruction, the only **nonpartisan** elected executive, heads the Department of Education. Education is a complex function in California with responsibilities divided among many state agencies and between the local, state, and national levels of government. The superintendent of public instruction administers several K–12 education programs including implementation of curriculum standards and statewide testing and accountability assessments.

THE LEGISLATIVE BRANCH

At the national level, the legislative function of formulating and legitimizing public policy is conducted by the U.S. Congress: the Senate and the House of Representatives. These are the only people whom Americans directly elect to national office. In a republic, representation is by geographic district. For the Senate, the geographic districts are the fifty states. Two senators are elected from each state for six-year terms in statewide at-large elections. The U.S. senators currently representing California are Dianne Feinstein and Barbara Boxer. Members of the House of Representatives are elected for two-year terms from political districts within the state. California's congressional delegation is 53 of the 435 seats in the U.S. House of Representatives, with each person representing one of the congressional districts shown in Exhibit 2-6. There are no term limits. Senators and representatives can continue in office as long as the voters in the state or district continue to periodically reelect them.

California's legislature consists of two houses, the assembly and the senate, which, like Congress, must concur on any **bill** in order to enact a new law. The assembly consists of 80 representatives elected by geographic district (see Exhibit 2-7). The state senate consists of 40 representatives elected by a larger geographic district (see Exhibit 2-8). Legislative elections are partisan. Democrats currently outnumber Republicans in both the assembly (48 to 32) and the senate (25 to 15). The overall legislative structure is summarized in Exhibit 2-9. The presiding officer of the assembly is the speaker—elected by the membership of the assembly at the beginning of each

See
color insert,
Exhibit 2-6

See
color insert,
Exhibit 2-7

See
color insert,
Exhibit 2-8

EXHIBIT 2-9		Assembly	Senate
California Legislature	Size	80 members	40 members
	Term of office	2 years	4 years
The **Big Five** *includes the governor, speaker of the assembly, president pro tempore of the state senate, and minority leaders in the assembly and senate. Name these politicians.*	Term limit	3 terms (maximum 6 years)	2 terms (maximum 8 years)
	Presiding officer	Speaker of the assembly	Lieutenant governor*
	Salary	$113,098[†]	$113,098[†]

*In practice, the president pro tempore is the leader and most powerful member of the senate. Elected by all senators at the beginning of each two-year session, the president pro tem chairs the Senate Rules Committee and presides over the senate in the absence of the lieutenant governor.

[†]Salary as of 2007 (set by the California Citizens Compensation Commission). The assembly speaker, senate president pro tempore, and the minority floor leaders of each house each receive $130,062 per year. The majority floor leaders of each house and the second-ranking minority leaders each receive $121,580. Each legislator also receives a daily allowance of $162 while the legislature is in session.

two-year session. Historically, California has a tradition of strong speakers who were just as powerful politically as the governor, such as Jesse Unruh (nine years, 1961–1970) and Willie Brown, an African American legislator from San Francisco, who served thirty-one years in the assembly including fifteen years as speaker (1980–1995). In recent years, leadership power has shifted more to the president pro tempore of the senate. Elected by the senate at the beginning of a two-year session, the president pro tem chairs the senate Rules Committee, a position so powerful that virtually no bill clears the legislature without his or her agreement.

Term Limits

In November 1990, Californians passed Proposition 140, establishing **term limits** for legislators and elected executives. Assembly members may be elected to three consecutive two-year terms (maximum of six years). Senators are limited to two consecutive four-year terms (maximum of eight years). Observers of California politics generally agree that Proposition 140 was a blatant move to oust Democrat Willie Brown as speaker.

A lively debate has ensued about the pros and cons of term limits, especially as the first legislators **termed-out** in the late 1990s. Supporters of term limits present several key arguments. It gets rid of deadwood.[4] It breaks up the relationships among legislators, special interest lobbyists, and governmental agencies. It also gets rid of entrenched legislators, such as Willie Brown, who by their seniority-determined status wield inordinate power. Perhaps without such domineering party influence,

---

[4]"In the time before term limits, California had lawmakers such as (Senator) Ralph Dills (D-Gardena), who was first elected to the Legislature when Franklin Roosevelt was president (1938). . . . He was finally forced from office in 1998, when he was 88 and could barely move around the Senate chambers. If not for term limits, his son was quoted as saying, 'You'd have to blast him out.'" Daniel Weintraub, "Tweaking California's Experiment with Term Limits," *Sacramento Bee*, 20 November 2001. The slogan for Dills's last election campaign was "Too Old to Retire."

legislators would vote their convictions, be more sensitive to public opinion, and be more responsive to their district constituents. Advocates also argue that term limit ensures turnover among legislators—disrupting deal-making with *special* interests, providing more electoral competition, and opening up opportunities for women and minorities. Term-limited legislators should be less susceptible to corruption. Regardless, they would be automatically out in a few years.

Term limit advocates also say that politicians should regard their office as a temporary period of public service rather than a career. Nevertheless, a set of career politicians has emerged. As they are termed-out of one elected office, they campaign for another—rotating through the California legislature and plural executive like a game of musical chairs.

The critics of term limits argue that term limits are inherently antidemocratic. Citizens should take responsibility for their democracy by either keeping politicians in office or voting them out. They also argue that under term limits we will have an inexperienced amateur legislature with less expertise in the legislative process and less institutional memory about previous public policy rationale, including the lessons of successes and failures. Strong party leaders and committee chairpersons cement legislative coalitions, promoting public policy consistency while avoiding fragmentation and dissension. Rather than reducing interest group influence, term-limited legislators are more susceptible to the advice of lobbyists and bureaucrats. Further, legislators will have a propensity for short-term, flash-in-the-pan legislation with less thoughtful policy analysis.

Redistricting

There is only one constitutional function for the census conducted in the United States every ten years, and that is to **reapportion** representation. The number of seats in the House of Representatives is fixed at 435. After Census 2000, California gained one congressional seat due to its increased population. Some states with decreasing population were correspondingly apportioned one or two fewer seats.

Every electoral district within a political jurisdiction must have an equal population. Once every ten years, after the decennial census, the boundaries of every legislative district within the state—congressional, assembly, senate, right down to city and county seats—are redrawn to meet this requirement, a process called **redistricting**. The official Census 2000 population of California was 33,871,648. So each of California's 53 congressional districts had to encompass 639,086 persons; each of the 80 assembly districts, 423,396; and each of the 40 state senate districts, 846,791. Redistricting is in the hands of the state legislature—with a Democratic Party majority. **Incumbent** politicians belonging to the majority party try to maintain a supportive constituency and design legislative districts to their party's advantage in order to win future elections.

Partisan redistricting is an important political act with a long tradition in the United States. It's called **gerrymandering**, after an early practitioner of partisan redistricting, Elbridge Gerry, a signer of the Declaration of Independence and later governor of Massachusetts and vice president under James Madison. Gerrymandering can yield some strange political maps. Examine the maps of California's congressional districts in Exhibit 2-6, assembly districts in Exhibit 2-7, and state senate districts in Exhibit 2-8. The districts were mapped to include neighborhoods where registered voters tend to favor one party or another, while meeting the equal population requirement. This resulted in many strange contortions and little rational relationship to the boundaries of existing cities and counties. Gerrymandering works. California Democrats and Republicans reached an implicit redistricting deal in 2001—to create "safe seats" and maintain the status quo. Thus, in November 2002 and again in November 2004, Californians elected 33 Democrats and 20 Republicans to represent them in Congress, 48 Democrats and 32 Republicans to the assembly, and 25 Democrats and 15 Republicans to the state senate. Every incumbent was reelected, and not a single legislative seat changed from one party to the other. In November 2006, party control of the seats in the legislature remained unchanged while only one congressional district changed party representation as Jerry McNerney (D) defeated Republican incumbent Richard Pombo in the 11th congressional district (Tracy).

This presents a fundamental question: Do Californians really choose their legislative representatives, or are they just being manipulated by the behind-the-scenes leaders of the Democratic and Republican parties? Whatever new political opportunities develop for women and minority legislators are less a result of term limits than a product of legislative redistricting. The 2001 redistricting cemented the status quo of safe Democrat and Republican districts and served to maintain the current demographic makeup of the legislature through the next decade. Latino, Asian American, and African American politicians may be competing against one another in relatively few districts.[5]

THE JUDICIAL BRANCH

See
color insert,
Exhibit 2-10

At the national level, the judicial function is fulfilled by the federal court system (see Exhibit 2-10). The federal courts have jurisdiction with respect to issues of federal law and crimes committed on federal lands. The first, lowest, level of the federal court system is the district trial court. There are four district courts in California that convene in various cities. California is part of the nine-state Ninth Circuit Court of Appeal—one of eleven multistate intermediate circuits. (Another circuit covers only Washington, DC. There are also several specialized courts.) The top rung in the federal judiciary is the U.S. Supreme Court.

The three-level structure of California's judicial system shown in Exhibit 2-11— trial courts, appellate courts, and supreme court—mirrors the federal structure. Trial courts, called superior courts, are located in each county and handle all civil and criminal cases, from small claims and traffic infractions to major civil suits and criminal misdemeanors and felonies. Some cases are appealed and reviewed by the appellate courts. Cases are not retried in the appellate courts. Rather, a panel of judges reviews the trial court record, hears arguments from attorneys, and decides whether appropriate judicial procedure and reasoning was applied in the trial court. The state supreme court is a final opportunity for appellate review. The work of the appellate courts and supreme court is important because their decisions become precedents. The accumulating body of case law precedents is the basis for judicial decisions and interpretations of **statutes** and the state constitution.

Unlike federal judges, who have lifetime appointments upon nomination by the president and confirmation by the U.S. Senate, all judges in California are elected. The system differs between the superior (county trial) courts and the appellate courts. Superior court judges are chosen in nonpartisan elections within each county for six-year terms. There are no term limits. Many judges start their judicial career by appointment by the governor to a vacancy on their county's superior court. Later they run for election to office as incumbents in nonpartisan elections—often unopposed.

---

[5]Dan Walters, "Could Redistricting Further Shrink African American Political Ranks?" *Sacramento Bee*, 23 November 2001.

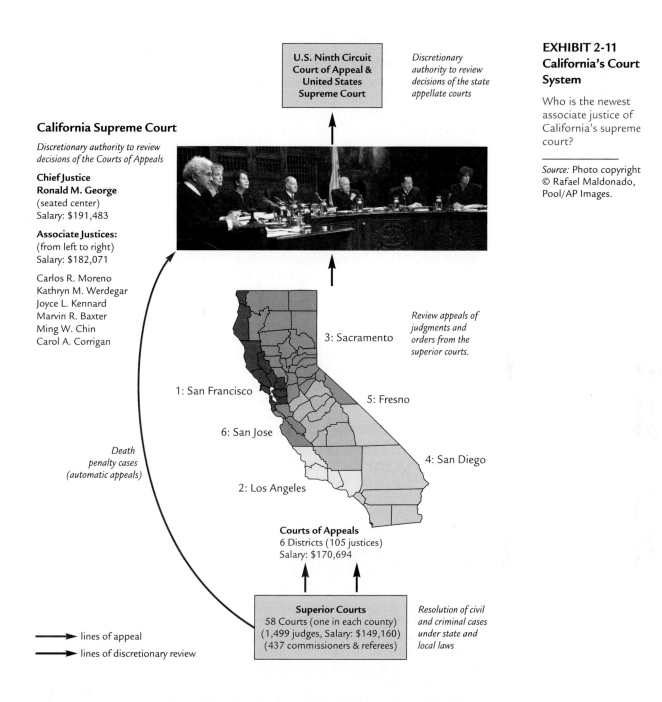

California Supreme Court

Discretionary authority to review decisions of the Courts of Appeals

Chief Justice
Ronald M. George
(seated center)
Salary: $191,483

Associate Justices:
(from left to right)
Salary: $182,071

Carlos R. Moreno
Kathryn M. Werdegar
Joyce L. Kennard
Marvin R. Baxter
Ming W. Chin
Carol A. Corrigan

U.S. Ninth Circuit Court of Appeal & United States Supreme Court

Discretionary authority to review decisions of the state appellate courts

3: Sacramento

1: San Francisco

6: San Jose

5: Fresno

4: San Diego

2: Los Angeles

Review appeals of judgments and orders from the superior courts.

Death penalty cases (automatic appeals)

Courts of Appeals
6 Districts (105 justices)
Salary: $170,694

Superior Courts
58 Courts (one in each county)
(1,499 judges, Salary: $149,160)
(437 commissioners & referees)

Resolution of civil and criminal cases under state and local laws

→ lines of appeal
→ lines of discretionary review

EXHIBIT 2-11 California's Court System

Who is the newest associate justice of California's supreme court?

Source: Photo copyright © Rafael Maldonado, Pool/AP Images.

State supreme court and appellate court vacancies are filled by **gubernatorial** appointments, subject to the approval of the state Commission on Judicial Appointments (composed of the chief justice of the supreme court, the attorney general, and the senior presiding judge on the Court of Appeals). They are then subject to a retention election (citizens vote yes or no as to whether they should continue in office) at the next general election and every twelve years thereafter. For example, in 2005, Governor Arnold Schwarzenegger appointed California Appellate Court Justice Carol A. Corrigan to the California Supreme Court, succeeding Justice Janice Rogers Brown, who was confirmed as a judge of the U.S. Circuit Court of Appeals for the District of Columbia earlier in the year. Justice Corrigan, retained by the voters in November 2006, will serve on the supreme court until another retention election in 2018. While appellate judges attract little public notice and easily win retention, there is an occasional rejection. This happened in 1986, when a majority of voters rejected Chief Justice Rose Bird for reelection on the basis of her consistent opposition to the death penalty. (She believed that the death penalty was applied disproportionately to blacks and other minorities.)

Many counties in California also have collaborative justice courts that specialize in interagency problem solving with respect to certain kinds of crimes and other offenses. These include different kinds of drug courts, domestic violence courts, youth courts, and mental health courts.

The state courts have jurisdiction with respect to issues of state law and crimes committed on all nonfederal land in California. Consider, for example, the case of Cory Stayner. In February 1999, Stayner murdered Carole Sund, 42, of Eureka; her daughter, Julie, 15; and family friend Silvina Pelosso, 16, near Yosemite National Park. Later, in the park, he murdered naturalist Joie Armstrong. He was tried and convicted in federal district court in Fresno of Armstrong's murder, because that crime occurred within the national park. He was tried for the Sund and Pelosso murders in state court.

If state law conflicts with federal law, federal law prevails. This principle was put to the test in 2005 in a case involving the medicinal use of marijuana. California's medical marijuana law, passed by voters in 1996, allows people to grow, smoke, or obtain marijuana for medical needs with a doctor's recommendation. Under the U.S. Constitution, Congress may pass laws regulating a state's economic activity so long as it involves interstate commerce. Although the marijuana in question was homegrown, and distributed to patients without charge and without crossing state lines, the U.S. Supreme Court ruled that Congress may regulate purely local activities if it determines that the total incidence of the activities may have a substantial economic effect on interstate commerce. Thus marijuana, a schedule I drug under the federal Controlled Substances Act, is illegal even for medicinal use.

CALIFORNIA LOCAL GOVERNMENT

Every Californian lives within overlapping jurisdictions of several governments, including county, city, school, and community college districts, and one or more special districts. Executive and legislative responsibilities are in the hands of boards of elected representatives. Local governments do not have judicial responsibilities—these stay with the state court system (the most local level of which is the superior court in each county).

Counties

California has fifty-eight counties. San Francisco is both a city and a county, whereas the city of Los Angeles is a separate entity within Los Angeles County. All counties elect a board of supervisors, sheriff, district attorney, and **assessor**. Day-to-day management of county services is in the hands of a hired professional chief administrative (or executive) officer. All counties provide three types of service: (1) agencies of the state, (2) countywide services, and (3) municipal services. The counties are, in effect, the local administrative arms of state government. They implement required state programs according to state policies, such as health services and social services. Countywide services include the jails, juvenile and adult probation, the offices of the district attorney and assessor (property tax collection), supervision of weights and measures, voter registration and elections, agricultural services (such as agricultural pest control), and optional services such as libraries. Counties also provide municipal-type services in areas outside of city limits, including fire protection, law enforcement (sheriff), road maintenance, and parks.

Cities

California has 478 **cities**. Most cities have a **council-manager** form of government. An elected five (or more)-member council is the policy-making authority of the city. The city council hires a city manager—a professional administrator who functions as the city's chief executive officer, overseeing all city departments. In some cities, council members compete in **at-large** citywide, nonpartisan elections. In other cities, council members represent political districts within the city. A city's mayor is usually elected at-large and serves as the presiding officer at city council meetings and as the official head of the city for legislative and ceremonial purposes. There is no statewide uniformity in the pay of city council members or mayors. City council pay can range from a few hundred dollars to over $40,000. Mayoral pay can range from a few thousand dollars to $100,000 or more.

Some of the largest cities in California (such as Los Angeles, San Francisco, and Oakland) have a **strong-mayor** form of government. In this form of government, the at-large elected mayor fulfills a management and policy role analogous to that of the president or governor—the political leader and the chief executive of the city (see Exhibit 2-12).

Special Districts

Special districts are local governments, separate from cities and counties, that provide services within a specified region. This area can range from a few acres with only a few thousand people to thousands of square miles and millions of people. California has more than 4,700 special districts. Over 80 percent are *single-function* districts, which provide only one service such as firefighting, library services, water delivery, waste disposal, mosquito abatement, or flood control. The rest are *multifunction* districts. For example, several *municipal utility* districts provide fire protection and

City	Mayor	EXHIBIT 2-12
Los Angeles	Antonio Villaraigosa	**Mayors: California's Largest Cities**
San Francisco	Gavin Newsom	
San Diego	Jerry Sanders	
Sacramento	Heather Fargo	*Which mayors are former legislators?*
San Jose	Ron Gonzales	
Oakland	Ronald V. Dellums	
Fresno	Alan Autry	

park services in addition to utility services. Fire protection districts often provide ambulance services, too. County Service Areas can provide a general range of municipal-type services. There are two types of governing structures for special districts. *Independent* special districts have their own elected governing boards. About two-thirds of special districts are independent. A county board of supervisors (or sometimes a city council) serves as the governing board for *dependent* special districts. Cemetery, Fire Protection, and Community Services Districts are mostly independent, whereas County Service Areas and Maintenance Districts are typically dependent.

About 30 percent of special districts are *enterprise* districts that operate facilities and provide services such as airports, electric utilities, harbors and ports, hospitals, transit, waste disposal, and water utility on a pay-as-you-go basis, much like businesses. *Nonenterprise* districts provide general benefits to entire communities or regions, such as fire or flood protection, libraries, cemeteries, and road maintenance, that do not lend themselves to user fees. They rely primarily on property taxes for their funding.

The "traffic cops" for this mélange of city, county, and special district government are the fifty-seven Local Agency Formation Commissions (one in each county except San Francisco). **LAFCO** membership is usually composed of two county supervisors selected by the Board of Supervisors, two city council representatives selected by a majority of the mayors in the county, two members representing special districts within the county, and one member of the public, selected by the other members. They regulate, through approval or denial, the boundary changes proposed by other public agencies or individuals. Typical applicants might include homeowners requesting annexation to a sewer district due to failing septic tanks; developers seeking annexation to cities in order to have water, sewer, and other municipal services extended to new housing and businesses; cities wishing to annex land for development or to consolidate county islands within the city; and special districts or cities seeking to consolidate two or more governmental agencies.

WEB LINKS

Federal Government—General
FedWorld: links to U.S. federal government **www.fedworld.gov**
FirstGov: a clearinghouse of links to the U.S. federal government **www.firstgov.com**
Thomas: U.S. Congress legislative information **thomas.loc.gov/**
United States Supreme Court **www.supremecourtus.gov/**

State and Local Government—General
Council of State Governments **www.csg.org**
International City/County Management Association **www.icma.org**
National Association of Counties **www.naco.org**
National Conference of State Legislatures **www.ncsl.org**
U.S. Conference of Mayors **www.usmayors.org**

California State Government
California courts **www.courtinfo.ca.gov**
California State Assembly **www.assembly.ca.gov**

California State Senate **www.sen.ca.gov**

Governor **www.governor.ca.gov/**

Governor's Gallery—a brief biography, official portrait, inaugural addresses, selected facts, and timeline of events in California, the United States, and the world **www.governor.ca.gov/govsite/govsgallery/h/index.html**

Governors of California **www.infospect.com/Governors.htm**

Legislative information **leginfo.public.ca.gov/**

State of California **www.ca.gov/**

California Local Government

California Association of Local Agency Formation Commissions **www.calafco.org/**

California Political Daily: news and views about California public policy, politics, and government—updated throughout the day **www.calpday.com**

California State Association of Counties **www.csac.counties.org/**

League of California Cities **www.cacities.org/**

Rough and Tumble: a daily online digest of newspaper articles relevant to California politics and government **www.rtumble.com**

PUBLICATIONS

Cannon, Lou. 2003. *Governor Reagan: His Rise to Power.* New York: Public Affairs.

Governing Magazine. **www.governing.com**

Rarick, Ethan. 2005. *California Rising: The Life and Times of Pat Brown.* Berkeley: University of California Press.

GLOSSARY

assessor   The government official responsible for determining the value of property.

at-large (local election)   The process by which every voter votes for as many candidates as there are seats to fill on the local governing board.

authority   The legitimate (by law or constitution) exercise of power.

bill   A proposed law introduced in either the assembly or the state senate.

city   The principal type of local government for an urbanized area.

council-manager (form of government)   A structure of government in which an elected board (such as a city council or county board of supervisors) performs legislative policy-making and oversight functions, and hires a professional manager as the chief executive officer to manage ongoing governmental activity.

democracy (representative democracy)   A system of government in which citizens participate directly by voting on proposed policies or indirectly by voting for representatives. See *republic.*

district (electoral or political)   A designated geographic area, the inhabitants of which elect a representative.

federalism   The legal/political/economic relationship in the United States between the states and the national government. The states and national government are separate sovereign entities. In general, they have different jurisdictions and responsibilities.

gerrymandering (partisan)   The drawing of electoral district lines in accordance with the known pattern of party registration of the population. Gerrymandered districts often have an elongated shape that does not correspond to existing jurisdictions or geographic features. Gerrymandering is an attempt to enhance the future electoral chances of one party versus another.

gubernatorial   A reference to the office of the state governor—for example, a *gubernatorial* election.

incumbent   The person who currently holds a public office by election or appointment.

jurisdiction   (1) The subject-matter authority of a governmental agency. (2) The geographic region within which a governmental entity has authority.

LAFCO   Local Agency Formation Commission. A regulatory agency within each county established to discourage urban sprawl and encourage the orderly formation and development of cities and other local government agencies. It must approve proposed boundary changes to cities and special districts.

mandate   A required action imposed on a unit of government by a higher level of government.

nonpartisan   Not affiliated with a political party.

plural executive   The process by which the executive power in California government is divided among several elected constitutional offices. In addition to the governor, Californians elect a lieutenant governor, attorney general, secretary of state, controller, treasurer, insurance commissioner, superintendent of public instruction, and Board of Equalization.

policy   (1) A statement of intended action; a prescriptive rule for behavior. A policy can usually be summarized as an if-then-else statement. If situation A exists, then B will be the response, or else C will be done. (2) A general statement of purpose or intent; a goal or a mission.

policy areas   A general subject-matter field of governmental jurisdiction and authority.

reapportion (reapportionment)   The process by which, after each U.S. census, the number of people in each election district (congressional, state, and local) is recalculated. The total population within the jurisdiction is divided by the number of representatives (districts). This is the principle of one person, one vote. See *redistrict*.

redistrict (redistricting)   The process by which, after each U.S. census, the boundary lines defining each election district (congressional, state, and local) are redrawn so that each district will have the same number of people as determined by the reapportionment calculation. See *reapportion*.

republic   A system of government in which citizens choose representatives to act on their behalf in accordance with a constitution. See *democracy*.

sovereign   Having independent authority.

special district   A type of local government that provides specific public services (such as fire protection, sewers, water supply, or street lighting) within a designated geographic area.

statute   A law. A bill becomes a statute after it is passed by both houses of the legislature and is signed (or neither signed nor vetoed) by the governor.

strong-mayor (form of government)   A structure of city government in which an elected representative (the mayor) also serves as the chief executive officer.

term limit   The maximum number of terms of office that a representative may serve. The term limits for the California legislature are two four-year terms for a state senator and three two-year terms for a state assembly member.

termed-out   The situation in which a representative has completed the maximum number of terms of office and therefore may not be a candidate for that office in the next election.

unitary form of government   The government principle that a level of government has only such power and authority as granted it by a higher level of government.

SUGGESTED ANSWERS TO EXHIBIT QUESTIONS

Exhibit 2-1: There are about *twice* as many K–12 school districts as cities in California.

Exhibit 2-2: Federal government: national parks, food and drug regulations, national defense, college loans; California state government: colleges and universities, state highways; local governments: streets, water, sewer, and garbage services, libraries, police and fire services.

Exhibit 2-3: Approximately 100 agencies are listed in this figure. The California State University is one of the Education Policy Boards. The Franchise Tax Board is in the State and Consumer Affairs Agency. The Employment Development Department is in the Health and Human Services Agency. The Department of Motor Vehicles and the California Highway Patrol are in the Business, Transportation, and Housing Agency. The Department of Parks and Recreation is in the Resources Agency. California's Environmental Protection Agency and Resources Agency both have major responsibility for dealing with the environment. Education is addressed by the Department of Education headed by the elected superintendent of public instruction, the governor-appointed secretary of education, and several independent boards and commissions.

Exhibit 2-4: Among recent California governors, Gray Davis had the shortest term in office; Earl Warren had the longest.

Exhibit 2-5: Eight California executive officials are directly elected. No federal executive officials are directly elected.

Exhibit 2-9: In 2006, the *Big Five* included Governor Arnold Schwarzenegger, Speaker of the California Assembly Fabian Núñez (D-Los Angeles), President pro tempore of the state Senate Don Perata (D-East Bay), Assembly minority leader George Plescia (R-San Diego), and Senate minority leader Dick Ackerman (R-Tustin).

Exhibit 2-11: Carol Corrigan is the newest associate justice of California's supreme court.

Exhibit 2-12: Ronald Dellums represented the Oakland area in Congress from 1971 to 1998. He succeeds Jerry Brown, a former California governor. Antonio Villaraigosa, the first Latino mayor of Los Angeles since 1872, represented the 45th district in the assembly from 1994 to 2000 (the term limit maximum), including serving as speaker from 1997 to 2000.

CHAPTER THREE

ELECTIONS

Vote, and the choice is yours. Don't vote, and the choice is theirs.[1]

To be free is to have choices—to have the opportunity to choose among competing candidates or alternative courses of action. Voting in elections is the way citizens make choices in a representative democracy. We choose representatives from among competing candidates, and in California, we vote *for* or *against* various policy propositions.

But do elections really present choices? Do elections matter? This chapter examines the election contest in terms of political parties, types of elections, campaigns, voting, and the nature of our participation.

POLITICAL PARTIES

Two major political parties, the **Democrats** and the **Republicans**, dominate American politics at the state and national levels. Every California state legislator, every California elected executive official,[2] and every congressional representative from California (186 offices altogether) is either a Democrat or a Republican, and the same applies to over 99 percent of the approximately 8,000 other state and national elected offices in the United States. A **political party** is an organization that nominates and supports candidates for elected office who will pursue policies consistent with that organization's espoused beliefs, **interests**, and **ideology** about public affairs. Political parties exist in a representative democracy for essentially two reasons. First, people fundamentally disagree with respect to social and economic values; these attitudes are generally summarized as **liberal** or **conservative** outlooks and are referred to as the "left" and the "right," respectively. A party helps people with similar interests and values act together to affect government and potentially gain the government's support for their common goals. A party organization provides the needed advocacy, representation, and cooperation. Second, political parties exist

---

[1] A common get-out-the-vote slogan.
[2] With the one exception of California's superintendent of public instruction.

because of the election "rules of the game." The rule is single-member-district **plurality voting,** winner-take-all. There is only one elected representative from each district, and *whoever gets the most votes wins*. This effectively sets up a contest between two major competitors and encourages voters to coalesce into two groups—parties—each sponsoring a candidate. Any third minor candidate draws support away from one or both of the others. Over time, a third party, always losing, will either remain a minor player or disappear as its discouraged supporters drift to one of the major parties (the wasted-vote syndrome). Unlike the proportional representation systems that are common to many other democracies, in which legislative seats are allocated by the percentage of the total vote, the losers get nothing.

The Republican Party is generally regarded as being in sympathy with people having a conservative outlook. However, there is a difference between *traditional* conservatives and the *New Right* or *Religious Right*. The New Right emphasizes moral issues, such as opposition to abortion and homosexuality, and advocates family values. Traditional conservatives focus on economic and social order issues—less government regulation, lower taxes, less spending for welfare and social programs, increases in military spending, growth of the private sector of the economy, and encouragement of more self-reliance and less dependence on government services.

The Democratic Party is not the ideological opposite of the Republicans. Instead of a *liberal* policy agenda, it is best characterized as having a coalition of interests that responds to women, African Americans, Latinos, union members, and the poor and middle class, as well as a general expectation that government programs can beneficially address societal problems.

Qualified political parties can automatically place candidates on the ballot for statewide elections. A party becomes qualified by having one of its candidates obtain at least 2 percent of the vote in a statewide election, or by having at least 1 percent of the statewide voter registration (and maintaining one-fifteenth of 1 percent of the statewide registration), or by submitting a petition signed by at least 10 percent of the number of voters in the previous gubernatorial election. California's five qualified minor parties—the American Independent Party, the Green Party, the Libertarian Party, the Peace and Freedom Party, and the Natural Law Party—are listed in Exhibit 3-1.

Qualified Party	Website	Percent of Registered Voters[†]
Democratic Party*	www.cadem.org	42.7%
Republican Party*	www.cagop.org	34.7
American Independent Party*	www.aipca.org	2.0
Green Party	www.cagreens.org	1.0
Libertarian Party	www.ca.lp.org	0.5
Peace and Freedom Party	www.peaceandfreedom.org	0.4
Natural Law Party	www.natural-law.org	0.2
Decline to state		18.2
Other		0.5

15,837,108 registered voters in October 2006—70 percent of the 22,652,190 Californians eligible to vote.
[†]Does not total exactly 100 percent due to rounding.
*These parties allow "Decline to state" voters to participate in their primary election.
Source: California secretary of state.

EXHIBIT 3-1

Qualified Political Parties in California

What percent of California voters decline to state a party or declare a third-party affiliation?

They advocate a variety of ideological positions, including less government regulation, environmentalism, rational decision making, fiscal responsibility, social justice, and opposition to war. Their principal function is to add their voice to ongoing policy debates. If one of their policy proposals begins to garner public support, it usually is taken up by the Democrats or Republicans seeking an electoral edge on the opposition. They currently have no one elected to California state or national office, although once in a while one of their adherents is elected to a nonpartisan local government office.

TYPES OF ELECTIONS

The political world works on two-year **election cycles**. In even-numbered years, all eighty California assembly seats, half of the forty state senate seats, and all of the U.S. House of Representatives seats are up for election. The governor of California and the president of the United States are elected in alternate election cycles. Presidential elections occur during leap years (years divisible by 4: 2004, 2008, 2012), and California gubernatorial elections are scheduled at the presidential midterm (2002, 2006, 2010). During each even-numbered year, there are two statewide elections: (1) a **primary election** in June and (2) a **general election** in November. Elections for local government offices may coincide with a general election or may be scheduled in an off year (that is, an odd-numbered year).

Primary Elections

A primary election has three purposes. The basic purpose is to narrow the field of candidates so that voters will have a clear choice in the November general election. In most of the world's democracies, partisan nominations are controlled by the party organizations. Party stalwarts choose the candidates behind closed doors in proverbial smoke-filled rooms. However, in California and most of the rest of the United States, voters choose party nominees in a primary election. Voters choose a political party at the time they register to vote (their party registration). The candidate of each political party who receives the most votes for a state elective office becomes that party's nominee for the November general election.

California currently has a *closed* primary election. In order to vote in the primary election for partisan offices, a voter must have identified a political party affiliation when registering to vote and can vote only for candidates of that party. If a voter declines to state a political party when registering, that voter is considered unaffiliated. In California, the American Independent, the Democratic, the Republican, and the Natural Law parties have agreed to let unaffiliated voters, if they wish, vote for their candidates. Otherwise, unaffiliated voters may vote only for candidates to nonpartisan offices and for initiative measures.

California's congressional, assembly, and state senate districts have been gerrymandered to virtually guarantee continuity by the Democratic and Republican parties. Political competition is more likely to occur in a primary election than in a general election. The winner of the primary in a safe-seat district does not have to worry about losing the general election. Relatively unknown politicians, seeking legislative or congressional office, need to compete within one of the major parties rather than attempting to form a third party. In order to organize support, gain recognition, and possibly win access to the general election ballot, a challenger may appeal to his or her party's strongest wing rather than the moderate center, reinforcing extremist rather than centrist, common-ground, compromise policy positions.

The second purpose of a primary is as an election venue for state and local non-partisan offices using the single-member-district with a runoff rule, called a two-round system (TRS). In a multicandidate election, anyone who receives a majority (more than 50 percent of the vote) in the first election (usually the primary election) wins the office. If no candidate receives a majority, a runoff is held (at the general election) between the top two vote getters.

The third purpose of a primary, in presidential election years, is to enable the parties to narrow the field of candidates to one candidate per party. They do this by having voters who are registered with the party choose delegates to a national party nominating convention. Each state has a certain number of delegates, proportional to its population. The Democratic Party allocates delegates two ways: Some are superdelegates, party officials who support the candidate of their choice; the rest are allocated to candidates in accordance with that candidate's share of the state's primary vote. Republicans use the winner-take-all rule. To win the party's nomination, a candidate needs a majority of the convention delegates. Primaries early in the presidential election year are important because they generate media coverage and are seen as a test of a candidate's electability. Primaries in large states such as California are important because they have clout in the delegate count. By June, the outcome is known, and the national party convention becomes a media event and political rally, kicking off the final presidential campaign toward the November general election.

General Elections

California voters choose their legislative representatives and executive officials in the biennial November general election. California has a long ballot. In addition to the state legislative and executive contests and congressional candidates, a general election ballot will include dozens of local government races, bond issue measures, and propositions. In the 2008 and 2012 general elections, the presidential election will be at the top of the ballot. In 2006 and 2010 (at the presidential midterm), the banner event is California's gubernatorial election. Other elected offices and propositions are "down-ballot" races.

There are interesting features to a presidential election from the state perspective. For starters, individual voters do not vote for the president of the United States. Nor is there only one presidential election every four years—there are fifty-one. The U.S. Constitution specifies that the president will be elected by electors chosen state by state (and also the District of Columbia). Each state is allocated a number of electoral votes equal to the size of its congressional delegation—its number of representatives in the House of Representatives and its two U.S. senators. There are 538 electors in total—the electoral college. The smallest states in population have three electoral votes; California, the largest state, has fifty-five. California, like nearly every other state, specifies that electors (nominated by the qualified political parties in the state) will be chosen in a winner-takes-all general election and consequently will vote as a block, with all the electoral votes of a state going to only one candidate (party).[3] Each political party has its own method for selecting presidential electors. In California's Democratic Party, the most recent party nominees for each congressional district and for each U.S. Senate seat are accorded the privilege of naming one Democratic Party elector. In California's Republican Party, the electors are the party leaders (the most recent party nominees for governor, lieutenant governor, treasurer, controller, attorney general, secretary of state, and U.S. Senate; the

---

[3]All states except Maine and Nebraska have a winner-takes-all system for electors. In those states, electoral votes are awarded proportionately.

state senate and assembly party leaders; elected officers of the state central committee; state party representatives to the national committee; and others).[4] The other political parties in the state pick their slates of electors at a nominating convention.[5] Shortly after the November election, the governor and secretary of state issue an official Certificate of Ascertainment to the National Archives and Records Administration (whose Office of the Federal Register administers the electoral college) naming the block of electors that won California's popular vote for president. In December, the electors representing the winning party assemble in the senate chambers of the state capitol in Sacramento to ceremoniously cast their votes for president and vice president.[6] The results are reported to the U.S. Senate in the form of an official Certificate of Vote. In January, the Congress meets in joint session to count the electoral votes and declare the president.[7]

Local Elections

There are approximately 20,000 local elected positions in California requiring about 5,000–10,000 elections in any given year. All local government elected officials, unlike state and national offices, are nonpartisan. This means that the ballot does not list the party affiliation of a candidate, and candidates receive no party funds for their campaigns. Local elections for school board, special district, city council, and county board of supervisors may use a couple of voting rules. Some jurisdictions elect governing board members by district or by designated seat using the two-round system.[8] Governing councils elected at large often use the multimember-district plurality rule, also called the "block vote" (BV). If there are N seats to be filled, each voter can vote for N people among the list of candidates on the ballot. The top N vote getters win.

Special Elections

A local government may occasionally schedule a **special election**—for example, to fill a vacant elected office or to vote on a local measure such as a bond issue and a regularly scheduled primary or general election is months away. The governor may also call a special election when an initiative has qualified for the ballot. California has had only eight statewide special elections since World War II, but two recent ones are of particular interest.

Soon after Gray Davis was reelected as governor in 2002, his popularity plummeted as the state's budget deficit climbed into the $30- to $40-billion range, and Californians faced an energy crisis with electricity outages. An antitax interest group

---

[4]No senator, or representative, or person holding an office of trust or profit under the United States can serve as an elector.

[5]The Libertarian and Natural Law parties specify a 50-50 ratio of men to women among electors.

[6]California law requires that electors vote for their party's candidate. In 1900, a so-called faithless elector in California voted for William Jennings Bryan when the state voted for William McKinley. Electors are paid $10 plus 5¢ per mile for the round trip from their homes to Sacramento.

[7]If no candidate receives a majority of the electoral college vote, the House of Representatives votes, with each state having a single vote, for the president. This happened a couple of times in the 1800s. For more information on the electoral college, see California Secretary of State, **www.ss.ca.gov**, and National Archives and Records Administration, **www.nara.gov/fedreg/elctcoll**

[8]Some jurisdictions are considering adopting the **instant runoff voting (IRV)** system. IRV allows voters to rank candidates as their first, second, third, and fourth choices and so on. If a candidate does not receive a clear majority of votes on the first count using each voter's top choice indicated on the ballot, a runoff count is conducted. The candidate who received the fewest first-place ballots is eliminated. The votes for the eliminated candidate are redistributed to each voter's second-choice candidate. All ballots are then recounted. This process continues until one candidate receives a majority; **www.fairvote.org/irv/**

initiated a recall of Davis. The recall petition and election, one of the good-government direct-democracy reforms in the early twentieth century (along with the lawmaking petition initiative), allows voters to remove and replace a state or local elected official midterm. The proponents of a recall are required to file a formal notice of intent and, within a specified time, obtain a certain number of signatures of registered voters. The signature requirements and time deadline vary by the office and the size of the district. If they succeed, obtaining what is called "certification of sufficiency," two questions are presented to the voters: (1) whether to remove the incumbent officeholder, and (2) who should replace that person. The recall effort languished until a well-heeled Republican, Darrell Issa (a congressman from the San Diego area who made his fortune in car alarms), reinvigorated things with a $500,000 infusion and the pledge of further funding. The Issa-funded petition drive—needing 900,000 valid signatures of registered voters—succeeded, and Davis scheduled a fall 2003 special election.

Every year there are several recall elections at the local government level, and once in a while a recall effort against a state legislator will reach the ballot. Prior to 2003, no recall drive had ever secured enough signatures to force a recall election for the governor or other statewide official. Davis lost the recall vote, and his successor, Arnold Schwarzenegger, was elected in a winner-takes-all contest among more than a hundred candidates. The 2003 recall special election showed the dominant influence of nominally Democratic Los Angeles County. Low voter turnout in the county was the key factor in Davis's defeat and the succession of Schwarzenegger.

Schwarzenegger called another special election in fall 2005 in order to advance a reform agenda of four propositions. The initiatives would have increased K–12 teacher tenure requirements (Proposition 74), restricted the use of public employee union dues for political campaign contributions (Proposition 75), set state budgetary spending limits (Proposition 76), and required middecade legislative redistricting (Proposition 77). Four other propositions regarding parental notification for abortions by minors (Proposition 73), prescription drugs (Propositions 78 and 79), and electric industry regulation (Proposition 80) were also on the 2005 ballot. Californians rejected all eight initiatives.

CAMPAIGNS

Suppose you have a yen for public service, envision a better state of affairs, and want to be at the center of the action and affect public policy. Then throw your hat in the ring as a candidate for public office. Why not? We need people of good will and good ideas in public office, and we can vote only for the candidates who are on the ballot. Placing your name on the ballot is fairly easy, and you can be a lot more influential as an elected official than at home.

Where do you start? If you want to get involved in public service, a good place to start is by getting appointed to a committee. There are dozens of voluntary advisory committees, commissions, boards, councils, and task forces in every city and county. They do important work and can give you invaluable experience and insight to government. You don't need party affiliation. All local government offices in California are nonpartisan. The city councils of small cities and seats on school boards and other special districts come closest to the ideal of representative democracy— public-spirited citizens putting forth their names as community leaders.

Okay, you have common sense and good ideas. You are interested in your community, and you have the support and encouragement of your friends and family.

You decide to run. Now you need to get elected. It is one thing to have good ideas based on relevant experience; it is quite another to get elected, and the first duty of a politician is to get elected.[9] All your good intentions are for naught if you don't win. How do you motivate people to vote for you rather than someone else? The formula is simple. To win you need:

- Name recognition
- Favorable reputation based on relevant experience
- Money—to spread your name and reputation so that enough voters will be motivated to place their vote next to your name on the election ballot

Sound like marketing and advertising? It is—except now it's called a **campaign**. The campaign needs to be planned and under way even before your first public action: taking out papers, that is, going to the city or county clerk's office and filing a declaration of candidacy.[10]

The first thing to do is make a self-assessment gut check. Ask yourself *why* you are seeking this office, and come up with a short, straightforward answer that makes sense and can potentially resonate with voters. Do you have relevant experience and something to contribute—some good ideas, both general and specific? Are you comfortable and basically articulate in public speaking? Can you think on your feet? Can you take criticism? Are you persistent, or are you easily discouraged? Can you tolerate potentially losing? Do you like meeting people—lots of people? Are you trustworthy? Who will vote for you—who is your *base* vote? Who is your *swing* vote—who can be persuaded to vote for you? Do you have any skeletons in your closet? Can you and your family afford the stress—financially, physically, emotionally, and in time away from family and job? Now try to assess your chances of winning: How widely are you known in the community? What is your reputation? Do you know any local movers and shakers or party leaders who might encourage, support, and endorse you? Voters are motivated by contrast—how do you differ from the other candidates? Will an incumbent be running again, or is this an open seat?

Second, develop a campaign plan. This is a fairly detailed schedule of what you will do between now and election day to make yourself known to district voters. The voters have competing choices between candidates and policy alternatives. Your job is to give them a favorable choice. You are not going to do this alone. Campaigning is a team effort. So you should sketch out a basic campaign organization, including a campaign manager, volunteer coordinator, and treasurer. Here are a few (and by no means exhaustive) basic elements of a campaign:

- *Develop a thirty-second sound bite and quotable quote.* Write, memorize, and practice a one-sentence sound bite about the key issue in the campaign and a slightly longer three-minute statement saying who you are, why you are running, and what you stand for.

---

[9]This adage is perhaps derived from Senator Everett McKinley Dirksen's Three Laws of Politics: "Get elected. Get reelected. Don't get mad, get even." Its corollary might be "The problem with political jokes is that they get elected" (Henry Cate).

[10]Once in a while you'll hear of a candidate who placed his or her name on the ballot almost as a lark, then kicked back, did nothing, and woke up the day after the election to find—much to his or her surprise—that they had won. This doesn't happen often.

- *Walk precincts.* It is one of the basics. Although this is inefficient in terms of time, it gives you a sense of the mood of the voters and the important issues. And you want to encourage the word-of-mouth reputation that you seek out and engage voters one on one in order to ask for their vote.

- *Make the rounds.* Meet opinion leaders, such as newspaper editorial boards, elected officials, League of Women Voters members, and civic clubs. Meet the people you will affect if elected, such as schoolteachers, farmers and growers, bureaucrats, small business owners, builders, and people on public assistance. Ask questions and listen to the answers.

- *Obtain campaign materials and media buys.* Large street signs, smaller yard signs, flyers, mailers, radio and cable TV and newspaper ads, Internet Websites, and direct mail flyers are necessary and expensive. Buy a line in an appropriate **slate mailer**—a type of direct mail campaign literature that endorses a set of candidates—a slate—for different public offices. A slate mailer might be prepared by an interest group, a political party, a few candidates pooling their resources and endorsing themselves, or a for-profit company seeking to make money from the election by, in effect, selling advertising space.

- *Take advantage of free media,* such as radio and cable TV call-in talk shows and newspaper interviews. Feed the media. Let them know what's going on.

- *Seek out elderly voters.* They often have nearly 100 percent voter turnout.

- *Raise funds.* People will want to support you, and financial contributions are a tangible expression of that support.

- *Attend candidate nights and debates.* Here, the most important member of the audience is the reporter who is writing the story for the next day's newspaper.

- *Tap absentee ballots.* An increasing number of people prefer to vote by absentee ballot rather than go to a polling place. If you encourage this, you may be able to bank a lot of votes before election day.

- *Open a bank account.* Keep careful records of contributions and expenditures. Carefully check local and state laws and regulations about campaign contributions and reporting requirements. Meet all the campaign filing and accounting deadlines.

Third, get some endorsements. An **endorsement** is a formal public statement of approval and support for a political candidate or ballot measure. Although the precise impact of endorsements is unknown, endorsements are often viewed as a political barometer of the breadth of support. An early endorsement from a respected source can inform the public and influence public opinion. For a relatively unknown candidate, an endorsement can enhance name recognition and signal potential electability. In an era of decreasing party line voting, endorsements can provide useful interest-oriented cross-party recommendations for various races—particularly those that get little attention from the media. It can be a news event, providing free publicity for the candidate as well as the endorser. Endorsements just before election day encourage and reinforce supporters. Many candidates subscribe to a slate mailer or publish an endorsement ad in the local newspaper containing a long list of residents who have pledged their vote.

CAMPAIGN FINANCE

"Money is the mother's milk of politics."[11]

Campaigns cost money. No candidate likes to continuously ask for money. But you have to plan a campaign budget and raise funds. Getting even basic information to voters requires advertisements, signs, and printing and distribution of campaign literature. A starting rule-of-thumb is that a campaign for a local government office will cost at least $1–2 per registered voter. So where does the money come from?

Sources of Funding

In 1992, Joan Darrah spent $130,000 in her campaign for reelection as mayor of Stockton. About $90,000 came from donors; relatives contributed $19,000; $15,000 was borrowed and repaid by subsequent fund-raising events; and the remaining $7,000 was her own money. The largest expenditure, nearly 40 percent, was for printing and targeted direct mail. About 10 percent went toward signs and media advertising, 10 percent to a campaign consultant, 15 percent to pollsters, 20 percent to salary and benefits for her campaign and volunteer coordinators, and 5 percent to the elections office for a statement in the voter pamphlet and voter lists.[12]

The nonpartisan campaigns for offices in larger cities or for county offices will have higher budgets and a paid campaign manager. For state partisan offices, the stakes are still higher, and the campaigns more costly. Interests begin to take a real interest. To have a real chance of winning requires significant financial support from a political party and interest contributors. Primary and general election campaign expenditures for a California legislative or congressional seat or one of California's statewide plural executive offices will be in the millions of dollars, and gubernatorial and U.S. Senate campaigns in the tens of millions.

The money is used to contact, inform, and win voters. In statewide campaigns, most of the campaign budget will be spent for media buys (television, radio, and newspaper advertisements) and direct mail advertisements. Campaign management (including the candidate's paid staff, campaign consultants, and public opinion polling) are smaller but still significant costs.

Elections are contests. Winning matters. Winning candidates become decision makers who will influence the laws and governmental actions that affect our lives. Political contributors want a winner who will represent their values and promote their preferred public policies. The purpose of campaign contributions is not enrichment. It is to obtain influence. Thus a politician basically has two constituencies: (1) voters who live in the district and (2) contributors who fund the campaign. Contributors are well-to-do individuals, interest groups, businesses, and, for partisan offices, the Democratic and Republican parties (and more specifically, the party leaders). Why do these people donate money? Are they merely public spirited? To contributors the return can be worth many times the amount of the contribution. They are making an investment—an investment in a person who will be sympathetic to their concerns, who will pay attention to them, and who will give careful consideration to their proposals. It's not a bribe. They are buying access and understanding—a sympathetic and potentially receptive outlook on governmental actions and public policy.

---

[11]Jesse Unruh, speaker, California Assembly, 1961–1968.

[12]Joan Darrah with Alice Crozier, *Getting Political: Stories of a Woman Mayor* (Sanger, CA: Quill Driver Books, 2002).

There is a lot of money invested in California state politics. During the 1997–1998 election cycle, in which California held gubernatorial, statewide executive, and state legislative races, $296 million was contributed to California state office candidates (about $120 million to all gubernatorial candidates, $100 million to legislative races, and the balance to candidates for other statewide offices). Another $81.2 million was contributed to California congressional candidates; $192.9 million went to support or oppose the various propositions that were on the 1998 ballot ($92 million in support of and opposition to Proposition 5, Tribal Casinos, alone).

Candidates for the legislature or other statewide office get most of their campaign money from three sources:

- Democratic and Republican parties
- Businesses (and associated political action committees)
- Labor union political action committees

A **political action committee (PAC)** is an organization that receives money and distributes campaign donations on behalf of a political interest. Labor contributions tend to be concentrated in a few PACs. Business contributions, although more than double those of labor in total, tend to be individually smaller and from many different industries (such as communications/electronics, tobacco, insurance, and agriculture). Small contributions (less than $200) from voters amount to less than 1 percent of the total. For major contributors, political contributions are generally good investments.

The analysis of California legislative and congressional campaigns allows us to state a few political axioms.

Gerrymandering creates safe seats. In the November 2004 general election, all 80 assembly, 20 state senate, and 53 congressional seats were on California ballots. Every incumbent candidate won, and no congressional or legislative seat changed parties.

Money follows power. Incumbents get money. Incumbents spend money. Money wins elections. Incumbent candidates significantly outspend challengers, and the winners outspend the losers by a large margin. Over time, the spending differential between winners and losers has increased—in both absolute dollars and spending ratio. The graphs in Exhibit 3-2 show the expenditures in races for the California Assembly from 1976 to 1998. In 1976, assembly winners outspent assembly losers by a ratio of less than 3 to 1. By the late 1990s, the ratio was approximately 14 to 1.

Legislators "dance with the one that brought them." A review of campaign contributions to California legislators by the Center for Public Integrity shows that 25 percent of California state legislators sit on a committee that regulates the industry of their largest contributor.[13] Who are these largest contributors? For the most part, they are PACs representing organized interests in California.

PACs representing well-defined interests are important: public employee unions, teachers, and Indians. Exhibit 3-3 shows the top contributors to California's legislative and initiative campaigns during the 2004 election cycle. Public employee labor unions, such as the Service Employees International Union (SEIU) and the California Teachers Association, are among the largest political contributors to California legislative candidates. As gerrymandering locks in safe districts and virtually

[13]Alex Knott, "California Awash in Campaign Cash, Potentials for Conflict of Interest," Center for Public Integrity, 25 January 2001, **www.publicintegrity.org/report.aspx?aid=318**

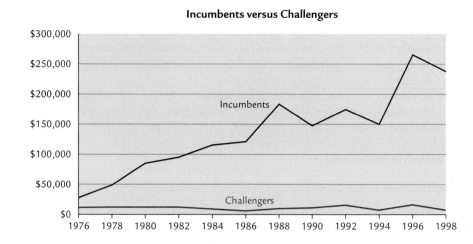

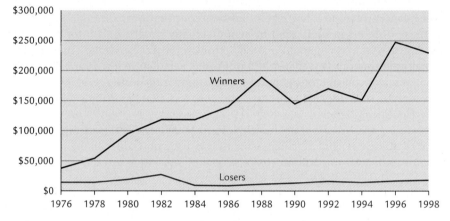

EXHIBIT 3-2   Expenditures in State Assembly Campaigns, 1976–98: Incumbents v. Challengers and Winners v. Losers

Incumbents significantly outspend challengers. Winners outspend losers. In 1976, assembly winners outspent assembly losers by the ratio of _____ to 1. By the late 1990s, the ratio was approximately _____ to 1.

_____

Source: California Secretary of State, Political Reform Division, **www.ss.ca.gov**

assures incumbent reelection, political dollars pour into value-laden "hot-button" initiative campaigns.

Parties are important. For statewide executive offices, the Democratic and Republican parties join the list of largest contributors. Political parties were the source of 13 percent of all contributions to California state candidates in 1997–1998 (about $40 million), 28 percent ($61 million) in 1999–2000, and 26 percent ($28 million) in 2003–2004.

Political power brokers attract money. Money is part of their power. A **power broker** is someone who exerts extraordinary influence in the public sector due to such factors as office, control of money, or the ability to deliver votes, affect public

Contributor Name	Interest Group, Policy or Candidate Supported or Opposed, and Outcome	Amount to Candidates	Amount to Ballot Measures
Agua Caliente Band of Cahuilla Indians	Tribal Government Pro Proposition 70 (lost)	$ 688,650	$13,700,000
California State Council of Service Employees International Union	Public Sector Union Pro Proposition 56 (lost) Pro Proposition 72 (lost)	1,014,315	12,818,278
California Democratic Party	Political Party Committee Largest recipients were Michael Machado (won) and Peg Pinard (lost)	11,413,588	1,010,525
San Manuel Band of Mission Indians	Tribal Government Pro Proposition 70 (lost)	955,520	11,000,000
California Teachers Association	Public Sector Union Pro Proposition 55 (won) Pro Proposition 56 (lost) Pro Proposition 72 (lost)	1,838,925	8,620,336
Schwarzenegger's California Recovery Team, Governor	Candidate Committee Pro Proposition 57 (won) Con Proposition 68 (lost)	0	10,178,721
Morongo Band of Mission Indians	Tribal Government Pro Proposition 70 (lost) Con Proposition 68 (lost)	1,251,600	8,334,600
Auburn Rancheria	Tribal Government Con Proposition 68 (lost)	83,800	8,285,047
Rumsey Band of Wintun Indians	Tribal Government Con Proposition 68 (lost)	97,000	8,244,241
California Republican Party	Political Party Committee Largest recipients were Gary Podesto (lost), Dean Gardner (lost), and Shirley Horton (won)	6,314,060	1,374,528
Pala Band of Mission Indians	Tribal Government Con Proposition 68 (lost)	47,300	6,693,293
Pechanga Band of Luiseno Indians	Tribal Government Con Proposition 68 (lost)	498,004	5,571,142
California Motor Car Dealers Association	Automotive Pro Proposition 64	453,456	5,304,911
Poizner Family Trust	Candidate self-finance Republican candidate 21st Assembly (lost)	5,313,732	0
Magna Entertainment Corp	Gambling & Casinos Pro Proposition 68 (lost)	54,200	4,800,008
SBC Communications	Telephone Utilities Con Proposition 67 (lost)	558,874	4,181,776

(continued)

EXHIBIT 3-3

Top 20 Contributors to California Campaigns, 2004

The top 20 contributors to candidates, party committees, and/or ballot measure committees accounted for 29 percent of the total contributions in the 2004 election cycle.

How much does a "seat at the table" cost?

Contributor Name	Interest Group, Policy or Candidate Supported or Opposed, and Outcome	Amount to Candidates	Amount to Ballot Measures
California Healthcare Association	Hospitals & Nursing Homes Pro Proposition 67 (lost) Pro Proposition 72 (lost) Pro Proposition 63 (won)	354,276	3,978,835
Viejas Band of Kumeyaay Indians	Tribal Government Con Proposition 68 (lost)	334,620	3,302,426
Pinnacle Entertainment	Gambling & Casinos Pro Proposition 68 (lost)	2,000	3,414,000
League of California Cities	Government Pro Proposition 1A (won)	0	3,109,888

Proposition 1A (November 2004):	Local property tax and sales tax revenues remain with local government (passed)
Proposition 55 (March 2004):	Education bond (passed)
Proposition 56 (March 2004):	State budget enaction with 55 percent legislative majority rather than the two-thirds vote currently required (lost)
Proposition 63 (November 2004):	Mental health services expansion: funding; tax on personal incomes above $1 million (passed)
Proposition 64 (November 2004):	Limits on private enforcement of unfair business competition laws (passed)
Proposition 67 (November 2004):	Emergency medical services: funding; telephone surcharge (lost)
Proposition 68 (November 2004):	Non-tribal commercial gambling expansion (lost)
Proposition 70 (November 2004):	Tribal gaming compacts: exclusive gaming rights (lost)
Proposition 72 (November 2004):	Health care coverage requirements (lost)

Source: The Institute on Money in State Politics, August 2006, **www.followthemoney.org**

opinion, or mobilize a constituency. During 2005–2006, senate president pro tem Don Perata raised more than $1 million for his candidate-controlled committee, Rebuilding California. The contributions were exempt from Proposition 34 campaign contribution limits, because Rebuilding California was an issue advocacy account—promoting a bond-funded capitol infrastructure rebuilding plan for California. New infrastructure, such as schools, roads, and water projects, benefits real estate developers and construction companies, and their investors. The three top donors to the committee, each at $100,000, were the insurance companies Ameriquest Capital and Mercury General, and John Moores, a University of California regent and owner of the San Diego Padres baseball team. The Tutor-Saliba and Albert Seeno construction companies along with Pacific Gas & Electric and Southern California Edison utilities each donated $50,000. Numerous other real estate and construction businesses gave $10,000–25,000. Rebuilding California funded a television and print advertising campaign extolling Perata's infrastructure plan, as an alternative to Governor Schwarzenegger's proposed bonds, under the guidance of campaign consultants Paul Hefner and Sandra Polka.

Individual deep-pocket contributors are important. Few Californians contribute to political campaigns, and even fewer are large donors (over $200). Only about 9 percent of Americans make a political campaign donation during an election cycle,[14]

[14]National Election Studies, **www.umich.edu/~nes/nesguide/nesguide.htm**

and very few are large donors. However, individual large donors can significantly aid campaigns, particularly in the early stages. A few names come up in California again and again: Ron Burkle (Yucaipa Companies), Jerry Perenchio (Univision), Alex G. Spanos (builder and developer, Stockton), and the Gallo family (E & J Gallo Winery, Modesto).

Businesses are important. Corporations make political investments as well. Insurance companies are especially active campaign contributors. Assembly member Thomas Calderon (D), a candidate for insurance commissioner in November 2002, received over $500,000 in campaign contributions from the industry, including $150,000 from the Mercury General Corporation (he lost to John Garamendi). The *Los Angeles Times* reported that in the 2003–2004 election cycle insurance companies donated more than $1 million to the campaigns of seventeen legislators who sat on the Assembly Insurance Committee. At the same time, insurance reform legislation written after the 2003 wildfires in Southern California—a set of six bills called a "homeowners' bill of rights," proposing more consumer information, easing claim documentation requirements for homeowners, and making it harder for companies to increase rates or cancel coverage after a claim—failed to clear the committee.[15]

Campaign Finance Reform

There is a strong relationship between money and politics because "the decisions that legislators make have multibillion-dollar consequences for affected interests."[16] What is the appropriate role of money in politics? Should money be limited in politics? Is it even possible to limit money in politics? These questions reflect an ongoing debate about political participation, capitalism, and representative democracy. One side argues that money is a form of speech and that restricting campaign donations restricts freedom. The other side counters that money is a form of power and influence by an unrepresentative set of wealthy individuals, special interests, and corporations. Both arguments are right. The question at hand becomes how to protect free speech while avoiding the inordinate leverage of money on public policy-making. There are two approaches: (1) reporting and disclosure, and (2) contribution limits.

California law, starting with the Political Reform Act of 1974 (Proposition 9), requires the disclosure of contributions and expenditures for political campaigns and lobbying. Since its passage, the law has been amended hundreds of times and now is a complex hodgepodge of rules and regulations regarding the reporting and disclosure of financial interests and transactions that affects about 100,000 elected and appointed officials and the individuals and organizations associated with these officials at both the state and local levels—basically, anything and everything in California dealing with money and politics. The primary responsibility for administering the act is divided between the Fair Political Practices Commission (FPPC) and the secretary of state. The commission interprets the Political Reform Act, issuing general regulations and interpretive opinions in specific situations. It enforces the act through investigation and administrative or civil prosecution of those who fail to follow the act's requirements.

Reporting and disclosure is one approach to regulating the relationship between money and politics. The secretary of state is the principal repository of financial transaction data. However, it is one thing to acquire data and quite another to have *useful* information. As the Internet develops, campaign and lobbying financial data are becoming more accessible, and watchdog groups such as the National Institute

---

[15]Jordan Rau, "Fire Victims Feel Burned by Lawmakers Tied to Insurers," *Los Angeles Times*, 27 February 2006.

[16]Dan Walters, "Money Limits Don't Cut It," *Sacramento Bee*, 2 May 1999.

on Money in State Politics, the Center for Responsive Politics, the Center for Public Integrity, Common Cause, and the Public Interest Research Group try to identify and publicize the relationships between who's giving, who's getting, and what public policy follows.

The second approach to regulating the money-and-politics relationship is to set donation and expenditure limits. In November 2000, voters passed Proposition 34. Written by legislators, ostensibly to strengthen political parties, Proposition 34 limits contributions to candidates for state office as summarized in Exhibit 3-4.[17] Contributions from individuals or PACs to legislative candidates are currently limited to $3,300 per election, but contributions to a political party can exceed $27,900 per year. There are no restrictions on the amount that party committees can give to candidates and are no restrictions on the amount that a politician can raise on behalf of an issue advocacy proposition campaign.

The rules favor the rich, the well-connected, incumbents, and the party faithful. A wealthy candidate may spend an unlimited amount from a personal fortune on his or her own campaign. Incumbents have a network of supporters among interest groups, businesses, and the affluent elite. Their money will keep coming through multiple donors (family, friends, and associates of the principal donor) and multiple political committees. Otherwise, donations will be channeled through the Democratic and Republican parties. Interest groups can mount independent campaigns in support of a candidate without donating to a candidate's campaign committee or being controlled by the candidate.

Campaign contribution limits, although seeming to control political influence, actually make it more difficult to track the myriad transactions that form the money–politics relationship. They favor incumbents while handicapping challengers—being out of power and relatively unknown, challengers are effectively denied access to an early infusion of seed money that can jump-start a campaign.

Basically, *money will find a way*. Rather than restricting contributions, the better approach is to open the money–politics relationship to public scrutiny by using the Internet to provide immediate and complete disclosure of all financial transactions.

VOTING

The Electorate

The **electorate** is that part of the resident population who can potentially vote in an election. The electorate comprises three parts—the eligible, the registered, and the voters.

The Eligible   You are eligible to vote in California if:

- You are a United States citizen.
- You are a resident of California.
- You are at least eighteen years of age (or will be by the date of the next election).
- You are not in prison or on parole for conviction of a felony. (One's right to vote is restored once sentence is completed.)
- You have not been judged by a court to be mentally incompetent to vote.

---

[17]Charter cities and counties may set limits for local campaigns.

EXHIBIT 3-4

California Campaign Contribution Limits

What is the maximum amount that you individually can contribute to a legislative campaign? How much can a political party contribute?

TO	FROM					Candidate (to another candidate)	Candidate (to self)	
	Individual	Political Action Committee	Small Contribution Committee	Registered Lobbyist	Political Party		Contribution	Loan
Candidate:								
State legislative	$3,300/ election	$3,300/ election	$6,700/ election	$0	No limit			
Governor	$22,300/ election	$22,300/ election	$22,300/ election	$0	No limit	$3,300/ election	No limit	$100,000
Other statewide	$5,600/ election	$5,600/ election	$11,100/ election	$0	No limit			
Political Action Committee	$5,600/year							
Small Contribution Committee	$200/year							
Political Party	$27,900/year	$27,900/ year						
Ballot Measure Committee	No limit					No limit		

Proposition 34 (2000)

The Fair Political Practices Commission (FPPC) can adjust contribution limits due to inflation every two years. The limits shown here are effective January 1, 2005.

Other statewide: lieutenant governor, attorney general, insurance commissioner, controller, treasurer, secretary of state, superintendent of public instruction, and Board of Equalization.

Example: An individual could donate $3,300 to a legislative candidate for the primary election and another $3,300 for the general election.

Source: State of California, Fair Political Practices Commission.

The Registered   However, in order to vote, you need to **register** at least fifteen days before an election. Only 70 percent of California's 23 million age-eligible electorate is registered. Under the federal Help America Vote Act (HAVA) of 2002, each state is responsible for maintaining a centralized voter registration database. In 2005, California became the first state in the nation to comply with the new voter database requirements.

Registration requires filling out a voter registration application form stating your name, address, and date of birth. In addition, you need to provide an identification number such as on your California driver's license or state identification card or the last four digits of your Social Security number. You are also asked to designate a political party affiliation. You can place a check by one of the seven qualified parties, fill in the name of another party, or check "I decline to state a political party."

The form goes to your county election office, where the registration form and an image of your signature are kept on file. The county must then verify your identity by matching your name and ID number with the Department of Motor Vehicles or the Social Security Administration. The county also checks the Department of Corrections and Rehabilitation's convicted-felon database and death records maintained by the Department of Health Services. If everything matches and clears, you are registered to vote. The purpose of registration and the HAVA requirements is to avoid vote fraud—ballot box stuffing such as described in the old political machine campaign slogan "Vote early and often." However, even though unregistered voters are not kept from voting—they can still vote a provisional ballot—the new identity requirements may slow the registration process and even dissuade new voters.

Voter registration is public information. Political campaigns, pollsters, and others purchase lists of registered voters in order to prepare mailings, develop contacts for public opinion polling, and launch get-out-the-vote efforts. Voter registration lists are combined with the list of licensed drivers in a county to form the jury pool from which potential jurors are called. Your voting history—which elections you voted in—is a matter of public record.

The Voters   The voters, of course, are those people, being registered, who actually do vote. Exhibit 3-5 shows significant differences in the electorate between the eligible, the registered, and the voters.[18] Key voter characteristics include the following:

- *Voters are predominantly white, but Latino voters are increasing.* California is a majority–minority state—Anglos (white non-Hispanics) make up only 57 percent of the eligible voters, 63 percent of those registered, and an overwhelming majority, 65 percent, of the voters. Latinos are a significant and growing demographic presence in California, and their influence is beginning to be felt in statewide elections. Whereas more than three-fourths of Anglos (73 percent) and 68 percent of African Americans are registered to vote (with about 70 percent of these groups voting), only about half of the Latino and Asian electorate are registered to vote (but 85 percent of those voted in 2004).

- *Voters are older.* Young people don't vote. Only half of the eligible 18- to 24-year-olds are registered, although 82 percent of that number voted in 2004. However, 77 percent of those age 65 and older are registered, and nearly all of them vote (95 percent). Nineteen percent of the 2004 general election votes were cast by voters age 65 and older.

---

[18]Sources of voter participation data include the Public Policy Institute of California, *Election 2000: Statewide Analysis*, November 2000, **www.ppic.org**; the Field Institute, *A Digest of California's Political Demography*, January 2002, **www.field.org**; and the U.S. Census Bureau, Current Population Survey, November 2004.

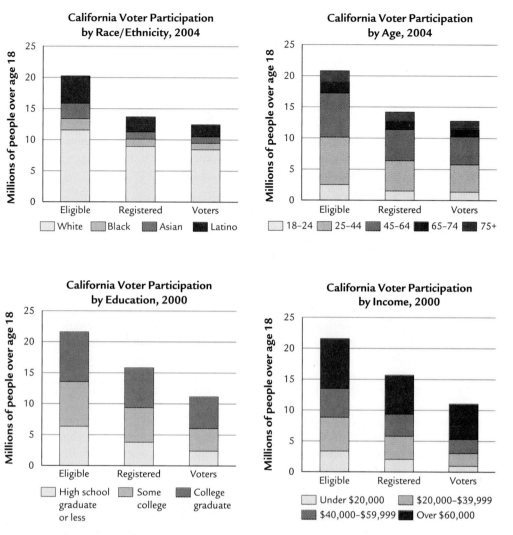

EXHIBIT 3-5   The California Electorate

Describe California's voters.

Note: Registered voters equaled 75 percent of eligible. Voter turnout in 2004 equaled 57 percent of eligible and 76 percent of registered voters.

- *Voters are better educated.* Forty-eight percent of voters are college graduates. Approximately 70 percent of those *not* registered to vote did not graduate from college.

- *Voters are more affluent.* Slightly more voters have incomes less than $40,000 per year (41 percent) than have incomes exceeding $60,000 per year (38 percent). However, on election day, 52 percent of the voters are in the $60,000-and-up bracket, whereas the under-$40,000 group accounts for only 27 percent.

Many other relationships can be discerned in the voter participation data. For example, men and women differ with respect to political party affiliation. About as many men report that they are Democrats (38 percent) as Republicans (39 percent). On the other hand, more women identify themselves as Democrats (51 percent) than Republicans (34 percent). In addition, one-fifth of all registered voters did not affiliate with either the Democrats or the Republicans. Most of these declined to state a party affiliation.

Voting Technology and Vote Counting

It is enough that the people know there was an election.
The people who cast the votes decide nothing.
The people who count the votes decide everything.[19]

Please let the winner win in a landslide.[20]

Americans learned a lot about voting technology and vote counting in the 2000 Florida presidential election—officially won by George W. Bush with a margin of merely 537 votes out of 5,861,785 votes cast in that state. We learned that vote counting is a demanding and exacting process; that elections are conducted by the counties throughout the United States; that several different kinds of voting equipment and ballots are used; and that there are errors in the system—errors operating or programming the voting equipment, errors on the ballots, errors by confused voters, errors in counting, and ambiguity in deciding what exactly is a vote, much less who that vote was cast for. Most of the time, these errors are irrelevant—the margin between winning and losing candidates usually exceeds the margin of error (about 1 or 2 percent) of the voting equipment and vote counting. Even if all the errors were counted in favor of the losing candidate, the election result would not change. But many times elections are close, and in a plurality, winner-takes-all election, every vote is important. Using Florida 2000 as an example, even if the voting systems were 99.9 percent error free, nearly 6,000 ballots would still be in question—ten times George W. Bush's official winning margin.

Elections seem simple. You mark or punch a ballot and drop it in a box. At the end of the day, poll workers deliver the box to the election office, where the ballots are counted under public inspection. However, California elections are complex and difficult operations. Counties are responsible for the administration and conduct of elections. In some counties, the elections department, headed by the registrar of voters, is an administrative office reporting to the county's chief executive officer and board of supervisors. In other counties, the elections department is under an elected executive (usually titled the county clerk-recorder). There are many political jurisdictions within a county—school districts, special districts, cities. They all have different boundaries, and many are further subdivided into wards or other geographic districts. In addition, many counties are crisscrossed by assembly district, senate district, and congressional district lines—none of which coincide. Many political boundaries changed in 2001 as a result of redistricting, but changes occur all the time due to development and annexations. One major function of the elections department is to maintain detailed maps of the political districts in the county. Once political jurisdictions have been determined, precincts of up to 1,000 registered voters are mapped out (1,250 voters in larger counties). Each precinct has a designated polling place such as a church, school, or fire

---

[19]Joseph Stalin, the dictator of the Soviet Union during much of the Cold War.
[20]An election official's prayer.

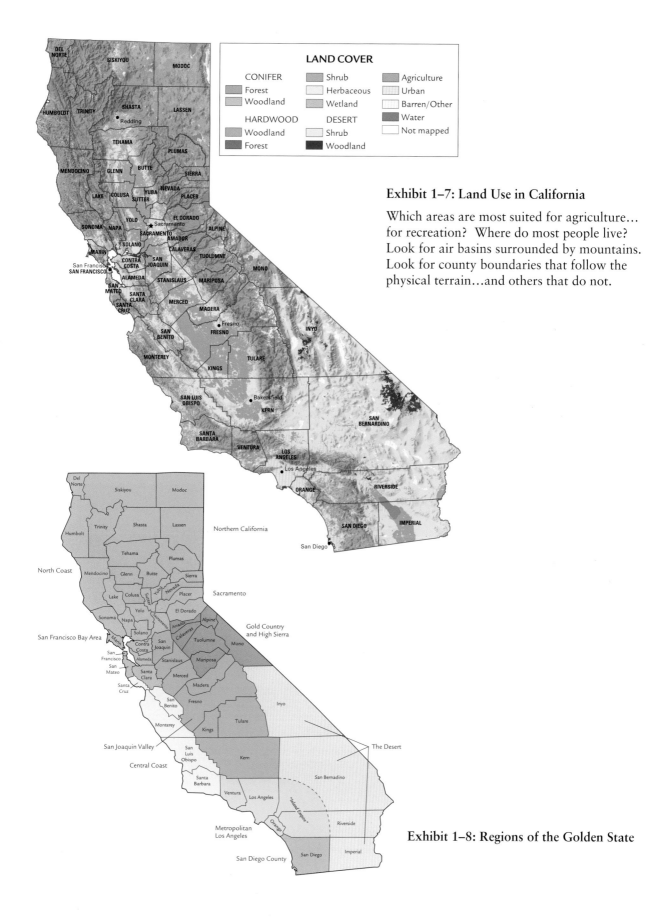

LAND COVER

CONIFER
- Forest
- Woodland

HARDWOOD
- Woodland
- Forest

- Shrub
- Herbaceous
- Wetland

DESERT
- Shrub
- Woodland

- Agriculture
- Urban
- Barren/Other
- Water
- Not mapped

Exhibit 1–7: Land Use in California

Which areas are most suited for agriculture... for recreation? Where do most people live? Look for air basins surrounded by mountains. Look for county boundaries that follow the physical terrain...and others that do not.

Exhibit 1–8: Regions of the Golden State

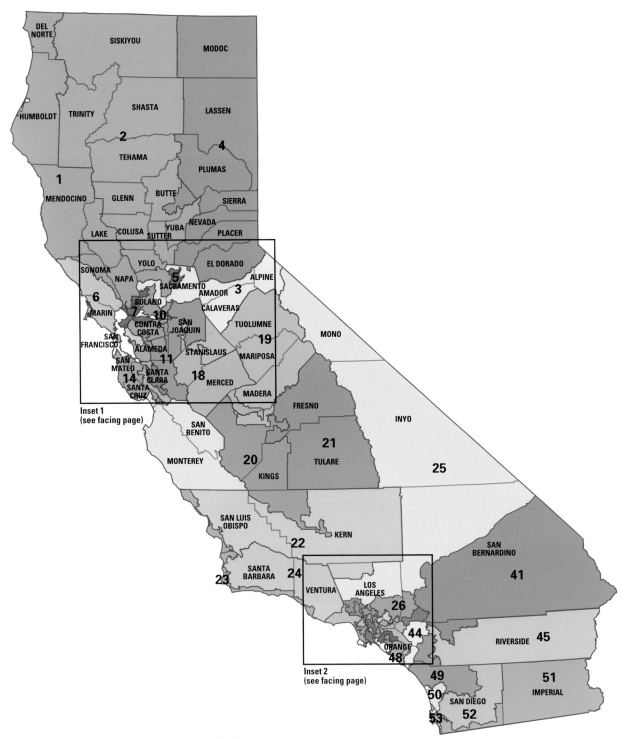

Exhibit 2–6: California Congressional Districts

Inset 1: San Francisco Bay Area

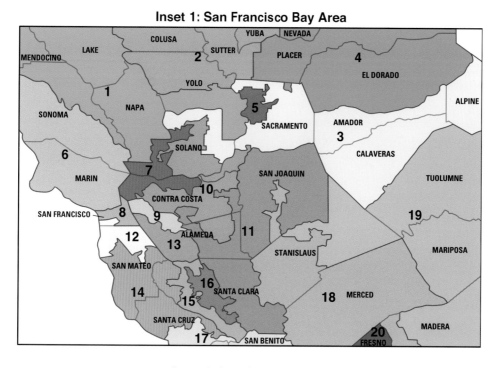

Inset 2: Los Angeles Area

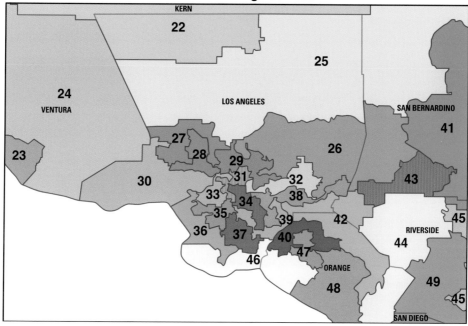

Exhibits 2–7: California State Assembly Districts

Inset 1: San Francisco Bay Area

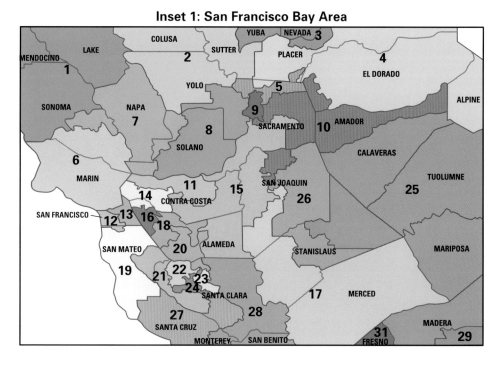

Inset 2: Los Angeles Area

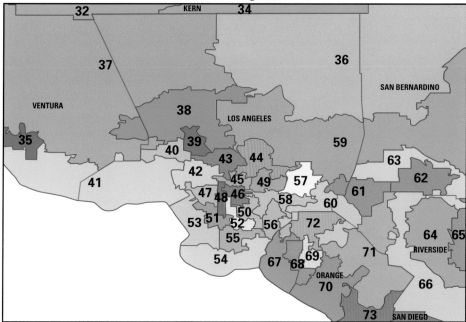

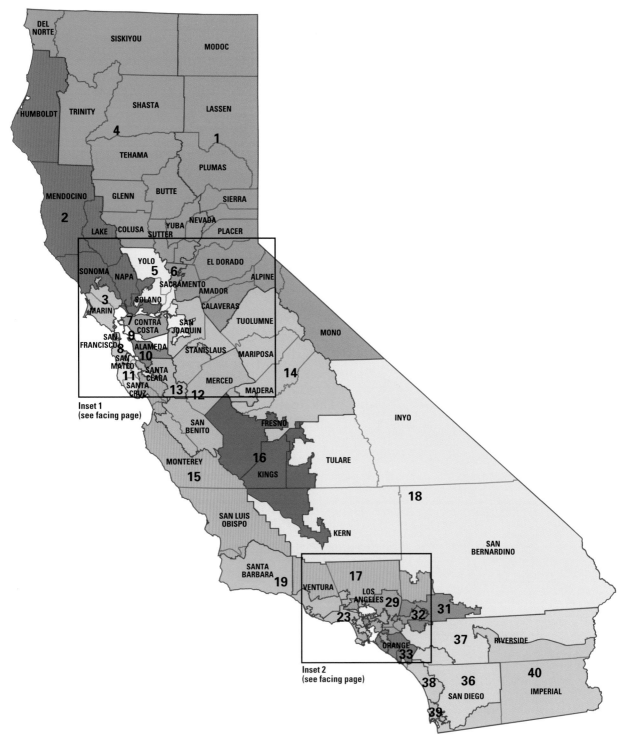

Exhibit 2–8: California State Senate Districts

Inset 1: San Francisco Bay Area

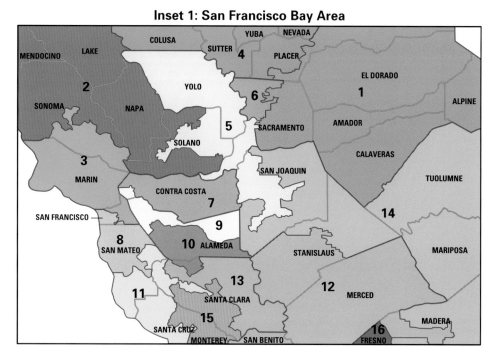

Inset 2: Los Angeles Area

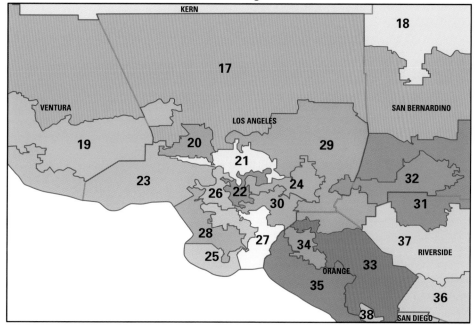

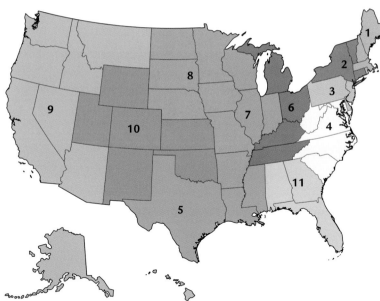

Geographic jurisdiction for the Federal Circuit Courts of Appeals (additional federal courts: U.S. Courts of Appeals for the Armed Forces, U.S. Court of Federal Claims, Federal Circuit, D.C. Circuit)

Eastern District (Redding, Sacramento, Fresno)

Northern District (Oakland, San Francisco, San Jose)

Central District (Riverside, Los Angeles, Santa Ana)

Southern District (San Diego)

Exhibit 2–10: U.S. Circuit Courts of Appeals and U.S. Federal District Courts in California

station. Voters in precincts with less than 250 voters do not have a polling place. Instead, they are sent a ballot by mail with a postage-paid return envelope.

Primary elections can be especially complicated. Separate ballots for each political party and political jurisdiction will list dozens of federal, state, and local candidates, as well as state and local propositions. To accommodate all the possible combinations, Sacramento County typically prints more than 100 different ballot-types, in two languages. Los Angeles County produces as many as 5,000 different ballot-types in nine languages.

Most Californians vote using an optical scan ballot. The state is gradually testing and certifying computer-based touch-screen, ATM-like devices for election day balloting. After the Florida 2000 dead-heat presidential election, there has been a call to upgrade voting technology by replacing outmoded punch card systems. A voting system needs to:

- Assure one-person, one-vote integrity.
- Assure ballot secrecy.
- Be inexpensive and easy to operate, store, maintain, and set up.
- Be accurate—counting every vote.
- Be auditable—allowing checks and recounts.
- Be trustworthy—providing public assurance that a ballot cast will indeed be counted.

By these criteria, current systems, though imperfect, are pretty good. New electronic technologies, although promising, still need development to meet every standard. There is no ideal system. A system for Los Angeles County, with 4 million registered voters and hundreds of political jurisdictions, is unnecessary in Siskiyou County, with just 26,000 voters. Nor is any system error free. Problems can occur within the voting system, such as confusing ballots that lead to intentional or unintentional voter undervotes or overvotes, and tabulation mistakes in the computer software. Problems can also occur outside the system due to errors in the printing and distribution of ballots to voters, voter authentication, and even the reporting of results (sometimes as simple as transposing digits when copying by hand).

Most people think that the election is over the day after election day. Not true! The final part of an election is the **canvass**. The canvass includes counting absentee and provisional ballots not previously processed, reconciling the vote count with the number of precinct polling place signatures and the inventory of ballots printed, accounting for all election material, and doing a hand count of all voted ballots from at least 1 percent of the precincts, including every office and measure. After the canvass, the election results are officially certified.

MAJOR TRENDS IN CALIFORNIA ELECTIONS

Decreasing Voter Participation

In a representative democracy, voting is regarded as the fundamental act of citizenship. There are two indicators: (1) **voter participation**, the percentage of the eligible population (citizens over age 18 and registered to vote) who vote in an election, and (2) **voter turnout**, the percentage of the registered voters who vote in an election.

EXHIBIT 3-6
Voter Participation

What was the lowest rate of voter participation in a California primary or general election?

Source: California Secretary of State and Federal Election Commission.

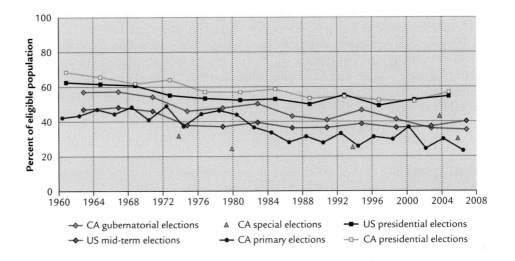

Voter participation has steadily declined in California and the United States over the past forty-five years (see Exhibit 3-6). Only 52 percent and 57 percent of eligible Californians voted in the 2000 and 2004 presidential elections, respectively. Only 25 percent participated in California's March 2002 primary election, 36 percent in the November 2002 gubernatorial (presidential midterm) election, 30 percent in the March 2004 primary, and 35 percent in the November 2005 special election.

Many political commentators bemoan this steadily decreasing participation in elections as some sort of failure, malaise, or crisis in American representative democracy. They cite a long list of possible reasons, including:

- *Fatigue and an excess of democracy.* The long ballot with dozens of local, state, and federal candidates and local and state ballot propositions confuses and intimidates voters. Between 2002 and 2007, California will have held eight statewide primary, special, or general elections.

- *Distractions.* People are too busy. People do not pay attention to elections because of the hectic pace of modern life and the demands and obligations of work and family.

- *Inconvenience.* One either has to go to a polling place or request an absentee ballot weeks in advance of an election.

- *Satisfaction with incumbents and the status quo.* Why vote if one is happy with the way things are?

- *Tyranny of the majority.* Why vote if one knows they are in the minority and will be on the losing side?

- *Cynicism.* Some people believe that all politicians are crooks.

- *Resignation, discouragement, apathy, or futility.* People may feel that it is not important or is no use—nothing changes. The system is fixed by the dominant political parties, incumbent politicians, the wealthy, and vested interests.

- *Alienation.* Not participating is a form of silent protest against a perceived unjust system.

- *Pocketbook issues.* People may not bother unless there is some immediate economic consequence.
- *The belief that it doesn't make any difference.* The candidates advocate inconsequentially small policy and ideological differences. Critics believe that in a representative democracy candidates should advocate clearly different policy choices so that voters have the opportunity to vote for a candidate whose values closely match their own. Instead, voters seemingly must choose the lesser of two evils, and, supposedly disgusted with having no real options, they choose not to vote at all. There is also the belief that an individual's vote is but one of hundreds, or thousands, or millions.

However, an alternate theory holds that low voter turnout is not the mark of a weak democracy—just the opposite. It could indicate a strong, functioning democracy in which competing candidates compromise *extreme* policy and ideological positions well before the election as they seek a voting majority. Even though the candidates proclaim their differences, they position themselves to appeal to the broadest range of public opinion. To most voters, each candidate presents a not-ideal but nevertheless acceptable middle-of-the-road compromise. They are perceived as "Tweedledum and Tweedledee"—marginally different and equally imperfect. Nevertheless, voter turnout remains an indicator of civic involvement and the relative political influence of various social and economic groups.

The Coastal-Inland Political Divide

Forty years ago, California politics pitted the urbane liberal north against the megalopolis conservative south as volatile issues regarding water, the Vietnam War, and civil rights rocked the state. Now the Coastal Range of mountains separates Democrat-voting San Francisco, Los Angeles, and the North Coast from the Republican-voting San Joaquin Valley, Inland Empire, and rural California. Exhibit 3-7a shows that more than two-thirds of California voters live in the coastal counties. These voters, large proportions of whom are college graduates, high income, and single, tend to register as Democrats or independents. Inland county voters average somewhat lower educational attainment and lower income. They have a higher rate of marriage and religious identification (especially born-again Christian), tend to register as Republicans, and identify with conservative public policies.[21] Therefore, California politics is dominated by its liberal coast, supporting Democratic candidates for statewide and national office, and liberal policies on everything from gay marriage, abortion rights, and environmental protection to the Iraq war. It's a sharp divide. Exhibits 3-7c and f show decisive plurality votes for Democratic gubernatorial and presidential candidates in general elections from 1998 to 2004, led by Los Angeles County and San Francisco Bay Area voters. The only recent significant statewide Republican wins were Arnold Schwarzenegger's successful gubernatorial campaign in the 2003 recall special election (because of low voter turnout in Los Angeles County) (see Exhibit 3-7g) and his subsequent reelection in 2006 (Exhibit 3-7b).

---

[21]Mark DiCamillo, "Three California Election Megatrends," *The Field Poll*, February 2006.

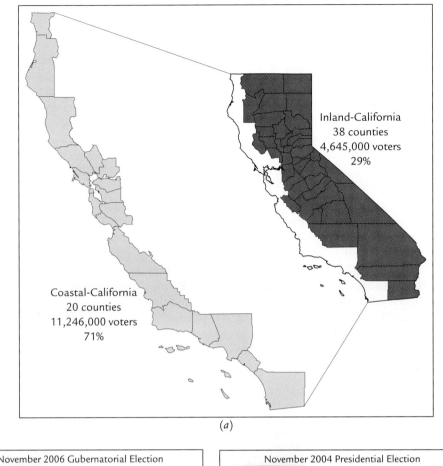

Inland-California
38 counties
4,645,000 voters
29%

Coastal-California
20 counties
11,246,000 voters
71%

(a)

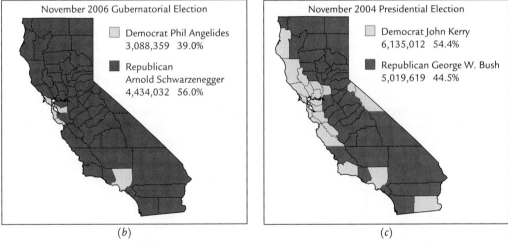

November 2006 Gubernatorial Election

Democrat Phil Angelides
3,088,359   39.0%

Republican
Arnold Schwarzenegger
4,434,032   56.0%

(b)

November 2004 Presidential Election

Democrat John Kerry
6,135,012   54.4%

Republican George W. Bush
5,019,619   44.5%

(c)

(continued)

Diminishing Democrat–Republican Identification

The Democratic and Republican parties have a lock on every state elected office. However, they are losing touch with new voters, and Exhibit 3-8 shows that their share of registered voters is declining. New voters overwhelmingly express themselves as nonpartisan and tend to favor middle-of-the-road policies and candidates between liberal and conservative extremes.

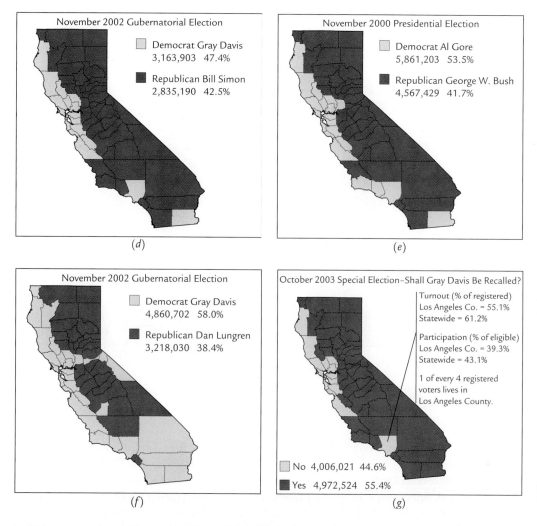

November 2002 Gubernatorial Election

☐ Democrat Gray Davis
3,163,903   47.4%

■ Republican Bill Simon
2,835,190   42.5%

(d)

November 2000 Presidential Election

☐ Democrat Al Gore
5,861,203   53.5%

■ Republican George W. Bush
4,567,429   41.7%

(e)

November 2002 Gubernatorial Election

☐ Democrat Gray Davis
4,860,702   58.0%

■ Republican Dan Lungren
3,218,030   38.4%

(f)

October 2003 Special Election–Shall Gray Davis Be Recalled?

Turnout (% of registered)
Los Angeles Co. = 55.1%
Statewide = 61.2%

Participation (% of eligible)
Los Angeles Co. = 39.3%
Statewide = 43.1%

1 of every 4 registered
voters lives in
Los Angeles County.

☐ No   4,006,021   44.6%
■ Yes 4,972,524   55.4%

(g)

EXHIBIT 3-7   California's Coastal-Inland Political Divide (continued)

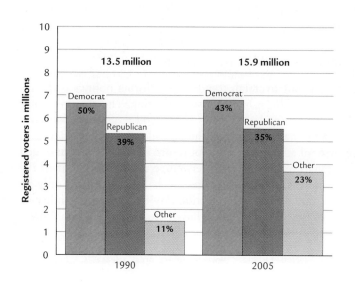

EXHIBIT 3-8

Diminishing Democrat–Republican Registration and Growth of Independents

Here's a math problem: The number of registered voters increased by 2.4 million between 1990 and 2005. What percent of these new voters registered as independents (a third party or decline to state) rather than as Democrats or Republicans?

EXHIBIT 3-9   Increasing Latino Electorate

What ethnic groups account for most of the new voters between 1990 and 2005?

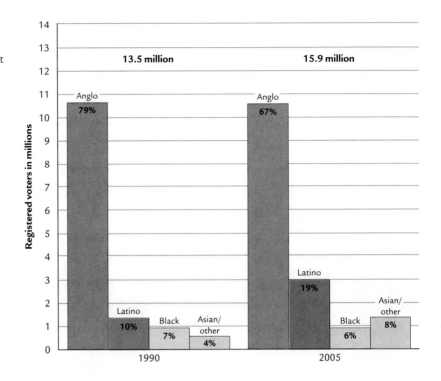

Growing Latino Electorate

Latinos are becoming an increasingly influential part of California's electorate. Exhibit 3-9 shows that their proportion of registered voters has nearly doubled from 10 percent in 1990 to 19 percent in 2005. Seventy percent of the 2.4 million new registered voters since 1990 are Latino. Three Latinos register as Democrats for every one that registers as Republican. Nearly one-fourth of Democratic party registrants, in contrast to less than 10 percent of Republican registrants, are Latino, and in recent general elections, Latinos have voted 2 to 1 for the Democratic presidential or gubernatorial candidate.[22] The political demography will continue to change as Latinos, who will soon make up a majority of the state's population, continue to increase their political participation.

Increasing Absentee Voting

One of the more popular, and controversial, trends in California politics is the increasing use of the mail-in ballot. This is called **absentee voting**. The absentee voter is sent a ballot by mail before election day, votes at home, and returns the ballot on or before election day either by mail (voter pays the postage) or by delivering it to the elections office. Vote-by-mail and absentee ballot return envelopes are bar coded to individual voters. The signature on the return envelope must match that of the voter to whom the ballot was sent. At one time, mail-in ballots were used only by voters who could not visit a polling place on election day because of disability or travel. However, requirements for absentee voting have eased over the years. Voters

---

[22]National Association of Latino Elected Officials, **www.naleo.org/press_releases/CA_Profile_02-04_fin.pdf**

There is literally no such thing as an idea that cannot be expressed well and articulately to today's voters in 30 seconds. —Dick Morris

What makes a news story? Here are a few characteristics that most newspapers, radio, and television stories have in common:

- Dramatic or personal events (Sometimes this is called political theater.)
- Conflict or scandal
- A story with two sides that can be presented as win-lose controversy
- A story that is new, strange, or unusual
- A story that fits a currently popular theme
- A story involving famous or familiar people
- A story that is simple to convey and can be summarized in short sound bites—one-sentence quotable quotes, quips, or catchy phrases
- A story with visual elements (especially for television)

MAJOR CALIFORNIA NEWSPAPERS

Los Angeles Times	www.latimes.com
Sacramento Bee	www.sacbee.com
San Francisco Chronicle	www.sfgate.com

REGIONAL NEWSPAPERS

Fresno Bee	www.fresnobee.com
Los Angeles Daily News	www.dailynews.com
Oakland Tribune	www.oaklandtribune.com
Orange County Register	www.ocregister.com

Riverside Press-Enterprise	www.pe.com
San Diego Union-Tribune	www.uniontrib.com
San Jose Mercury News	www.mercurycenter.com

NATIONAL NEWSPAPERS WITH SIGNIFICANT CALIFORNIA COVERAGE

Wall Street Journal	www.wsj.com
New York Times	www.nytimes.com
Washington Post	www.washingtonpost.com
USA Today	www.usatoday.com

DAILY DIGESTS OF CALIFORNIA POLITICAL NEWS

Rough and Tumble	www.rtumble.com
California Political Daily CALpDay	www.calpday.com
New America Media	www.newamericamedia.org

CALIFORNIA POLITICAL BLOGS

Calitics	www.calitics.com

For a complete list of California media, see Newslink.

Newspapers:	newslink.org/canews.html
Television:	newslink.org/catele.html

Source: Anthony Pratkanis and Elliot Aronson, *Age of Propaganda: The Everyday Use and Abuse of Persuasion* (San Francisco: W.H. Freeman, 2001).

no longer have to state a reason for the absentee request, and the last day for requesting an absentee ballot has been moved closer to election day. A California voter can now register as a permanent absentee who will receive a mail-in ballot for each election (as long as he or she continues to vote). Despite declining voter turnout overall, absentee voting is becoming more popular. Forty percent of California voters cast absentee ballots in the 2005 special election (see Exhibit 3-10).

However, absentee voting remains controversial. For one thing, it changes the nature of campaigning. Election day becomes just a deadline for the elections office to receive mail, and political campaigns phase out during the absentee-voting period rather than build to a climactic finish. In addition, vote counting actually takes longer as each absentee ballot is signature-checked. Uncertainty about the outcome of close, cliffhanger contests may extend for several days. Further, last-minute events sometimes affect an election, and absentee votes cast days or weeks before election day do not reflect such developments. Everybody is not acting on the same information about current events. On the other hand, public opinion surveys conducted

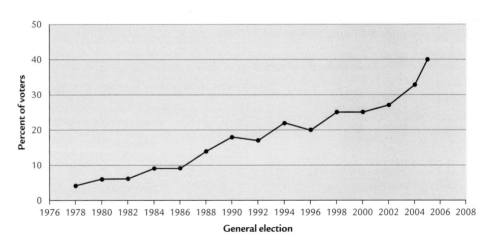

shortly before election day may presage who's leading and influence voter turnout and results. Also, there may be two election technologies—very likely a computer-based one at the polls on election day and an old optical-scan system for mail-in absentee voting. Lastly, absentee voting removes an important civic expression of freedom—the public act of going to a polling place and casting a ballot.

WEB LINKS

Political Resources Online
California Voter Foundation **www.calvoter.org**
Campaign Finance Information Center **www.campaignfinance.org**
Center for Public Integrity **www.publicintegrity.org**
Center for Responsive Politics **www.opensecrets.org**
Center for Voting and Democracy **www.fairvote.org**
Common Cause **www.commoncause.org**
Field Institute **www.field.com**
Hoover Institution: Campaign Finance **www.campaignfinancesite.org**
National Institute on Money in State Politics **www.followthemoney.org**
PoliData: population and election result maps **www.polidata.org**
PoliticalMoneyLine **www.fecinfo.com/**
Political information **www.politicalinformation.com**
Politics 1: a comprehensive list of links to parties, issues, and candidates **www.politics1.com/**
Public Policy Institute of California **www.ppic.org**
Statewide database **swdb.berkeley.edu**
Tools for Candidate, Issue, and Corporate Campaigns **www.politicalresources.com**

California
Fair Political Practices Commission **www.fppc.ca.gov**
Secretary of state **www.ss.ca.gov**

PUBLICATIONS

Baldassare, Mark. 2002. *A California State of Mind: The Conflicted Voter in a Changing World*. Berkeley: University of California Press.

Bosley, Gary O. 2000. *Campaigning to Win*. Philadelphia: Xlibris.

Darrah, Joan. 2003. *Getting Political: Stories of a Woman Mayor*. Sanger, CA: Quill Driver Books.

Faucheux, Ronald A. 2003. *Running for Office: The Strategies, Techniques and Messages Modern Political Candidates Need to Win Elections*. New York: M. Evans.

Grey, Lawrence. 1999. *How to Win a Local Election: A Complete Step-by-Step Guide*. New York: M. Evans.

Guzzetta, S. J. 2003. *The Campaign Manual*, 4th ed. Anaheim, CA: Political Publishing.

Mills, Fetzer, Jr. 2001. *Grassroots: How to Run Your Own Campaign and Win!* Philadelphia: Xlibris.

Shea, Daniel M., and Michael John Burton. 2006. *Campaign Craft: The Strategies, Tactics, and Art of Political Campaign Management*, 3rd ed. New York: Praeger.

Thomas, Robert J., and Doug Gowen. 1999. *How to Run for Local Office*. Westland, MI: R & T Enterprises.

GLOSSARY

absentee voting   Vote by mail. A voter receives a ballot by mail well in advance of election day and returns it either by mail or in person.

campaign   An organized effort to win an election or advance public policy.

canvass   The period after election day during which absentee and provisional ballots are counted, the vote count is reconciled with the number of precinct polling place signatures and the inventory of ballots printed, election material is accounted for, and a hand count is conducted of all voted ballots from at least 1 percent of the precincts, including every office and measure. After the canvass, the election results are officially certified.

conservative   A political ideology that favors defending the economic status quo while enforcing personal virtue and responsibility.

Democrats   One of the two major political parties in the United States.

election cycle   The two-year term between elections for representatives to the state assembly and U.S. House of Representatives.

electorate   The people who are eligible to vote, by virtue of age and citizenship.

endorsement   A formal public statement of approval and support for a political candidate or ballot measure.

general election   A statewide election to choose officeholders and vote on propositions.

ideology (political)   A comprehensive and consistent set of beliefs about personal virtue and societal institutions, especially the most appropriate role for government. See *conservative* and *liberal*.

instant runoff voting (IRV)   A system of voting in which voters rank their candidate preferences. If no candidate receives a majority of first choices, the instant runoff begins. The candidate with the fewest first-place choices is eliminated, and the votes for that candidate are reassigned to the voters' second-place choices. This continues until one candidate receives a majority of the votes.

interest (political)   A cause or endeavor in which a group has a stake, concern, or responsibility.

liberal   A political ideology that favors government programs and regulations to increase individual and society well-being while minimizing governmental concern with personal behaviors and values.

plurality voting   The process by which the candidate with the most votes wins, even if that number is not a majority.

political action committee (PAC)   An organization that receives money and distributes campaign donations on behalf of a political interest.

political party   An organization that nominates and supports candidates for elected office who will pursue policies consistent with that organization's espoused beliefs, interests, and ideology with regard to public affairs.

power broker   A person who exerts extraordinary influence in the public sector due to such factors as office, control of money, or the ability to deliver votes, to affect public opinion, or to mobilize a constituency.

primary election   The process by which voters who have identified a political party affiliation when registering choose party candidates for the general election.

register (to vote)   The act by which a citizen over age 18 files a signed document with the local county stating his or her name and address and identification number (and, optionally, political party affiliation) in order to vote in an election.

Republicans   One of the two major political parties in the United States.

slate mailer   A type of campaign literature mailed to households that endorses a set of candidates—a slate—for different public offices. A slate mailer might be prepared by an interest group, political party, a few candidates pooling their resources and endorsing themselves, or a for-profit company seeking to make money from the election by, in effect, selling advertising space.

special election   An election called for a specific purpose, such as filling a vacant elected office

voter participation   The percentage of the eligible population who vote in an election.

voter turnout   The percentage of the registered voters who vote in an election.

SUGGESTED ANSWERS TO EXHIBIT QUESTIONS

Exhibit 3-1: 22.8 percent of California voters decline to state or declare a third-party affiliation.

Exhibit 3-2: In 1976, assembly winners outspent assembly losers by 4 to 1. By the late 1990s, the ratio was approximately 24 to 1.

Exhibit 3-3: A seat at the table costs at least $500,000, election cycle after election cycle.

Exhibit 3-4: Individual contributions to a legislative campaign are limited to $3,300 per election. There are no limits on contributions from a political party.

Exhibit 3-5: California's voters are predominantly Anglo, 45–64 years old, and college graduates, and have a relatively high income.

Exhibit 3-6: The lowest rate of voter participation in a California primary or general election, 23.4 percent of the eligible population, occurred in the June 2006 primary election.

Exhibit 3-7: Democratic strongholds are concentrated in Los Angeles County and the San Francisco Bay Area.

Exhibit 3-8: Of the 2.3 million new voters registering between 1990 and 2005, 90.5 percent registered as independents—either declining to state a party or affiliating with a third party.

Exhibit 3-9: The growth in California voter registration between 1992 and 2005 is accounted for by new Asian and Latino voters.

Exhibit 3-10: More than 40 percent of voter turnout is absentee.

CHAPTER FOUR

LAWMAKING

*There ought to be a law! Law and order! This is a
government of law, not of men! No man
is above the law!*[1]

L aws and lawmaking are central to our society and government. What are laws?
Why are they so important? How are they made?

A **law** is a formal written expression of public policy. Laws establish rules that
order and structure our lives. They affect nearly everything in our lives—travel, consumer products, banking, employment, school, even many aspects of personal relationships. Only government, through lawmaking procedures, has the power and
authority to create laws and enforce compliance—all for noble purposes, of course:
peace, order, stability, justice, prosperity, and so forth.

Laws attempt to resolve public problems. Political scientist Charles O. Jones defined a public problem as "a need, deprivation, or dissatisfaction, self-identified or
identified by others, for which relief is sought."[2] In other words, lawmaking begins
with discontent and a desire to change the status quo. This perception is shared and,
through communication and organization, may lead to a demand (as expressed in
the First Amendment to the U.S. Constitution) for redress of grievances.

This sounds like a bottom-to-top process, from the people to the government;
sometimes it is, but not always. The initial dissatisfaction might be on the part of
individuals or established social or economic interests, or even governmental political and administrative authorities themselves.

Lawmaking requires **power** and is an expression of power—the power of con-
stitutionally defined governmental institutions and procedures. Lawmaking focuses
on a specific proposed policy—a written rule—that, if adopted, would exert influence, change the status quo, modify behavior, relieve the perceived distress, and
achieve an intended outcome. It requires a formal act—voting—the express approval by a majority of either elected representatives or the people themselves on a
matter presented to them in a general election. This might be a *simple* majority, 50
percent plus one, or a *super* majority, such as two-thirds.

---

[1]The first two phrases are common expressions. The third phrase is often attributed to ancient Roman
governance. The fourth phrase is a partial quotation from Theodore Roosevelt: "No man is above the
law and no man is below it; nor do we ask any man's permission when we ask him to obey it." *Man* is
a generic term.

[2]Charles O. Jones, *An Introduction to the Study of Public Policy* (Belmont, CA: Wadsworth, 1970).

If passed, the policy, now a law, is implemented, applied, and interpreted. Often, further rule making—administrative regulations, procedures, and court cases (all having the force of law)—expands on the literal text of the policy. Eventually, new reactions and perceptions lead to new public problems and an ongoing cycle of new policy and law.

The first part of this chapter addresses lawmaking by legislation. The second part reviews four other ways law is made at the state and local levels in California: initiative, administrative rule making, judicial decisions, and executive orders.

LAWMAKING BY LEGISLATION

On the surface, lawmaking by **legislation** follows a step-by-step procedure—introduction of **bills,** committee reviews, voting, and bill signing. Behind the scenes, the legislative process involves demands, pressure, debate, compromise, party politics, bargaining, trade-offs, and negotiation—all in search of a voting majority coalition, issue by issue, bill by bill. "The essential feature of American . . . government is that a governing majority must be assembled, issue by issue, by some combination of party demands, electoral pressure, personal ideology, rhetorical skills, political bargaining and vote exchanges."[3]

California's Legislative Procedure

Legislative lawmaking at the state level occurs in the halls of the California State Legislature in Sacramento. The process is not quick or easy. Legislative lawmaking involves multiple reviews first in one, and then the other, house of the legislature. The legislature has a two-year session, and bills advance according to a legislative calendar. As Exhibit 4-1 shows, the legislative procedure begins when a proposed law is brought to the attention of a senator or assembly member and that legislator decides to author (sponsor or carry) the proposal as a bill. The legislator sends the proposal to the legislative counsel, where it is drafted into the language of a proposed law. Then in January or February, the senator or assembly member introduces the bill in that legislator's house, where it is assigned a number and "read" for the first time. (That is, the clerk reads the bill number, the name of the author, and the descriptive title of the bill to the senate or assembly.)[4]

We can track, for example, the progress of a typical piece of legislation, SB 19, authored by Senator Martha Escutia (D-Norwalk, District 30).[5] Senator Escutia introduced SB 19 in the California Senate on 4 December 2000. SB 19 proposed improved nutritional standards for food served in California's public schools. "The state of California and its schools have a responsibility not to sell out our children's health to the fast-food companies, the snack-food companies, and the soft-drink companies," Escutia said. "How can we teach our young children about good nutrition in the classroom and then shove junk food at them at lunchtime?"[6]

---

[3]James Q. Wilson, "Pork Is Kosher Under Our Constitution," *Wall Street Journal,* 15 February 2000.

[4]The number begins with AB for Assembly Bill or SB for Senate Bill. A bill is conventionally identified by its number and author's last name, such as SB 19, (Escutia). The maximum life of a bill is two years—the length of a legislative session, from the first Monday in December of each even-numbered year until November 30 of the next even-numbered year. No bill may be acted upon for the first thirty days after its introduction.

[5]The print media often provide a parenthetic identification for legislators, including party affiliation and the city in which they live.

[6]Bradley Weaver, "Junk Food on Campuses Under Fire," *North County Times,* 25 March 2001.

**EXHIBIT 4-1
Lawmaking: The
Legislative Procedure
in California (to be
completed within a
two-year legislative
"session")**

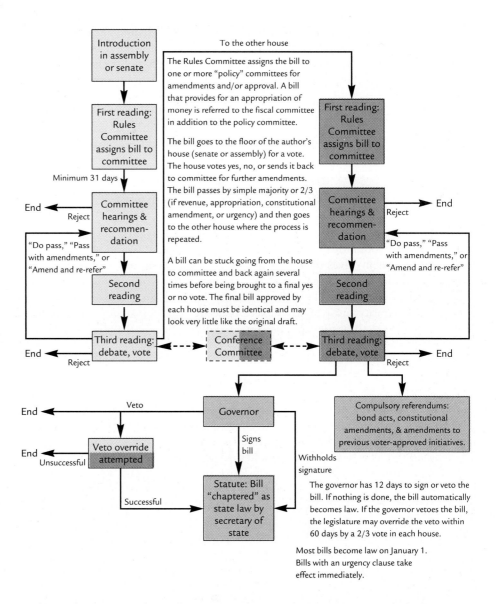

After first reading, the bill goes to the house Rules Committee, where it is assigned to one or more of the policy committees listed in Exhibit 4-2, consistent with the subject matter of the bill. The senate's Rules Committee referred SB 19 to two policy committees: Health and Human Services, and Education.

Policy committees hold hearings and take testimony and evidence from supporters and opponents of a bill. The committee then votes (by simple majority) on the bill: "do pass," "do pass as amended," or "do pass and re-refer to another committee"; or it votes against the bill. Bills can be amended and reconsidered several times. Bills that require the expenditure of funds will also be reviewed in the respective **fiscal** committees of each legislative house: the Senate Appropriations and Assembly Appropriations committees.[7] Policy committees need to finish their work

---

[7]Before a bill is heard in committee, a bill analysis is prepared that explains current law, states the bill's intent, and gives some background information. It also usually lists organizations that support or oppose the bill. The analysis is updated as the bill makes its way through the process.

EXHIBIT 4-2

Senate	
Agriculture	Health
Banking, Finance, and Insurance	Human Services
Budget and Fiscal Review	Judiciary
Business, Professions, and Economic Development	Labor and Industrial Relations
	Local Government
Education	Natural Resources and Water
Elections, Reapportionment, and Constitutional Amendments	Public Employment and Retirement
	Public Safety
Energy, Utilities and Communications	Revenue and Taxation
Environmental Quality	Transportation and Housing
Governmental Organization	Veterans Affairs
Government Modernization, Efficiency, and Accountability	

Assembly	
Aging and Long-Term Care	Jobs, Economic Development, and the Economy
Agriculture	
Budget	Judiciary
Business and Professions	Labor and Employment
Education	Local Government
Elections and Redistricting	Natural Resources
Environmental Safety and Toxic Materials	Public Employees, Retirement, and Social Security
Governmental Organization	
Health	Public Safety
Higher Education	Revenue and Taxation
Housing and Community Development	Transportation
Human Services	Utilities and Commerce
Insurance	Water, Parks, and Wildlife

Standing (Policy) Committees in the California Legislature

Each house also has a Rules Committee that assigns bills to the appropriate policy committees and an Appropriations Committee, the fiscal committee that reviews all bills containing proposed expenditures.

Which committees might review a bill proposing new air pollution regulations?

by May (and fiscal committees by June). A bill must pass its house of origin by mid-June. A bill that fails to advance is considered either a dead bill or a two-year bill, which means that further consideration of the bill will be postponed to the second year of the session. Policy committees need to finish consideration of the other house's bills by mid-July (and fiscal committees by the end of August). The legislative lawmaking deadline is mid-September. There is always a last-minute crush of hundreds of bills rushed to a final vote and delivery to the governor before the legislature adjourns for the fall elections and the holidays.

The Senate Health and Human Services Committee heard SB 19 in March 2001. It was amended several times and then re-referred to the Education Committee with a "do pass as amended" recommendation. Education heard the bill in May, amended it, voted "do pass as amended," and referred the bill onward to the Appropriations Committee. In June 2001, Appropriations amended it again and also voted "do pass as amended."

Bills passed by committees proceed to a second and then a third reading in the house of origin. Then the bill goes to floor debate and a roll call vote. Bills that require an **appropriation** or that take effect immediately (an urgency measure) require a two-thirds majority to pass (27 votes in the senate, 54 votes in the assembly). Other bills generally require a simple majority (21 votes in the senate, 41 votes in the assembly). Even if a bill is defeated, the author may seek reconsideration and another vote. Later in June 2001, SB 19 was read a second and third time and passed by the senate.

After a bill has been approved by one house, it proceeds to the other house, where the whole procedure is repeated. An identical bill must pass both the senate and the assembly. If a bill is amended in the second house, the house of origin must vote on it again. If agreement cannot be reached, the bill is referred to a six-legislator conference committee (three senators and three assembly members) to resolve differences and then returned to both houses for a vote on the compromised version.

Having been passed by the senate, SB 19 came to the assembly, where it was assigned to two policy committees: Health and Education. It failed passage in the Health Committee in July, was amended and reconsidered, and in August was approved "do pass as amended" and re-referred to Education. The Assembly Education and Appropriations committees, after further amendments, voted "do pass as amended." In September, SB 19 finally went to the floor of the assembly. Upon second reading, and another amendment, it was re-referred to the Appropriations Committee. With another "do pass" recommendation, SB19 was read the third time and passed by the assembly on September 12. The next day, the senate voted to concur with all the assembly amendments to SB 19. An identical bill having passed the senate and assembly, SB 19 went to the governor. Governor Gray Davis signed SB 19 on 24 September 2001.[8] It became law on 1 January 2002.

When a bill has been passed by the legislature and enacted into law, it is called a statute. The secretary of state chapters the statute, assigning it a number in the order in which it became law. SB 19 was chaptered as Chapter 913, Statutes of 2001.

Legislative Behavior

Most legislators are motivated by the calling of public service—a sincere desire to represent the people in their district. Of course, there may be other motivations too: ego, power, public attention. The downside is always being on the public stage, subject

---

[8]SB 19, Escutia, sets nutritional standards for foods sold in elementary schools. Any snacks sold outside the federal meal program must obtain no more than 35 percent of its calories from fat, obtain no more than 10 percent of its calories from saturated fat, and be no more than 35 percent sugar by weight. The only beverages that may be sold to students are milk, water, or juice that is at least 50 percent fruit juice with no added sweeteners. In middle schools, carbonated beverages may be sold only after the end of the last lunch period. High schools and middle schools may elect to take part in a pilot program that implements the nutritional standards for all foods and beverages sold outside the federal meal program. The bill increases the reimbursement rate for free and reduced-price meals in elementary and middle schools from the current 13¢ to 23¢. Meals purchased at full price by children will be reimbursable at a rate of 10¢ per meal. Districts with elementary schools, middle schools, or high schools participating in the pilot program may apply for planning grants to be used for developing other policies related to nutrition and physical activity. Funds may be used for costs associated with developing and adopting these policies, including paid release time for teachers and school employees, publication costs, and costs associated with holding a public hearing. Anticipated costs are $5 million each year in the first two years for grants and technical support, $30 million in the third year, and $60 million per year thereafter for increased reimbursement rates.

to scrutiny and criticism; always having to prepare for the next campaign; and always having to appeal to supporters for campaign contributions.

A legislator has multiple roles. A legislator can be a delegate, trustee, champion, opponent, mediator, or ombudsman—all at the same time. As a delegate, the legislator speaks for and acts on behalf of his or her district constituents. In the trustee role, the legislator, although sensitive to public opinion in the district, tries to decide what is best both for the district and for the state. Sometimes a legislator acts as a champion—a policy innovator—sponsoring and advocating public policy in the form of legislation and leading the effort toward forming a majority coalition for its passage. As an opponent, the legislator seeks to defeat other legislation. Legislators are often risk averse. Rather than taking a firm pro or con position, they will often seem aloof, waiting for competing and conflicting interests to settle their differences and present a compromise. They seek reassurance of public acceptance before committing to a position on an issue. In this role, legislators see themselves as brokers, mediators, or facilitators. In addition, legislators act as ombudsmen, attempting to assist constituents in their dealings with public agencies. This casework can often speed resolution of individual problems with the state's bureaucracy.

Legislators actually spend very little time in the house chamber voting. The real legislative work is in committees. About 80 percent of a legislator's time during the legislative session is spent in committees. Each assembly member has three or four committee assignments; each state senator, five or six. It is during the committee phase of legislation that a majority coalition is built and deals are struck to win support or placate opponents. Each legislator, alone, represents the voters in a district. It would seem, then, that each legislator is an independent actor. However, legislation occurs only by majority action. Therefore, legislators need to work together to build a voting majority coalition bill by bill. Some people decry the behind-the-scenes tactics and stratagems in the legislature—the compromises, negotiation, **quid pro quo** trade-offs, and arm-twisting. However, vote trading (called **logrolling**) and deal making to benefit a legislator's constituents (called **pork**) are essential for cooperative action. These behaviors may be criticized as shortsighted, ill-planned, expedient measures, but they are the stock-in-trade of the legislative process. Over time, benefits are distributed and interests addressed throughout the state.

Personal abilities in persuasion, bargaining, and deal making are important. But a legislator's political party and party loyalty, and the leadership of that party, are more important. Political party, political ideology, and a legislator's voting record go together. Democrats expound a *liberal* ideology, and Republicans a *conservative* one. Liberals desire an activist government that attempts to increase individual and societal well-being through government programs and regulation while being tolerant of diverse personal behaviors and values. Conservatives favor governmental regulation to enforce personal virtue and responsibility and only such programs that defend the economic status quo. "In essence, liberals and conservatives disagree over what are the most important sins. For conservatives, the sins that matter are personal irresponsibility, the flight from family life, sexual permissiveness, the failure of individuals to work hard. For liberals, the gravest sins are intolerance, a lack of generosity toward the needy, narrow-mindedness toward social and racial minorities."[9] The Democratic and Republican parties differ sharply on political ideology. Voting records show that the most conservative Democrat is more liberal than the most liberal Republican.

---

[9]E. J. Dionne, Jr., *The War Against Public Life: Why Americans Hate Politics* (New York: Simon & Schuster, 1991).

The party with the most members is called the majority party.[10] The majority party in each house elects the house leaders (speaker of the assembly and president pro tempore of the senate), controls the key committees (Rules and Appropriations), and holds most of the policy committee chairs. In other words, the majority party controls the flow of legislation—what bills get heard in committee and reported out to floor votes. Legislators vote the party line (party ideology and legislative priorities) most of the time. The Democrats and Republicans vote as blocks, with the party leadership voicing and enforcing the party line. Party leaders can reward a legislator's loyalty (or discipline disloyalty) through committee assignments and appointment of committee chairs (particularly to "juice" committees in which monied interest groups direct campaign contributions to committee members); support (or not) for the consideration of the member's bills; and even such matters as office assignments (some are better situated and larger than others), staff, and parking spaces. Party leaders and committee chairs are also important because they are magnets for campaign contributions and can transfer money to aid the reelection campaigns of members they favor.

The minority party is not powerless. The key number to remember about the California legislature is two-thirds. A two-thirds vote in each house is required to pass any bill calling for new revenue (taxation or fees). A two-thirds vote in each house is required to pass any bill having an appropriation (expenditure). A two-thirds vote in each house is required to pass an urgency measure (a law that takes effect immediately). And a two-thirds vote in each house is required to override a gubernatorial veto. Because most important legislative proposals have fiscal implications, a minority party that has at least one-third of the seats can significantly influence legislation. A simple 50-percent-plus-one majority is not enough. In order to have a two-thirds voting majority coalition, some minority party legislators must join the affirmative vote—otherwise, it can effectively block legislation that it opposes.[11]

Interests and Lobbying

A political *interest* is a cause or endeavor in which a group has a stake, concern, or responsibility. Politics has been described as a process of competing and conflicting interests. Legislation is proposed (or opposed), influenced, and advocated by special or **vested interest** groups—people or organizations who see themselves affected by proposed legislation—that might potentially gain or lose something important, whether it be tangible, such as money, or intangible, such as perceived freedom.[12]

There are hundreds, perhaps thousands, of interest groups active in California. Many are national groups interested in this state's issues. Most have local state chapters. Others are home grown, originating within the state and focusing on state issues. For the most part, groups' interests can be categorized by subject: government, health, manufacturing/industrial, finance and insurance, education, professional/trade, utilities, oil and gas, labor unions, real estate, entertainment and recreation, agriculture, transportation, legal, public employees, merchandise/retail, lodging/restaurants, political organizations. In addition, a number of interest groups have a very

---

[10]In each house, the members of the majority party sit on one side of the chamber and the minority party members on the other—hence the expression "the other side of the aisle" when referring to one party versus the other.

[11]After the November 2002 general election, the state senate had 25 Democrats (2 shy of two-thirds) and 15 Republicans. The assembly had 48 Democrats (6 shy of two-thirds) and 32 Republicans.

[12]All interests are *special*. There are no *general* interests.

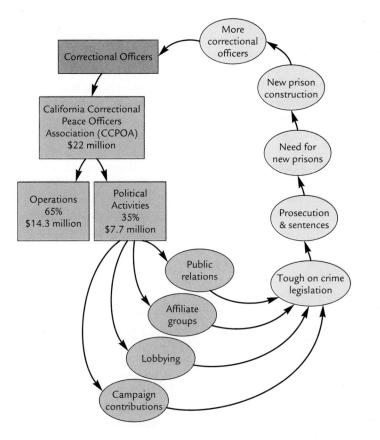

**EXHIBIT 4-3
An Interest
Group:
California
Correctional
Peace Officers
Association**

What are the
interests of this
interest group?

Source: Center for
Juvenile and Criminal
Justice, San Fran-
cisco, CA. Used with
permission.

specific single-interest policy agenda, such as pro- or anti-abortion (so called pro-choice or pro-life) or anti–drunk driving.[13] Exhibit 4-3 depicts one such interest group, the California Correctional Peace Officers Association (CCPOA), that has had considerable success advocating legislation that benefits its members.

Interest groups influence public policy by participating in political campaigns for politicians and initiatives through endorsements and campaign contributions, and by **lobbying**—advocating or opposing legislative bills.

Interest groups lobby in two ways: (1) *inside*, working the legislative rooms and offices of the state capitol in Sacramento; and (2) *outside*, stimulating public opinion. Inside lobbying is most often conducted by professional lobbyists, working either for a particular interest group or for a lobbying firm representing a number of clients. They meet with lawmakers and legislative staff, provide analysis and information to committees and legislative offices, testify in committee hearings, and negotiate the deals with politicians and other interest groups that are part of the legislative policy-making process. The largest interest groups employ professional lobbyists. Either they have their own staffs working full-time in a government relations office in Sacramento, or they hire a lobbying company to represent them (just like contracting for the services of a law firm or an advertising company).

Outside lobbying activities include press relations (such as news releases, editorial board visits, and assisting reporters with stories), visits by constituents (interest group

---

[13]Pro-abortion: California Abortion and Reproductive Rights Action League. Anti-abortion: California Pro-Life Council. Anti–drunk driving: Mothers Against Drunk Driving.

members) to their legislators, letter-writing campaigns, and rallies. Large interest groups, particularly those with an active membership, attempt to coordinate outside and inside lobbying to achieve legislative objectives.[14] You may very well find yourself occasionally involved in outside lobbying. Perhaps a news article on a public issue will stimulate you to call or e-mail a legislator. An interest group to which you belong may ask you to write a letter to your assembly member or state senator, participate in a rally at the state capitol building, or visit a legislator or staff at their Sacramento or district offices. Besides elections, these are the most fundamental actions in a representative democracy.

Lobbying is a big business in Sacramento—more than 2,000 organizations either directly employ lobbyists or hire one of nearly 400 firms that specialize in lobbying. In total, more than 1,000 individuals are registered as lobbyists—ten times the number of state legislators. Who lobbies? Everybody—that is, everybody who is potentially affected and has a stake in the public policies of California. Teachers, nurses, truck drivers, doctors, lawyers, farmers, students, business owners—the list is endless, even including government itself. All have interest groups that represent them. Exhibit 4-4 lists California's top lobbying organizations by interest area. In the 2003–2004 two-year legislative session, lobbying expenditures totaled over $400 million. The largest lobbying organizations—each spending more than $5 million—were the Western States Petroleum Association, Pacific Telesis Group, California Teachers Association, and California Chamber of Commerce.

What is the largest interest group lobby in California? Is it insurance? Health care? Education? Agriculture? Business and industry? These are all important lobbies in Sacramento, but the answer is, None of the above. The largest lobby is government itself—local government advocating and protecting its interests with respect to state government—spending more than $69 million in this effort in 2003–2004.

There are two political science concepts of the role of lobbying in the legislative process. One model is called **iron triangles** or subgovernments. This model sees tight, long-lasting relationships between (1) vested interests that have a stake in public policy and are most knowledgeable about the issues, (2) governmental administrative organizations (such as regulatory agencies) in the policy area, and (3) legislators, relevant legislative policy committees, and legislative staff. Not only does each component of the triangle support the other two, but there also can be career movement of individual participants from one component to another—an interest group lobbyist might be appointed to a regulatory agency, and a retiring politician might become a lobbyist. From time to time, various political observers have perceived iron triangles involving the insurance industry (see Exhibit 4-5 on p. 76), agriculture (the dairy industry), education (K–12 teachers), and the state bar association (lawyers).

An extreme example a few years ago involves former California Insurance Commissioner Chuck Quackenbush. Quackenbush, a Republican, was elected with the help of the insurance industry in 1994 and again in 1998. Nineteen ninety-four was also the year of the Northridge (Los Angeles area) earthquake. Quackenbush and the insurance department that he headed were accused of doing nothing "while insurance companies low-balled settlements or tied [homeowners] up in court for years."[15] Rather than pursuing lawsuits and penalties, Quackenbush allowed the insurance companies (including the 21st Century Insurance Group) to pay a nominal fine and donate several million dollars to a nonprofit foundation, run by Quackenbush,

---

[14]The Democracy Center, **www.democracyctr.org**

[15]"Earthquake Scandal Shakes California Insurance Chief, *CNN.com*, 17 May 2000, **www.cnn.com/2000/US/05/17/calif.quake.scandal/**

Category	Top Lobbyist Employers	Expenditures	Total
Agriculture			$6,100,000
	California Farm Bureau Federation	$1,320,000	
Education			$28,200,000
	California Teachers Association	$5,340,000	
	California School Boards Association	1,720,000	
	Association of California School Administrators	1,340,000	
Entertainment/Recreation			$7,890,000
	Motion Picture Association of America, Inc.	$544,000	
	Walt Disney Company	522,000	
Finance/Insurance			$34,700,000
	Blue Cross of California	$2,610,000	
	California Bankers Association	2,250,000	
	Association of California Insurance Companies	1,480,000	
	California Credit Union League	1,050,000	
Government			$69,700,000
	California State Association of Counties	$2,560,000	
	Los Angeles, County of	2,190,000	
	League of California Cities	2,100,000	
	San Bernardino, County of	1,710,000	
	Alameda, County of	1,680,000	
	Orange, County of	1,680,000	
	San Diego, County of	1,520,000	
	Los Angeles, City of	1,400,000	
	Metropolitan Water District of Southern California	1,300,000	
	Redding, City of	1,200,000	
	Association of California Water Agencies	1,150,000	
	State Bar of California	1,110,000	
	San Diego, City of	1,100,000	
	Regional Council of Rural Counties and its joint powers authority (RCRC)	1,080,000	
Health			$46,400,000
	California Healthcare Association, et al.	$2,560,000	

(continued)

EXHIBIT 4-4

Lobbying Activity, 2003–2004 Legislative Session

EXHIBIT 4-4

Lobbying
Activity,
2003–2004
Legislative
Session
(continued)

Category	Top Lobbyist Employers	Expenditures	Total
Health (continued)	Kaiser Foundation Health Plan, Inc.	1,550,000	
	Johnson & Johnson Services, Inc.	1,280,000	
	Alliance of Catholic Health Care	1,230,000	
	California Dental Association and iIts wholly owned subsidiaries	1,130,000	
	Blue Shield of California	1,110,000	
	California Association of Health Plans	1,110,000	
Labor unions			$17,600,000
	California State Council of Service Employees	$3,310,000	
	California State Council of Laborers	2,220,000	
	California Labor Federation, AFL-CIO	1,970,000	
	California Professional Firefighters	1,020,000	
	California Federation of Teachers	1,010,000	
Legal			$7,110,000
	Consumer Attorneys of California	$3,050,000	
	California Applicants' Attorneys Association	1,250,000	
Lodging/restaurants			$2,120,000
	California Restaurant Association	$1,220,000	
Manufacturing/Industrial			$41,700,000
	Alliance of Automobile Manufacturers	$3,040,000	
	California Manufacturers & Technology Association	2,260,000	
	Calpine Corporation	1,490,000	
	California Forestry Association	1,120,000	
	Philip Morris USA, Inc., by its Service Company, Altria Corporate Services, Inc.	1,070,000	
Merchandise/retail			$7,430,000
	California Retailers Association	$1,430,000	
Miscellaneous			$51,800,000
	California Chamber of Commerce	$5,280,000	
	California School Employees Association	2,830,000	

(continued)

Category	Top Lobbyist Employers	Expenditures	Total
Miscellaneous (continued)	National Federation of Independent Business	1,310,000	
	California Council for Environmental & Economic Balance	1,060,000	
	California Transit Association	1,050,000	
Oil and gas			$14,500,000
	Western States Petroleum Association	$5,400,000	
	Chevron-Texaco Corporation	2,540,000	
	BP America	2,240,000	
	Shell Oil Products U.S.	1,290,000	
Political organizations			$931,000
	California National Organization for Women	$307,000	
Professional/Trade			$24,900,000
	California Building Industry Association	$2,440,000	
	California Medical Association	2,430,000	
	California Cable & Telecommunications Association	1,050,000	
Public employees			$5,660,000
	California State Employees Association (CSEA)	$1,280,000	
Real estate			$11,500,000
	California Association of Realtors	$1,730,000	
Transportation			$8,250,000
	Los Angeles County Metropolitan Transportation Authority	$704,000	
	California Electric Transportation Coalition	567,000	
Utilities			$27,100,000
	Pacific Telesis Group SBC	$5,370,000	
	Edison International	3,860,000	
	AT&T	1,580,000	
	Verizon Communications, Inc.	1,560,000	
	Los Angeles Water and Power Department, City of	1,110,000	
	California Wind Energy Association	1,090,000	
Total			$413,591,000

EXHIBIT 4-4

Lobbying Activity, 2003–2004 Legislative Session (continued)

EXHIBIT 4-5   An Iron Triangle of Interest Group–Bureaucratic–Legislative Relationships

What are the quid pro quo relationships on each side of this "iron triangle"? (*Quid pro quo* is Latin for "this for that.")

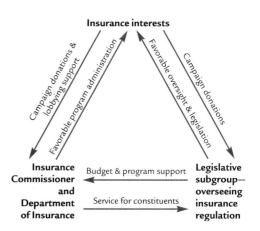

"some of which was later used for television commercials featuring the commissioner."[16] When these questionable relationships, on this and similar matters, were described in the news media and legislative investigations in 2000, Quackenbush resigned to avoid impeachment.

A second model of interest group influence is called **issue networks**. Issue networks are the set of people in lobbying groups, legislative staffs, universities, public policy think tanks (often titled institutes or centers), and the print and broadcast media that are engaged in addressing a public policy issue. The coalitions and alliances may vary from issue to issue and from bill to bill—allies at one time can be opponents another. Consider the interest group network about SB 19 as sketched in Exhibit 4-6. The school nutrition bill was supported by a coalition of education, child nutrition, and health interest groups; soft-drink manufacturers and distributors opposed it. However, the Association of California School Administrators, an education interest group, joined the opposition. Why? These contracts may be worth hundreds of thousands of dollars of additional *free, unrestricted* revenue to school and district administrators. School administrators thus have a vested interest in maintaining the sale of sugar water to their students.

Some interest groups publish legislative scorecards. Each year they identify several bills that are important to them and list the voting record of each assembly member and state senator on these bills, scoring the legislator from 0 to 100 percent. More than anything else, the scorecards reflect the ideological stance of the interest group and the respective party affiliation of each legislator (Democrat or Republican—in effect, liberal or conservative).[17]

Local Ordinances

Elected local governments in California, such as a city council or county board of supervisors, can take two kinds of actions: legislative or adjudicatory. Legislative acts involve the formulation of new policies in the form of laws, called **ordinances**,

---

[16]Virginia Ellis and Dan Morain, "GOP Hid Insurance Firm Donations in Tight Races," *Los Angeles Times*, 6 March 2003.

[17]Interest groups maintaining legislative scorecards include politically conservative organizations such as the California Chamber of Commerce, Gun Owners of California, and the California Taxpayers Association, and politically liberal organizations like the California League of Conservation Voters, the California Public Interest Research Group, and California NOW (National Organization for Women).

EXHIBIT 4-6   A Partial Issue Network for SB 19 (2001), Escutia, School Nutrition

Why do you suppose the Association of California School Administrators joined with the candy and soft drink lobbies in opposing SB 19?

California School Food Service Assn.

California Nurses Assn.

California Food Policy Advocates

California Dental Assn.

California Teachers Assn.

SB 19 (2001)
Senator Martha Escutia
(D-Whittier)
School Nutrition

Assn. of California School Administrators

California Distributors Assn.

California-Nevada Soft Drink Assn.

Jelly Belly Candy Co.

Grocery Manufacturers of America

■ Support   ■ Oppose

to be applied within the local jurisdiction. In general, ordinances are introduced at one council meeting and adopted by a simple majority vote at a second meeting at least five days later. A new ordinance must be published in a local newspaper of general circulation within fifteen days after adoption. It becomes effective thirty days after adoption.[18] Adjudicatory acts involve decision making—the application of existing policy to a specific situation. For example, decisions regarding conditional-use permits, variances, planned unit development applications, subdivision map approvals, and employee discipline and appeals are adjudicatory. Adjudicatory decisions are based on a motion—a proposal, introduced by one of the elected members, that the council or board take a certain action or express itself as holding certain views.[19] Motions are approved or denied by a simple majority vote.

Most ordinances address such seemingly mundane (but nevertheless locally important) matters as parking, use of city and county parks, and tree maintenance. The most important local ordinance is the city or county general plan, which prescribes land use and the course of future commercial and residential building and development. Sometimes a local ordinance can have broad effect. In 1996, San Francisco passed an Equal Benefits Ordinance, which "requires companies doing business with the city to provide the same benefits to domestic partners, including same-sex couples, that they do for married couples."[20] This was the first such law in the country. Since then, over 4,000 companies, colleges and universities, and local governments have announced that they will extend health insurance coverage to the domestic partners of their employees. In 2001, the city of Oakland introduced a similar ordinance for vendors to that city, and Governor Gray Davis signed a law (AB 25, Migden) extending health care benefits, and estate planning and adoption rights to domestic partners—becoming only the second state government (Vermont was first) to provide these employee benefits.

---

[18]From the city of Santa Maria, **www.ci.santa-maria.ca.us/201.html,** and the city of San Pablo, **www.ci .san-pablo.ca.us/faqs/faqsmain.html**

[19]A resolution is a more formal presentation of a motion.

[20]Christopher Heredia, "Equal-Benefit Law in S.F. Has Big Impact Across U.S.: Firms Recognize Domestic Partners," *San Francisco Chronicle*, 4 November 2001.

Lawmaking by Initiative

Lawmaking by legislation, with all of its attendant formal procedures and informal coalition building, can be bypassed by the **initiative**. Sometimes called direct democracy, an initiative presents a proposal for a new law or constitutional amendment to a vote of the people (a plebiscite).[21] An initiative presents the policy *as is*—exactly as the author wrote it—without any of the reviews, compromises, or amendments associated with legislation. Instead of lobbying, supporters and opponents of the initiative wage election campaigns fighting for a majority vote. Anyone can author an initiative and bring it to a vote. All it takes is money.

The initiative process starts with a proposed policy idea. An individual or interest group drafts the policy and submits it to the attorney general along with a $200 filing fee. The attorney general creates an official title and summary, and an estimate of the financial implications of the proposed policy is prepared by the Department of Finance and the legislature. The attorney general then sets the schedule for submitting the qualifying petitions. The proponent has 150 days to obtain signatures from registered voters on petitions favoring placing the initiative on the ballot. The number of valid signatures differs by the intent of the initiative. For a proposed statutory initiative—a new state law—this number is 5 percent of the total votes cast in the last gubernatorial election.[22] For a proposed amendment to the state constitution, this number is 8 percent of the last gubernatorial vote.[23] The proponents, of course, must gather substantially more than the minimum in order to make up for signatures by unregistered voters and other mistakes. If the petition deadline is met, the signatures are counted and checked, after which the initiative is *qualified* by the secretary of state and placed on the next statewide general election ballot (at least 131 days hence) as a proposition (see Exhibit 4-7).[24]

Lawmaking by initiative, like term limits, is favored by the public. However, also like term limits, the initiative process in California is controversial. Initiatives often deal with policy issues that reflect fundamentally conflicting political and social values. Initiatives tend to address broad societal issues that present conflicts of ideological values or "pocketbook" issues such as taxes, crime, insurance, gambling, and pollution. The supporters of the initiative process argue that initiatives act as a safety valve for the public, providing an alternate means of lawmaking when legislators, whether due to timidity, insensitivity, or ignorance, are unresponsive to the public will and reluctant to act. They argue that initiatives stimulate public participation in democratic governance, lessen alienation, and provide legitimacy to laws and constitutional amendments that address important, often controversial, public problems. Critics of lawmaking by initiative say that many initiatives reflect fads,

---

[21]An initiative proposes new policy. A **referendum** calls for voters to ratify or repeal an existing act of the legislature. The most common referenda are *compulsory*—meaning that they are automatically placed on the statewide election ballot: bond acts (legislation that calls for the state to borrow money by selling bonds), legislature-proposed constitutional amendments, and legislative amendments to any initiative previously passed by the voters.

[22]For 2002, 419,260 signatures were required to qualify a statute initiative.

[23]For 2002, 670,816 signatures were required to qualify a constitutional amendment initiative.

[24]Propositions are numbered consecutively. Once in a while, the legislature resets the numerical sequence or emphasizes a proposition by giving it a special number.

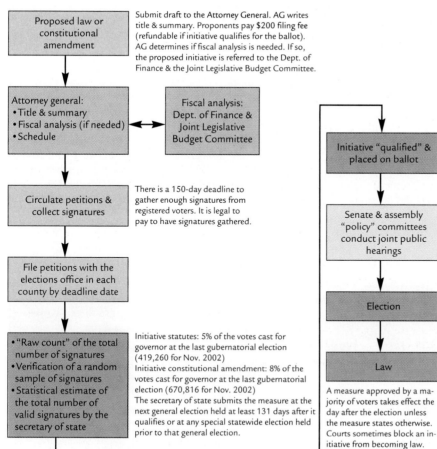

Proposed law or constitutional amendment

Submit draft to the Attorney General. AG writes title & summary. Proponents pay $200 filing fee (refundable if initiative qualifies for the ballot). AG determines if fiscal analysis is needed. If so, the proposed initiative is referred to the Dept. of Finance & the Joint Legislative Budget Committee.

Attorney general:
• Title & summary
• Fiscal analysis (if needed)
• Schedule

Fiscal analysis: Dept. of Finance & Joint Legislative Budget Committee

Circulate petitions & collect signatures

There is a 150-day deadline to gather enough signatures from registered voters. It is legal to pay to have signatures gathered.

File petitions with the elections office in each county by deadline date

• "Raw count" of the total number of signatures
• Verification of a random sample of signatures
• Statistical estimate of the total number of valid signatures by the secretary of state

Initiative statutes: 5% of the votes cast for governor at the last gubernatorial election (419,260 for Nov. 2002)
Initiative constitutional amendment: 8% of the votes cast for governor at the last gubernatorial election (670,816 for Nov. 2002)
The secretary of state submits the measure at the next general election held at least 131 days after it qualifies or at any special statewide election held prior to that general election.

Initiative "qualified" & placed on ballot

Senate & assembly "policy" committees conduct joint public hearings

Election

Law

A measure approved by a majority of voters takes effect the day after the election unless the measure states otherwise. Courts sometimes block an initiative from becoming law.

moods, or fears of the day. Further, despite popular support, many initiatives are unconstitutional. Also, some initiatives have long-term adverse consequences that are hard to correct. In general, the critics say that initiatives undermine representative democracy, diminish the role of the legislature, and provide an escape whereby elected legislators can avoid addressing tough, value-laden issues. Legislation, they say, with successive committee reviews, interest group lobbying, and opportunities to amend a pending bill, makes better laws.

Exhibit 4-8 lists a series of important initiatives that have significantly changed California governance. First on the list, and most important, is Proposition 13, passed in 1978. At the time, California state and local government financing relied on the property tax. The tax was a fixed percentage of the assessed market value of property. When real estate values escalated in the late 1970s, so did property assessments and every homeowner's tax bill. Renters were also affected, because property taxes were indirectly reflected in rents. Property taxes are unpopular. They can be financially burdensome because they are, in effect, taxes on unrealized capital gains rather than on income and often need to be paid in a lump sum. Property reassessments, based on the changing market value, increased taxes and fueled taxpayer anxiety and anger.

Proposition 13, authored by Howard Jarvis and Paul Gann, replaced the fixed-percentage tax with an acquisition-value assessment. It provided that property was to be assessed at its value when acquired through a change of ownership or by new

EXHIBIT 4-8

Important
California Ballot
Initiatives

Proposition Number	Date	Description
13	6 June 1978	Property tax. Replaced the fixed-percentage property tax with an "acquisition-value" assessment. It provided that property was to be assessed at its value when acquired through a change of ownership or by new construction, at which time property taxes were limited to no more than 1 percent of the assessed value. Thereafter, the "taxable value" of the property could increase by no more than 2 percent per year. It also required that all state tax rate increases be approved by a two-thirds vote of the legislature and that new local taxes be approved by a two-thirds vote of the electorate in the district.
98	8 November 1998	School funding. Guaranteed a minimum amount of funding for elementary and secondary schools and community colleges based on state revenue.
140	6 November 1990	Term limits. Limited the number of terms that an elected state official can serve in the same office. As regards the legislature, assembly members are limited to three two-year terms and state senators to two four-year terms.
184	8 November 1994	"Three strikes and you're out." Increased sentences for repeat felons. Persons convicted a second time for a serious or violent crime were to be sentenced to double the usual term. Criminals with two or more such "strikes" who committed any new felony were sentenced to triple the usual prison term or twenty-five years to life, whichever was greater.
187	8 November 1994	"Save Our State." Withheld education and medical care from undocumented immigrant children and their families.
209	5 November 1996	"California Civil Rights Initiative." Eliminated state and local government affirmative action programs in the areas of public employment, public education, and public contracting to the extent that these programs involve "preferential treatment" based on race, sex, color, ethnicity, or national origin.
215	5 November 1996	Medical use of marijuana. Exempted patients who possess or cultivate marijuana for medical treatment recommended by a physician from criminal laws. Physicians who prescribe marijuana are exempt from sanctions.
227	2 June 1998	"English for the Children." Required all public school instruction be conducted in English.
5	3 November 1998	Indian tribe casinos. Required the state to make compacts with Indian tribes permitting specified gambling activities on Indian lands, in facilities owned and regulated by the tribes themselves, with limited state oversight.
22	7 March 2000	Limit on marriages. Provided that only marriage between a man and a woman is valid or recognized in California.
36	7 November 2000	Drug treatment. Mandated probation with "treatment" for all "nonviolent drug offenders" until their third conviction, then limited incarceration to a maximum of thirty days.

Source: California Ballot Propositions, Santa Clara University, School of Law, **www.scu.edu/law/library/ballot_propositions.html**

construction, at which time property taxes were limited to no more than 1 percent of the assessed value. Thereafter, the taxable value of the property could increase by no more than 2 percent per year. This shielded property owners from rapidly skyrocketing taxes during a booming real estate market. If sold, the property was reassessed at 1 percent of the new market value, with the 2 percent yearly cap placed on this new assessment.[25] In addition, Proposition 13 required that all state tax rate increases be approved by a two-thirds vote of the legislature and that new local taxes be approved by a two-thirds vote of the electorate in the district.

Proposition 13 had the immediate direct effect of dropping California from fourth to twenty-fourth among the states in state and local government taxation.[26] On the other hand, Proposition 13 had several significant indirect and unanticipated consequences.[27] Local government officials began to pay more attention to the public finance implications of land use decisions. Growth and development were encouraged. Developments that generated sales tax revenues in addition to property taxes, such as big-box, Wal-Mart-type retail stores and car dealerships, gained greater favor among city council members and county supervisors. Redevelopment was used to trigger new construction and property reassessments. New development fees offset the cost of municipal infrastructures. New public finance techniques, such as investment pools, were adopted. In 1994, an Orange County investment pool managed by Bob Citron, promising returns 2 percent higher than the comparable state pool, leveraged its entire portfolio in risky derivative securities. Citron bet that interest rates would stay low or even. When interest rates suddenly increased, the pool lost $1.6 billion, and Orange County declared bankruptcy.

Proposition 13 allowed for gradual property reassessment in a booming real estate market. But what if the real estate market is flat for a while? The cost of governmental programs and services does not vary with the real estate market. Some counties treated Proposition 13's 2-percent reassessment limit as an average over time rather than a year-by-year cap. For example, they raised home assessments by 4 percent if the market had not justified a reassessment in the previous year, thus recouping *lost* property tax revenue. The courts have recently ruled against the counties on this issue, which only places a further financial constraint on local government.

Many initiative-created policies are thrown into the courts for interpretation and what amounts to de facto judicial lawmaking. Proposition 184 (the "Three Strikes and You're Out" initiative) passed in 1994. Californians were incensed by the highly publicized arrest of Richard Allen Davis, a career criminal with prior violent crime convictions, for the kidnapping and murder of 12-year-old Polly Klass. Proposition 184, which had been languishing, suddenly received overwhelming public support. It was a no-compromise, no-discretion, tough-on-crime, zero-tolerance law. Persons convicted a second time for a serious or violent crime were to be sentenced to double the usual term. Criminals with two or more such strikes who committed any new felony were sentenced to triple the usual prison term or 25 years to life, whichever was greater. The law made no distinction with respect to third-strike offenses. A felony was a felony, regardless of whether it was a property crime or a crime against a person, or whether it was a violent or nonviolent offense. Judges and prosecutors began to act as their own umpires—deciding what should be fairly counted as a strike. Some judges claimed that preexisting law gave them the power

---

[25]Howard Jarvis Taxpayers Association, **www.hjta.org**

[26]Total tax revenue of state and local government per $1,000 of personal income dropped from about $158 to $120; **countingcalifornia.cdlib.org**

[27]Jeffrey I. Chapman, *Proposition 13: Some Unintended Consequences* (San Francisco: Public Policy Institute of California, 1998), **www.ppic.org/main/publication.asp?i=116**

to ignore a past strike. Some differentiated between violent and nonviolent crimes. Others considered the time since the last offense, as well as the nature of the current offense. Many times, in the interest of justice, felony strike charges were reduced to misdemeanors.[28]

Unlike in most other states, the California legislature cannot amend initiative statutes (unless the measure provided for it). Another initiative is needed to amend the first. For example, Proposition 39, passed in 2000, reduced the majority necessary to approve local school bonds from Proposition 13's two-thirds to 55 percent.

Some initiatives are unconstitutional. Californians passed ninety-four statute and constitutional amendment initiatives between 1986 and 2000. Forty were petition initiatives and fifty-four were legislative compulsory referenda. Twenty-six (65 percent) of the petition initiatives were challenged in court, and of these, thirteen (50 percent) were invalidated in whole or in part. Four of the legislative propositions were challenged, and only one was ruled unconstitutional.[29] The implication is that many initiatives, although receiving a majority vote, are ill considered and violate either federal law, basic constitutional principles of federalism, or constitutional rights.

Sometimes, legislators work around an initiative. In 2000, California voters passed Proposition 22, which provided that only marriage between a man and a woman is valid or recognized in California. Since then, state law and local ordinances have extended the same benefits to domestic partners as are afforded married couples in most areas of the law.

Other times, an initiative is used to work around lawmakers. For example, politicians don't want to appear "soft" on drugs; the safe stance is to pass stiff criminal penalties. However, some liberal factions sensed that the public did not regard marijuana in the same class as other illegal drugs and frowned on criminalizing first-offense, private behavior with respect to possessing small quantities of marijuana and other drugs. They qualified and persuaded voters to pass Proposition 215 (1996), allowing the medical use of marijuana, and Proposition 36 (2000), providing for drug treatment rather than incarceration upon a first or second conviction for simple drug possession.

Obtaining hundreds of thousands of valid signatures to qualify an initiative may be a daunting task for a grassroots volunteer interest group. However, a wealthy individual or well-heeled interest group can spend a few million dollars and easily qualify an initiative by employing a signature-gathering firm to carry the petitions to shopping malls, supermarkets, and college campuses throughout the state. One individual or one group with enough money can move their particular issue and policy proposal to center stage, buying their way around the legislative route to policy making, with all of its give-and-take filtering, and promote their agenda directly to voters statewide with a television campaign. Critics say the ensuing initiative campaign war wastes a lot of money and dissipates a lot of energy that would be better invested in formulating sound policy by legislative lawmaking.

In 2006, Hollywood movie producer Steve Bing proposed his solution for reducing California's oil and gasoline consumption: a $4 billion program of alternative

---

[28]The U.S. Supreme Court has held that California's three-strikes law is constitutional: "State legislatures enacting three strikes laws made a deliberate policy choice that individuals who have repeatedly engaged in serious or violent criminal behavior, and whose conduct has not been deterred by more conventional punishment approaches, must be isolated from society to protect the public safety." *Ewing v. California*, No. 01-6978, March 2003, and *Lockyer v. Andrade*, No. 01-1127, March 2003.

[29]David J. Jung and Janis M. Crum, *Ballot Measures and Judicial Review: 1985–2000* (San Francisco: Hastings College of the Law, Public Law Research Institute, Fall 2000), **www.cainitiative.org**

energy incentives funded by a tax on California oil producers; hence, Proposition 87. Bing put up over $40 million to qualify and promote the initiative, the record by one person in support of a single ballot measure in California. In opposition, the campaign battle was joined by the Chevron Corporation, Aera Energy, and Occidental Oil and Gas Corporation. They matched Bing's spending dollar for dollar. Spending by both sides eventually exceeded $113 million. In the end, the initiative was defeated. Who benefited from the fight except campaign consultants and media outlets?

Initiative advocates point out that Californians tend to scrutinize and reject most initiatives, and that financial support does not guarantee passage. Over the years, nearly 1,200 initiatives have been proposed for statutes or constitutional amendments. Only one-fourth of these proposals obtained enough signatures to qualify and be placed on a statewide ballot. Only one-third of these propositions were passed by the voters (about 100 altogether).

Lastly, it is argued that the initiative process, rather than being reserved for voters to redress problems unattended to by the legislature, can be, and has been, effectively hijacked by ideological interests to promote their own agendas. Jewelle Taylor Gibbs and Teiahsha Bankhead of the University of California, Berkeley, make this argument in their book *Preserving Privilege: California Politics, Propositions, and People of Color.*[30] They examine four initiatives: Proposition 184 ("Three Strikes and You're Out," passed in 1994); Proposition 187 ("Save Our State," also passed in 1994), which withheld education and medical care from undocumented immigrant children and their families; Proposition 209 ("California Civil Rights Initiative," passed in 1996), which dismantled affirmative action; and Proposition 227 ("English for the Children," passed in 1998), which severely limited bilingual programs in schools. With the exception of Proposition 209 (largely financed by conservative Republican Ron Unz), these initiatives all received significant support from the Republican Party. Gibbs and Bankhead maintain that these initiatives were an orchestrated effort by political conservatives, facing the demographic reality of a nonwhite majority, to protect their way of life and prerogatives. "Those four initiatives have come to symbolize the struggle between the old guard and the new majority emerging in California politics, the conflict between liberals and conservatives, and the widening gulf between the powerful and the powerless."[31] Because the majority rules in passing initiatives and because, despite demographic change, about 70 percent of the voting electorate is still white and older, initiatives can be used to override some minority interests.

An initiative at the local government level is called a **measure**.[32] Measures may be placed on the ballot for a local election either by citizen petition or by action of the local governing body (city council or county board of supervisors). Measure M, on the ballot for citizens of Modesto in November 2001, is an example. In 1997, the state enacted legislation mandating the fluoridation of public water systems with at least 10,000 service connections. The city of Modesto was required under state law to fluoridate its water when outside funding sources became available to install fluoridation equipment and to operate and maintain it. Funding was available for the equipment, but there was no such outside funding for ongoing system operation and maintenance. The city had to decide whether to fluoridate its drinking water. It became a local controversy. The city council determined to let the voters decide the issue by voting on the following question: "For the purpose of dental health, shall

---

[30]Jewelle T. Gibbs and Teiahsha Bankhead, *Preserving Privilege: California Politics, Propositions, and People of Color* (New York: Praeger, 2001).

[31]Gibbs and Bankhead, p. 2.

[32]The referendum procedure to repeal a recently enacted ordinance is also available locally.

the City of Modesto fluoridate its drinking water in accordance with the standards set by the State of California, and raise water rates by up to two percent (2%) to support the operation and maintenance costs of fluoridation?" The voters answered no.

Lawmaking by Administrative Rule Making

Have you been to one of California's water slide amusement parks? You anticipate a day of fun in the sun with friends and expect the slides to be perfectly safe. This wasn't the case in June 1997, when dozens of teenagers crowded aboard a water slide in Concord. The slide collapsed, killing one teenager and injuring thirty-two. Now you see at least one park employee at the top of the slide keeping order and controlling the timing of people starting the slide, and another employee, certified in lifesaving, at the splash pool. Why? Is there a law? The answer is that the law (passed soon after this 1997 incident) authorizes the government to adopt safety **regulations** having the force of law. Most laws express general policy and intent. The specifics of precisely how to accomplish a policy objective or implement a program are left to **administrative rule making** by governmental agencies. This process, as shown in Exhibit 4-9, can take considerable time. Rule making is overseen by the Office of Administrative Law, an independent office within the executive branch of the government of the state of California. The office reviews proposed regulations and ensures that the public has an opportunity to comment and that the appropriate agency considers the comments during the development of the regulations. In California, the regulations are codified in the **California Code of Regulations**. Those amusement park employees are doing their jobs because of regulations about the operation of water slides issued by the California Occupational Safety and Health Agency.[33]

Lawmaking by Judicial Decisions

Sometimes judges make law. The usual role of the judiciary is to apply existing law to resolve disputes between two specific parties. However, in a dynamic society, judges can be presented with new fact situations that call for interpreting or extending the law or expressing new principles and public policy. They do this in three ways: judicial review, case law, and common law. These **judicial decisions** establish precedents—in effect, new law.

Consider these issues: (1) In 1997, the California legislature passed a law providing that a young woman (under age 18) must have parental consent in order to abort a pregnancy. (2) In 1989, after an individual armed with an AK-47 semiautomatic weapon opened fire on a Stockton schoolyard, killing five children and wounding one teacher and twenty-nine children, the California legislature passed a law prohibiting the manufacture, possession, sale, transfer, or import into the state of a specified list of semiautomatic weapons.[34] All laws must be consistent with the U.S. and California constitutions. So, were the two laws passed by the California legislature allowable? The process of deciding the constitutionality of a law and determining constitutional principles is called **judicial review**. In deciding such cases, courts consider not only the exact wording of statutes or regulations but also historical context, contemporary traditions and practices, and public policy.

---

[33]Proposed regulation: Department of Industrial Relations, Division of Occupational Safety and Health, Title 8 Permanent Amusement Ride Safety Orders, Chapter 4, Subchapter 6.2. Permanent Amusement Ride Safety Orders, Art. 10 Water Parks, Sec. 3195.13 Operation and Maintenance (c)1; **www.dir.ca .gov/oshsb/aquaticdevices.html**

[34]California Penal Code, Sec. 12275.

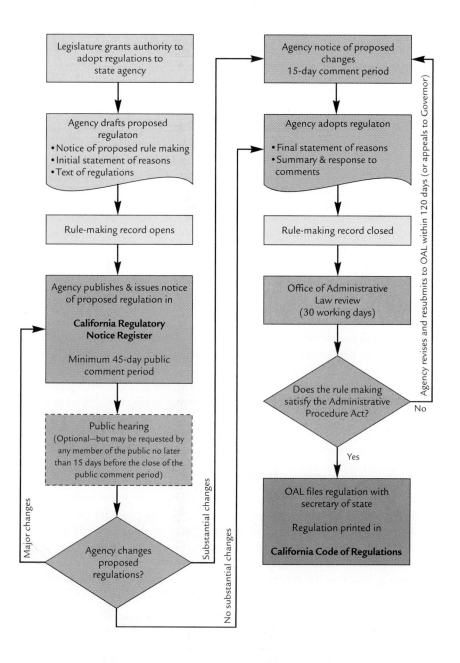

EXHIBIT 4-9   Administrative Rule Making

Privacy is not specifically mentioned in the U.S. Constitution. But the California Constitution (Art. I, Sec. 1) states: "All people are by nature free and independent and have inalienable rights. Among these are acquiring, possessing, and protecting property, and pursuing and obtaining safety, happiness, and privacy." The California Supreme Court held that the statute mandating parental consent in abortions involving young woman under age 18 was an unconstitutional infringement on the right to privacy. The state failed to show a compelling state interest in requiring parental consent that would justify such an invasion of personal autonomy.[35]

---

[35]*American Academy of Pediatrics v. Lungren*, 16 Cal. 4th 307, 66 Cal. Rptr. 2d 210; 940 P.2d 797 (1997).

The Second Amendment to the U.S. Constitution states: "A well regulated Militia, being necessary to the security of a free State, the right of the people to keep and bear Arms, shall not be infringed." In an eighty-six-page decision, including a comprehensive historical review of the origins of the Second Amendment, the Ninth Circuit Court of Appeals concluded:

> We believe that the most plausible construction of the Second Amendment is that it seeks to ensure the existence of effective state militias in which the people may exercise their right to bear arms, and forbids the federal government to interfere with such exercise. . . . What the drafters of the amendment thought "necessary to the security of a free state" was not an "unregulated" mob of armed individuals such as Shays's band of farmers, the modern-day privately organized Michigan Militia, the type of extremist "militia" associated with Timothy McVeigh and other militants with similar anti-government views, groups of white supremacists or other racial or religious bigots, or indeed any other private collection of individuals. To the contrary, "well-regulated" confirms that "militia" can only reasonably be construed as referring to a military force established and controlled by a governmental entity. . . . The historical record makes it plain that the Amendment was not adopted in order to afford rights to individuals with respect to private gun ownership or possession.[36]

Having rejected the principle of an individual right to ownership of semiautomatic weapons, the court extended the law by ruling that an exception allowing retired police officers to own assault weapons had no *rational basis* in terms of serving a public purpose. This, of course, is not the final word on the gun ownership issue. It sets the stage for the U.S. Supreme Court to further interpret the meaning of the Second Amendment.

Case law is the interpretation and application of existing statutes to unique situations. The courts sometimes provide an avenue to make new law when rigid bureaucracies, reluctant legislators, or public bias forestall government attention to needed policies. Consider the case of Ryan Thomas, a 5-year-old boy with AIDS. At school one day, Ryan bit another boy without breaking the skin. In response to community alarm, the school board suspended Ryan. Existing law provides that the government may not interfere with an *otherwise qualified* handicapped person's enrollment in regular school programs on any basis other than medical necessity.[37] The U.S. District Court for the Central District of California ruled that AIDS was a disability under the law, that the means of transmission was virtually always by sexual intercourse or infected blood, and that contact between children in a school setting (even an altercation involving biting) posed no medical risk. Court decisions in hot-button issues such as this provide political cover for administrators and politicians who are wary of public criticism.

The **common law** consists of rules and principles evolved by long-standing tradition and practice. Judges can make law by extending common law principles to new problem situations. One example of common law is the doctrine of public trust. This doctrine, dating back hundreds of years, holds that certain resources, such as air, running water, the sea, and the seashore, should be available to all. Navigable waterways were declared to be "common highways, forever free." Under the public trust doctrine, the state is guardian of the public's access to these resources. The California

---

[36]*Silveira v. Lockyer*, Ninth Circuit Court of Appeals, No. 01-15098 (2002).

[37]Donna Shestowsky, "When Courts Legislate: How the Judiciary Established a National Anti-Discrimination AIDS Policy in Schools," *The Yale Political Quarterly* 17(2), April 1996. Section 504 of the Rehabilitation Act of 1973, 29 U.S.C. Section 794, *Thomas v. Atascadero Unified School District*, 662 F. Supp. 376 (1986).

Supreme Court has held that the public trust doctrine protects not only such traditional uses as navigation, commerce, wildlife, and fishing but also new uses such as ecological units for scientific study, open spaces, habitats for birds and marine life, and environments that favorably affect the scenery and climate of an area.[38]

Lawmaking by Executive Order

Executive orders are declarations of public policy by the governor. By executive order, the governor can direct administrative action, establish policy priorities, allocate resources, reorganize executive branch departments and responsibilities, or express public policy and administrative goals. For example, in March 2004, Governor Arnold Schwarzenegger ordered the development of hydrogen-powered vehicles as a policy goal for state agencies; in June 2005, he established targets for the statewide reduction of greenhouse gas emissions; in March 2006, he ordered the California Department of Water Resources to immediately begin twenty-four critical levee erosion repair projects on the Sacramento River; and in April 2006, he established the executive position of crime victim advocate to improve the coordination of victim services programs.

WEB LINKS

Around the Capitol: a very useful one-stop Website, maintained by education lobbyist Scott Lay, linking political blogs, the California legislative directory, the California Code, and information about elections, pending legislation, and lobbying **www.aroundthecapitol.com**

Ballot Initiative Strategy Center **www.ballot.org**

California ballot propositions, Santa Clara University **www.scu.edu/law/library/ballot_propositions.html**

California secretary of state: provides information regarding ballot initiatives, candidates, campaign contributions, and lobbying activity **www.ss.ca.gov**

California Voter Foundation **www.calvoter.org**

Democracy Center: founded in San Francisco in 1992 to strengthen the advocacy work of nonprofit and community groups in California, as well as NGOs in countries around the world **www.democracyctr.org**

Howard Jarvis Taxpayers Association **www.hjta.org**

Initiative and Referendum Institute **www.iandrinstitute.org**
Ballot Watch is the Initiative and Referendum Institute's report on what's on the ballot and what may be headed there. This site provides regularly updated status reports on every effort under way to qualify an initiative or referendum for a statewide ballot. **www.ballotwatch.org**

Institute of Governmental Studies Library, UC Berkeley **www.igs.berkeley.edu/library/**

Legislative Analyst's Office: provides nonpartisan fiscal and policy analysis to the California legislature **www.lao.ca.gov**

---

[38]*National Audubon Society v. Superior Court of Alpine County*, 33 Cal. 3d 419 (1983).

Legislative Counsel: posts the statutes, bills, analyses, votes, legislative histories, and the California Code **www.leginfo.ca.gov**

Office of Administrative Law **www.oal.ca.gov**

Online municipal codes for many (not all) California cities **www.bpcnet.com/codes.htm#CA**

National Conference of State Legislatures: compares California with other states; **ncsl.org**

Political news in the states **www.stateline.org/**

Speaker's Commission on the Initiative Process **www.cainitiative.org**

U.S. term limits **www.termlimits.org**

PUBLICATIONS

Allswang, John M. 2000. *The Initiative and Referendum in California, 1898–1998*. Stanford, CA: Stanford University Press.

Basham, Patrick. 2001. *Assessing the Term Limits Experiment: California and Beyond*. Policy Analysis (Cato Institute), No. 413. **www.cato.org/pubs/pas/pa413.pdf**

Broder, David S. 2000. *Democracy Derailed: Initiative Campaigns and the Power of Money*. Orlando, FL: Harcourt.

Dubois, Philip L., and Floyd Feeney. 1998. *Lawmaking by Initiative: Issues, Options and Comparisons*. Edison, NJ: Agathon Press.

Gerber, Elisabeth R., ed. 2000. *Stealing the Initiative: How State Government Responds to Direct Democracy*. Englewood Cliffs, NJ: Prentice-Hall.

Gibbs, Jewelle T., and Teiahsha Bankhead. 2001. *Preserving Privilege: California Politics, Propositions, and People of Color*. New York: Praeger.

Goddard, Taegan D., and Christopher Riback. 1998. *You Won—Now What?* New York: Scribner.

Guyer, Robert L. 2003. *Guide to State Legislative Lobbying*. Gainesville, FL: Engineering THE LAW.

Michael, Jay, and Dan Walters. 2002. *The Third House: Lobbyists, Power, and Money in Sacramento*. Berkeley, CA: Berkeley Public Policy Press.

Mills, James R. 1987. *A Disorderly House: The Brown-Unruh Years in Sacramento*. Berkeley, CA: Heyday Books.

Schrag, Peter. 1999. *Paradise Lost: California's Experience, America's Future*. Berkeley: University of California Press.

Silva, J. Fred. 2000. *The California Initiative Process: Background and Perspective*. San Francisco: Public Policy Institute of California.

GLOSSARY

administrative rule making The process of establishing rules (policies) by governmental agencies that have the force of law in order to implement or enforce existing statutes. See *regulations*.

appropriation   A legislative bill or provision within a bill that authorizes a state agency to expend (or obligate) a certain amount of money for a specified purpose.

bill   A proposed law introduced in either the assembly or the state senate.

California Code of Regulations   The compendium of regulations for all California state agencies.

case law   The interpretation of existing statutes in light of unique situations.

common law   Rules and principles developed over time by judges deciding cases and gradually extending judicial reasoning to new, but similar, problem situations.

executive order   A decree issued by the president or governor directing administrative action and having the force of law.

fiscal   A reference to public finance.

initiative (proposition)   Lawmaking by plebiscite—a vote of the electorate.

iron triangle   A long-lasting, mutually supportive, relationship between (1) a vested interest that has a stake in public policy, (2) governmental administrative organizations (such as regulatory agencies) in the policy area, and (3) legislators, relevant legislative policy committees, and legislative staff.

issue network   The set of people in lobbying groups, legislative staffs, universities, public policy think tanks, and print and broadcast media who are engaged in addressing a public policy issue.

judicial decision (lawmaking)   A ruling by an appellate court that establishes public policy.

judicial review   The review of existing laws for compliance with California and U.S. constitutional principles.

law   A formal statement of public policy (usually enacted by legislation or initiative). Compliance is enforceable by the government.

legislation   Lawmaking by elected representatives. See *initiative*.

lobbying   The process of influencing legislation.

logrolling   Vote trading among elected representatives. Logrolling is named after the lumberjack sport in which two people must cooperate to maintain their balance on a floating log as they spin it with their feet.

measure   A ballot initiative, usually at the local government level.

ordinance   A local law applying only within an individual city or county jurisdiction.

pork (pork barrel)   Appropriations or projects with local economic and political benefits uniquely favoring the district of one legislator.

power   The potential ability to influence thought or behavior.

quid pro quo   "Something for something" or "this for that" (Latin); what a vested interest gets from elected officials in return for that interest's endorsement or campaign contribution (such as a tax break, subsidy, appointment, regulatory exemption, or favorable legislation).

referendum   A ballot measure that calls for voters to ratify or repeal an existing act of the legislature.

regulations   Rules (policies) adopted by a state agency to implement, interpret, or make specific the laws (statutes) enforced or administered by it, or to govern the agency's procedures. See also *administrative rule making*.

rule making   See *administrative rule making.*

vested interest (special interest)   A person or group with a stake (often financial) in a pending public policy decision.

SUGGESTED ANSWERS TO EXHIBIT QUESTIONS

Exhibit 4-2: Legislative committees that might review a bill proposing new air pollution regulations: Senate: Environmental Quality; Natural Resources and Wildlife. Assembly: Environmental Safety and Toxic Materials; Natural Resources

Exhibit 4-3: The CCPOA is primarily interested in the employment salary, benefits, and security of its members.

Exhibit 4-5: Possible quid pro quo relationships include (1) campaign donations to an elected insurance commissioner in expectation of lax regulation, (2) campaign donations to legislators in expectation of favorable legislation, and (3) budgetary support to an agency that provides services to a legislator's constituents of key donors.

Exhibit 4-6: It seems that soft-drink manufacturers cut deals with school districts, especially high schools, for the exclusive sales of their products in school cafeterias and campus vending machines, providing welcomed revenue for budget-tight school administrators.

Exhibit 4-7: Anyone can author an initiative and bring it to a vote. All it takes is money.

CHAPTER FIVE

IT'S YOUR MONEY

Modern government's primary function, when you come down to it, is to take money from some people and give it to others.[1]

Everything costs money: schools and colleges for child and adult education; health care for children, the indigent, and the aged; police and fire departments for public safety; highways and trains for transportation. Directly or indirectly, we all pay for government programs and public facilities by the **taxes** and **fees** we pay to federal, state, and local governments (see Exhibit 5-1). The total tax burden for a Californian is 32.8 percent—$21.90 in federal taxes and $10.90 in state and local taxes per $100 personal income.[2] For this, the governments provide benefits (payments such as Social Security or MediCal) and services. Some of the taxes and fees we pay to one level of government are actually spent by another. Some public money is transferred from the federal to state and local governments; from the state to cities, counties, and special districts; and even from one local government to another.

Government accounting is basically the same as yours. On a year-to-year basis, if annual income (revenue) exceeds spending (expenditure), one avoids debt and may even be able to carry some money forward to the next year. If expenses exceed revenue, one incurs a **deficit**. The only differences are in scale—the government accounts for billions of dollars—and in the twelve-month year. And rather than the January-to-December calendar year, California government uses a 1-July-to-30-June **fiscal year**.[3] Government spending is summarized in the table below Exhibit 5-1 on the following page.

---

[1]Daniel Weintraub, "Reversing Robin Hood: State Takes from the Poor," *Sacramento Bee*, 14 March 2002.

[2]2006 estimate: Tax Foundation, **www.taxfoundation.org**. California ranks ninth in total tax burden. The average among the states is 31.6 percent. Connecticut is highest at 35.9 percent, and Alabama is lowest at 27.5 percent. California ranks fifteenth in state and local tax burden—close to the national average of 10.6 percent. Maine is highest at 13.5 percent, and Alaska is lowest at 6.6 percent.

[3]For various reasons—including election schedules, school calendars, and even agricultural and meteorological seasons—it is convenient to use a fiscal year rather than a 1-January-to-31-December calendar year for financial accounting. The federal government uses a 1-October-to-30 September fiscal year.

EXHIBIT 5-1   The Flow of Public Money

Source: Dollars & Democracy, 1999. Reprinted by permission of California Budget Project.

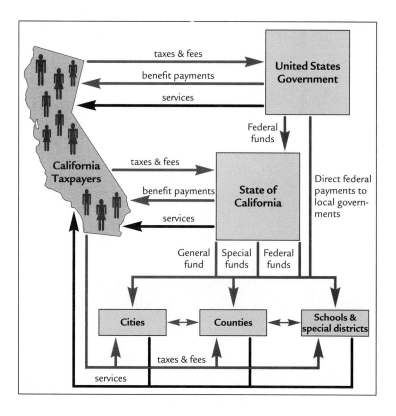

Revenue	–	Spending	=	Surplus or (Deficit)
Taxes and fees		K–12 education		
Borrowing		Health and human services		
Intergovernmental funds		Higher education		
		Corrections		
		Other		

But why do we need to know about such matters as revenues, expenditures, and budgets? Because, despite all the statements of good intentions, political rhetoric, and comprehensive plans, money is the final and most basic expression of public policy—what the government will do and how it will do it.

The public money comes from you and, curiously enough, eventually comes back to you—not person by person, or dollar for dollar, and not usually as cash, but in the form of public services and facilities. This chapter explores how this process works: (1) how the public money is obtained and (2) how it is spent.

WHERE THE MONEY COMES FROM

The California State government is a more than $140-billion-a-year operation. As shown in Exhibit 5-2, most of this money, about $100 billion, comes from direct payment of taxes and fees by Californians to the state—a **per capita** average of $3,000. Californians also pay about $24 billion to local governments—an average of $700 per capita.

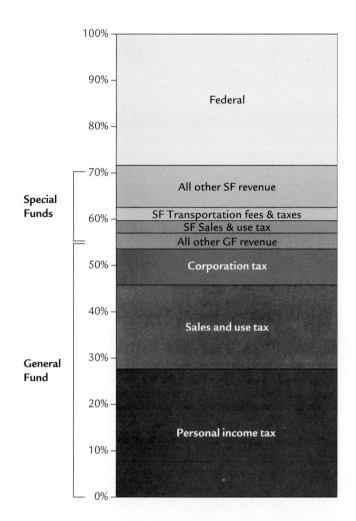

EXHIBIT 5-2   California State Government Revenues, 2004–2005

Total revenues:	$148.1 billion
Total general fund revenue:	$84.5 billion
Total special funds revenue:	$20.7 billion
Total federal revenue:	$42.9 billion

What is the largest source of general fund revenue to California state government?

Source: State of California, *Comprehensive Annual Financial Report,* for the year ending June 30, 2005, controller of the state of California, December 2005.

Public money is deposited into accounts called funds. Some income sources and expenditure purposes are connected by law—including all federal funds and about $21 billion in state taxes and fees. This is designated as restricted income, and the money is deposited into one of several **special funds** dedicated for specific purposes. The rest of the income, nearly $85 billion, is undesignated and goes into the state's **general fund**.

Taxes

Personal Income Tax   Both the federal government and the state of California levy a personal income tax (PIT). The PIT is the largest source of tax revenue for California.[4] It applies to almost all sources of employment, business, and investment income, including wages and salaries, interest, dividends, and **capital gains** earned by individuals (as well as estates, trusts, sole proprietorships, and partnerships). It is also paid by nonresidents on that part of their income earned in California. The state and

---

[4]Forty-three other states and Washington, DC, also have a PIT. Most of these taxes, like California's, are progressive. A few states use a flat tax. For example, Pennsylvania's PIT rate is 3.07 percent for everyone, regardless of income.

federal PIT rates vary by a taxpayer's filing status (single, married-filing-separately, married-filing-jointly, surviving spouse, or head of household) and income. California has six income brackets within each filing status, with tax rates ranging from 1 percent to 9.3 percent. The federal PIT rates vary from 10 to 35 percent. Exhibit 5-3 shows these brackets for a single taxpayer and married-filing-jointly taxpayers.

California 2005 Tax Rate Schedule X	IF TAXABLE INCOME IS:		COMPUTED TAX IS:	
	Over—	But Not Over—	Base Amount Plus:	Of Amount Over:
Use if your filing status is Single or Married filing separately. If Married filing jointly, double all the dollar figures.	$ 0	$ 6,319	$ 0.00 + 1.0%	$ 0.00
	6,319	14,979	63.19 + 2.0%	6,319
	14,979	23,641	236.39 + 4.0%	14,979
	23,641	32,819	582.87 + 6.0%	23,641
	32,819	41,476	1,133.55 + 8.0%	32,819
	41,476	and over	1,826.11 + 9.3%	41,476

Federal 2005 Tax Rates	If Taxable Income Is Over—	But Not Over—	The Tax Is:
Schedule X—Single	$ 0	$ 7,300	10% of the amount over $0
	7,300	29,700	$730 plus 15% of the amount over 7,300
	29,700	71,950	$4,090.00 plus 25% of the amount over 29,700
	71,950	150,150	$14,652.50 plus 28% of the amount over 71,950
	150,150	326,450	$36,548.50 plus 33% of the amount over 150,150
	326,450	no limit	$94,727.50 plus 35% of the amount over 326,450

Schedule Y-1— Married Filing Jointly or Qualifying Widow(er)	If Taxable Income Is Over—	But Not Over—	The Tax Is:
	$ 0	$ 14,600	10% of the amount over $0
	14,600	59,400	$1,460.00 plus 15% of the amount over 14,600
	59,400	119,950	$8,180 plus 25% of the amount over 59,400
	119,950	182,800	$23,317.50 plus 28% of the amount over 119,950
	182,800	326,450	$40,915.50 plus 33% of the amount over 182,800
	326,450	no limit	$88,320.00 plus 35% of the amount over 326,450

EXHIBIT 5-3   Personal Income Tax Schedules

What are the California and federal tax rates for someone with a taxable income of $30,000?

Source: U.S. government and state of California.

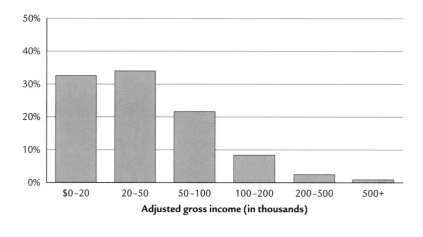

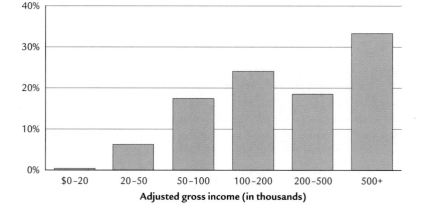

Adjusted gross income (in thousands)

EXHIBIT 5-4   California Personal Income Tax: Tax Returns and Liabilities by Income, 2003

13.6 million tax returns. Total PIT liability: $30.4 billion.

What percent of taxpayers have an annual income below $50,000? What percent of California's personal income tax do they pay? What percent of taxpayers have an annual income over $500,000? What percent of California's personal income tax do they pay?

Source: Franchise Tax Board, *2004 Annual Report,* **www.ftb.ca.gov**

The state's PIT is a progressive tax, meaning that the more you earn, the more you pay. Those who can afford to pay have a higher tax burden. As shown in Exhibit 5-4, only 10 percent of California taxpayers make over $100,000 a year—but they pay 75 percent of the tax. Less than 8 percent of California's PIT revenues come from taxpayers with incomes below $50,000; those making less than $20,000 pay virtually no PIT.

Well-to-do taxpayers derive more of their income from businesses and investments than from salaries. High-end taxpayers can control the timing and amount of such income by deciding when to exercise stock options and when to realize capital gains from asset sales. As shown in Exhibit 5-5, wage and salary income is fairly steady from year to year, but reported income from stock options and capital gains can fluctuate significantly and rapidly as the economy and stock market go through boom and bust cycles.

Policy questions regarding California's PIT include the following:

- California's highest PIT rate of 9.3 percent is above that of most other states. Does this discourage work and investment? Its lowest PIT rate is lower than that in most other states. Is it fair to "soak the rich" to finance state government?

- California's PIT is based on the federal definition of adjusted gross income. Is this computation too complicated? Is California tied too closely to federal PIT policy?

- California's revenue from the PIT can vary significantly from year to year. Yet the PIT accounts for over half of the state's general fund. Is California government overreliant on the PIT?

EXHIBIT 5-5   Personal Income Volatility

Nonwage income is principally stock options and capital gains.

Why did personal income drop in 2000–2001?

Source: California Legislative Analyst's Office, *The 2006–07 Budget: Perspectives and Issues,* February 2006. Used with permission.

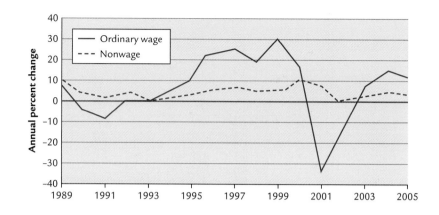

Sales and Use Tax   The sales and use tax (SUT) is the second-largest tax imposed by the state. The SUT is applied to final consumer purchases of personal property, such as clothing, household furnishings, appliances, and motor vehicles. Services, for the most part, are not subject to the SUT, and utilities (water, gas, and electricity), food, medicine, and a few other items are exempt. The use tax applies to items purchased out of state and brought into California.[5]

The basic state SUT rate is 7.25 percent (see Exhibit 5-6). For every $100 of taxable purchases, a consumer pays an additional $5.00 to the state's general fund, $1.00 to the local city government, and $1.25 to three state-administered special funds that aid local government. Some counties and cities levy an additional SUT— as much as 1.25 percent—to fund local transportation, libraries, or other programs. Thus the SUT varies somewhat by locations at which you make your purchases.[6]

The SUT is a *regressive* tax—the less you earn, the higher your tax burden. The rich and poor alike pay the SUT at the same rate. Low-income individuals tend to live from paycheck to paycheck and, in addition to housing and food, to spend their income on taxable goods. Individuals with higher incomes spend a lower percentage of their income on taxable goods than on nontaxed services.

Following are some policy questions regarding California's SUT:

- The SUT accounts for about 16 percent of total state revenue (compared with an average of 8 percent in other states) and about one-fourth of the state general fund. How large a role should the SUT play in financing state and local government operations?

- The SUT taxes the acquisition and use of tangible goods. Should intangible property (such as the transfer of a computer program by e-mail) and services be taxed as well?

- The SUT is usually not applied to Internet and mail-order transactions because the state cannot regulate out-of-state vendors. Should this be addressed, and if so, how?

---

[5]Motor vehicles and some mail-order items. Because of enforcement issues, the SUT is not applied to most Internet transactions.

[6]7.25 percent is a relatively high rate. However, due to the exemptions, the sales tax burden on Californians is near the average of the forty-five states with an SUT. The law provides that the state SUT be reduced by 0.25 percent whenever it is projected that state reserves will exceed 3 percent of general fund revenue. The rate is restored when that excess is not forecasted. California's base SUT changed from 7 percent in 2001 to 7.25 percent in 2002.

Destination	Amount	Restrictions	EXHIBIT 5-6
State general fund	5¢	Unrestricted except for motor fuel sales, which are restricted to transportation	**Allocation of 7.25 percent Statewide California's Sales and Use Tax**
State local revenue fund	$1/2$¢		
State local public safety fund	$1/2$¢	Restricted for public safety	*For every dollar of taxable purchases, you pay sales tax to _____.*
State fiscal recovery fund	$1/4$¢		
City or county jurisdiction in which sale occurred	$3/4$¢	Local government operations	
County	$1/4$¢	Restricted for transportation	

Note: A city or county may levy additional sales and use tax. Therefore, the SUT varies in California from 7.25 to 8.75 percent.

Corporation Tax   The corporation tax (CT), the third-largest tax imposed by the state, applies to corporations that do business in California. The basic rate is 8.84 percent. Nonprofit corporations (such as churches and charitable organizations) are exempt, as are insurance companies (which instead pay a gross premiums tax). Corporations doing interstate and international business are taxed on the California share of their profits. Banks and financial institutions pay a 10.84 percent bank tax. Some policy questions regarding California's CT follow:

- Despite significant growth in the economy during the 1990s, CT revenues remained relatively flat. Some experts attribute this to creative corporate accounting. What is the future role for this tax in financing California? How should it be administered and enforced?

- Various CT exemptions, exclusions, deductions, and credits—nearly $4 billion annually—can be regarded as business subsidies and incentives. Should this be a part of CT policy?

Property Taxes   Property taxes are based on the dollar value (**ad valorem**) of real property (land and buildings) and certain personal property (such as machinery, boats, and aircraft, but not cars). Local county assessors determine property values. Prior to the adoption of Proposition 13 in 1978, cities, counties, school districts, and other local governments separately established their own property tax rates and received the tax revenues. Proposition 13 eliminated locally set real-property taxes and replaced them with a state-determined tax set at 1 percent of the 1975–1976 value of the property.[7] The assessed value of the property could increase up to 2 percent

---

[7]Jeffrey I. Chapman, *Proposition 13: Some Unintended Consequences* (San Francisco: Public Policy Institute of California, 1998).

each year. Property could be revalued only upon a change of ownership or new construction. Currently, cities receive an average of 11 percent of total property tax revenues, counties approximately 19 percent, school districts 52 percent, and other local entities 18 percent.

Consider the two residences shown in Exhibit 5-7: two homes—both built in 1974, having the same square footage, located in the same neighborhood. One was purchased soon after it was built and has been owned by the same persons ever since. The other was recently resold. Proposition 13 created an acquisition-value system for property tax assessment. Longer-term owners pay lower taxes, reflecting historical property values, whereas newer owners pay higher taxes, reflecting more recent values. Property taxes for the home that resold are about 2.5 times more than the property taxes on the first home. Is this unequal treatment a denial of the equal protection principle? The courts, including the U.S. Supreme Court, held that Proposition 13 did not violate the equal protection principle. They reasoned as follows:

(a) Unless a state-imposed classification warrants some form of heightened review because it jeopardizes exercise of a fundamental right or categorizes on the basis of an inherently suspect characteristic, the Equal Protection Clause requires only that the classification rationally further a legitimate state interest.

EXHIBIT 5-7
Two Homes, Unequal Taxes

Is this fair? These two 1,300-square-foot Fremont (Alameda County) homes were built in the same neighborhood in 1974. Why, in 2001, do the new owners of house *A* (top) pay about $4,500 per year in property taxes, whereas the property taxes for house *B* (bottom), still held by the original owners, are about $600 per year?

Source: Photos copyright © Kim Komenich/*The San Francisco Chronicle*, 2001. Used with permission.

(b) In permitting longer-term owners to pay less in taxes than newer owners of comparable property, [Proposition 13's] assessment scheme rationally furthers at least two legitimate state interests.

   a. First, because the state has a legitimate interest in local neighborhood preservation, continuity, and stability, it legitimately can decide to structure its tax system to discourage rapid turnover in ownership of homes and businesses.

   b. Second, the state legitimately can conclude that a new owner, at the point of purchasing his property, does not have the same reliance interest warranting protection against higher taxes as does an existing owner, who is already saddled with his purchase and does not have the option of deciding not to buy his home if taxes become prohibitively high.[8]

Other Taxes   California imposes a variety of other taxes, each contributing only a few percentage points but altogether accounting for almost 25 percent of state government revenue. These include taxes on the insurance industry, estates, alcoholic beverages, motor vehicles, gasoline and diesel fuel, and tobacco products. In addition, California operates a state lottery and taxes businesses and employees to fund the state's disability and unemployment insurance programs.

- *Insurance tax.* A 2.35 percent tax is levied on insurance company net premiums—the periodic payments for an insurance policy—and investment dividends.

- *Estate tax.* This is sometimes called the estate pickup tax. Federal law allows for a credit against the federal estate tax for any state estate taxes paid. California's rate is set equal to the maximum allowable federal credit. Thus the state is able to pick up these revenues for itself, at no additional cost to taxpayers. However, federal estate taxes are gradually being reduced.

- *Fuel taxes.* The state levies an **excise tax**—a tax on a specific product—on motor vehicle fuels (gasoline, diesel, ethanol, or natural gas) of 18¢ per gallon, which goes to a transportation special fund. This revenue is in addition to the federal excise tax of 18.3¢ per gallon and the state SUT. A constitutional amendment (Proposition 42) approved by voters in March 2002 requires that the SUT on gasoline be spent solely on transit and highway improvements.

- *Tobacco-related taxes.* State excise tax is imposed on all kinds of tobacco products. Taxes, of course, are passed on to consumers by increasing the price of the product. Some of the proceeds go to the state's general fund although most is **earmarked** for special programs such as breast cancer research. Because this represents a sin tax on an unpopular product, there is little public opposition to squeezing as much revenue as possible out of tobacco products.

- *Alcoholic beverage taxes.* Other excise sin taxes are imposed on the sale of liquor ($3.30 per gallon for less than 100-proof, double for higher proof), beer, and wine (20¢ per gallon, 30¢ per gallon for champagne—about 11¢ per six-pack and 4¢ per bottle of wine).

- *Gambling-related revenue tax.* California allows gambling in the form of the state lottery, card rooms, horse racing, bingo and other games for charity, and Indian **gaming**. California's state lottery was established by Proposition 37

---

[8]*Nordlinger v. Hahn*, 505 U.S. 1 (1992).

in 1984. Half of the proceeds are returned to bettors, up to 16 percent reserved for administrative expenses, and at least 34 percent earmarked for education at all levels. Lottery gambling is estimated to total about $3.6 billion a year, of which about $1.2 billion goes to K–12 education. This may seem like a lot, and lottery proponents tout the aid to education, but lottery revenues amounted to less than 3 percent of state-sourced K–12 school funding. It is a poor bet, anyway. It has been estimated that if someone purchases fifty Lotto tickets each week, he or she will win the jackpot about once every 5,000 years.[9] Indian tribes pay up to 13 percent (depending on the number of slot machines) of their net win to the Indian Gaming Special Distribution Fund.

- *State disability insurance tax.* California is one of six states to operate a publicly funded state disability insurance (SDI) program. The SDI tax is levied on almost 12 million workers in the form of payroll deductions. SDI provides short-term insurance benefits to offset, in part, lost wages due to non-job-related illnesses, injuries, and pregnancy. For 2006, the SDI contribution rate was 0.8 percent of the first $79,418 of an employee's annual income.

- *Unemployment insurance tax.* The unemployment insurance (UI) tax is levied on employers. All states have a federally mandated UI program, but rates and provisions vary. Tax revenues provide partial wage replacement to unemployed workers looking for new work. Employers pay unemployment taxes from 1.5 percent to 6.2 percent on to the first $7,000 in annual wages paid to each worker. The actual tax rate varies for each employer, depending in part on the amount of UI benefits paid to former employees. An employer may earn a lower tax rate when fewer claims are made on the employer's account by former employees.

Cities and counties impose and collect a variety of local taxes. Altogether, these compose only 10–15 percent of their income, but they are nevertheless important because the revenues are unrestricted. Most common are a utility users' tax on electricity, gas, cable television, water, and telephone bills; a business license tax based on gross receipts (or sometimes just a flat fee); a transient occupancy tax on guests renting motel, hotel, or similar overnight accommodations; and a property transfer tax on the sale of real estate.

Borrowing

There are two basic ways for state and local governments to borrow money: (1) bond financing and (2) **certificates of participation**. Bond financing is long-term borrowing. State and local governments get money by selling bonds to investors that are repaid with interest. Just as you would borrow money from a financial institution to buy a house (a mortgage), governments use bond financing to pay for the purchase of property and construction of costly facilities—such as parks, prisons, and school and college buildings—that will be used for many years. Most of the bonds the state sells are **general obligation bonds** (GO). GO bonds are a form of public debt backed by the full faith, credit, and unlimited taxing power of the state government. Payments of principal and interest come from the state's general fund.

---

[9]Mike Orkin, *Can You Win? The Real Odds for Casino Gambling, Sports Betting and Lotteries* (New York: W.H. Freeman, 1991).

All general obligation bonds are placed on the ballot by legislative action or by initiative and must be approved by a majority of voters. The state also issues **lease payment bonds** (also called lease revenue) and **revenue bonds**, which do not require voter approval. Lease payment bonds are repaid out of rent payments to bond holders by the public agency. Revenue bonds are backed by a specific revenue source, such as bridge tolls or student fees. As of October 2005, the state had about $42 billion of general fund bond debt—$35 billion in general obligation bonds and $8 billion in lease payment bonds. Payments on this debt will total about $4.3 billion in 2006–2007 (about 4 percent of general fund spending). A certificate of participation (COP) is somewhat analogous to a line of credit. The local or state legislative body creates a nonprofit entity that sells COPs. The nonprofit uses the money to build the desired building, purchase the capital equipment, or acquire other permanent infrastructure. The legislative body rents the asset from the nonprofit with periodic payments from its general fund, and the nonprofit repays the COP holders. COPs are attractive because they do not require voter approval and, not technically being government debt, are not included in the total and legal limits on public debt.

Intergovernmental Grants

Californians send about $250 billion in taxes and fees each year to the federal government. A large part of this (the Tax Foundation estimates 79 percent) comes back to California as intergovernmental grants from the federal to the state government. These grants-in-aid are designated for specific, congressionally authorized programs. Most of the funds go to health care and social service programs such as Medi-Cal, California's version of Medicaid, which pays for health and long-term care for eligible low-income citizens and legal residents, and CalWORKS, California's implementation of the federal Temporary Aid to Needy Families (TANF) welfare program. Other federal grants provide educational assistance for disadvantaged children and aid highway planning and construction. The state, in turn, allocates most of the federal-source education and welfare funds to the counties, which actually administer the programs at the local level. Additional federal grants go directly to local government.

Fees and Assessments

At one time, cars were included as taxable personal property. This was replaced by the state-imposed vehicle license fee (VLF)—actually a tax—based on the depreciated value of each vehicle. In general, such ad valorem per-unit levies are regressive. However, lawmakers figure that higher-income taxpayers are more likely to own newer and pricier vehicles and thus can afford a higher VLF, whereas lower-income taxpayers will tend to drive older vehicles having a lower VLF. The VLF is a form of **revenue sharing**. Proposition 47 (1986) requires that nearly all VLF revenue be transferred to city and county governments on a per-capita basis. The legislature controls both the tax rate and allocation percentages. The state collects the tax and distributes it to cities and counties. About three-fourths of the VLF funds can be used for any spending purpose. The remaining quarter of local government VLF funds is restricted to funding various health, mental health, and social services programs. Between 1999 and 2000, the VLF was reduced by two-thirds. The revenue reduction to local governments was **backfilled** by the governor and the legislature from the general fund. One of Governor Arnold Schwarzenegger's first acts was to cancel the planned restoration of the VLF to pre-1999 levels.

Other fees, also called service charges, are imposed by state and local governments on virtually any activity or transaction that provides a personal user benefit. The state imposes fees on such things as visits to state parks, university applications and course registration, and liquor licenses. City and county service charges include fees for utilities (such as water, sewers, and waste disposal), transportation (airports and harbors), and recreation (stadiums, sport fields, parks, and golf courses). A minor component of state income, they provide about 12 percent of county revenue and more than one-third of city revenue. **Assessments**—per-parcel charges on real property—are a common method of financing the creation and maintenance of public facilities. Basically, a local government designates a geographic area—an assessment district—within which property owners will be charged for benefit improvements. Assessments are usually added to the property tax bill. There are thousands of such districts throughout the state that finance landscaping, street lighting, sewers, flood control, public transit, and many other projects. Proposition 218, passed in 1996, limits assessment fees and requires voter approval for new assessment districts.

Local Government Realignment

In the 1980s and 1990s, local government financing in California underwent a radical transformation that has come to be called the **realignment**. Over the course of twenty-four years, a succession of ballot initiatives and legislative statutes significantly shifted the sources and allocation of local government revenues. After Proposition 13, the state assumed the task of distributing property tax receipts among the local governments within each county. At the same time, property tax revenues declined sharply. Exhibit 5-8 shows that within three years the school districts' share of property tax receipts fell from an average of over 50 percent to about 30 percent. The state took over primary responsibility for funding K–12 education from local school boards, allocating money throughout the 1980s from the general fund to offset the **shortfall**.

The rest of the realignment is summarized in Exhibit 5-9. The passage of Proposition 98 in 1988 locked in a minimum funding level for K–12 and community college districts based on a funding formula that guaranteed a share (approximately 40

EXHIBIT 5-8
Property Tax Allocation over Time: Percent of Property Taxes Allocated to Local Agencies

How did the allocation of property tax revenues change with the realignment of local government financing?

Source: California Legislative Analyst's Office, *The 2004–05 Budget: Perspectives and Issues.*

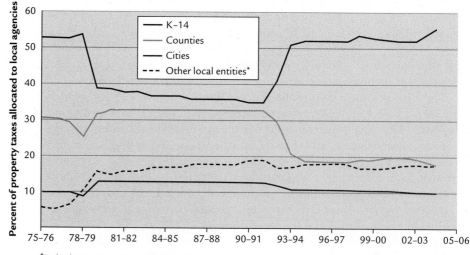

*Redevelopment agencies and special districts.

1978	Proposition 13. Established one tax rate, 1 percent of the 1975–1976 property value, with assessment increases limited to 2 percent per year unless the property was sold.
	SB 154 provided "block grants" to local governments to cover revenue losses and provided a formula for allocating property taxes.
1979	AB 8 allocated property taxes and provided state-source funding of health and human services programs.
	Proposition 4. Set state and local government spending limits—modified by later initiatives.
1982	First Certificate of Participation issued
	Passage of Mello–Roos Act
	Proposition 6. Prohibits state gift and inheritance taxes except for "pickup" tax qualifying for federal tax credit.
	Proposition 7. Requires indexing of state personal income tax brackets for inflation.
1984	Proposition 37. Establishes state lottery and dedicates revenue to education. Places prohibition of casino gambling in State Constitution.
1986	Proposition 62. Requires a simple majority of the voters for a general tax and a two-thirds margin for a special tax (initially held unconstitutional).
1986	Proposition 47. Requires that nearly all vehicle license fee revenue be transferred to city and county governments.
1988	Proposition 98. Established a formula for earmarking about 40 percent of state general fund revenue to education.
	Proposition 99. Imposes a 25¢-per-pack excise tax on cigarettes and other tobacco products. Limits use of tax revenue, primarily to augment health-related programs.
1990	Proposition 111. Established formulas for state and local government spending limits.
	SB 2557 authorized counties to charge cities jail-booking fees. (Cities subsequently reimbursed by the state.)
1992	Proposition 162. Limits the legislature's authority over California's Public Employee Retirement System (PERS) and other public retirement systems.
	Proposition 163. Repealed "snack tax" and prohibits any future sales tax on food items, including candy, snacks, and bottled water.
	Proposition 172. Imposes one-half-cent sales tax and dedicates the revenue to local public safety programs.
1992–1994	Property tax shift to help state budget (establishment of county Educational Revenue Augmentation Funds).
1995	Proposition 62 upheld by California Supreme Court.
1996	Proposition 218. Limits authority of local governments to impose taxes and property-related assessments, fees, and charges. Requires majority of voters to approve increases in all general taxes and reiterates that two-thirds must approve special taxes.
1997	Trial court financing reform

(continued)

EXHIBIT 5-9

**The Realignment:
A Chronology of
Governmental
Financing in
California
(continued)**

1998	Proposition 10. Imposed a 50¢-per-pack excise tax on cigarettes and higher tax on other tobacco products. Limits use of revenues, primarily to augment early childhood development programs.
	Proposition 11. Authorized local governments to voluntarily shift sales tax revenues among themselves by a two-thirds vote of the local city council or board of supervisors rather than requiring a majority vote of the people in each affected jurisdiction. (Attempt to reduce city–county competition for projects generating sales tax revenues.)
1998–2000	Vehicle license fee reduced by two-thirds. City and county revenues "backfilled" from the general fund.
2000	Proposition 39. Changed the required majority for local voter approval of public school and community college general obligation bonds from two-thirds to 55 percent of the votes.
2002	Proposition 42. Required revenues from state sales and use taxes on the sale of motor vehicle fuel to be used for transportation purposes.

Source: After Jeffrey I. Chapman, *Proposition 13: Some Unintended Consequences* (San Francisco: Public Policy Institute of California, 1998), and *1998 Cal Facts: California's Fiscal Structure* (Sacramento, Calif: Legislative Analyst's Office).

percent) of the state general fund. When the economic recession of the early 1990s hit, the state did not have enough income going to the general fund to meet all of its post–Proposition 13 and post–Proposition 98 commitments. The state solved the crisis by reallocating a significant proportion of property taxes away from cities—and especially counties—to a countywide Educational Revenue Augmentation Fund (ERAF) for K–12 and community college education. The **ERAF shift** brought the property tax distribution close to pre–Proposition 13 percentages, but it decimated the financial structure of counties. To remedy this crisis, the state backfilled. It added a half cent to the state SUT and earmarked that for county public safety expenditures (an action voters made permanent through Proposition 172 in 1993). During the 1990s, the state also assumed most trial court funding that previously had been a county responsibility. On the average, these measures largely made up for the ERAF shift for counties. However, the offsets are very uneven. Some counties break even or even realize small gains (Butte and Orange counties, for example); others are still left with substantial losses (Calaveras, Merced, and San Joaquin counties, for example).[10]

Local government's fiscal realignment has had four principal consequences that raise serious long-term policy issues for California: fiscalization of land use, intergovernmental dependence, innovative financing, and entrepreneurial activity.

Fiscalization of Land Use   Cities and counties control land use with their general plans and zoning ordinances. Their goals include new development to provide affordable housing, well-paying jobs, environmental protection, and efficient transportation. "Fiscalization of land use" refers to the increasingly important objective of encouraging development that provides a revenue stream to local government.[11] There are only two ways to do this: (1) expand the city to increase the property tax

---

[10]*Shifting Gears: Rethinking Property Tax Shift Relief* (Sacramento: Legislative Analyst's Office, 1999).
[11]Dean Misczynski, "The Fiscalization of Land Use," in *California Policy Choices*, vol. 3, pp. 73–106, ed. John J. Kirlin and Donald R. Winkler (Sacramento: University of Southern California, 1986).

base, which also incurs additional infrastructure and service costs, or (2) promote retail commercial development, which is relatively compact, demands few services, and provides 1¢ of unrestricted income for every dollar of taxable sales. The most valuable commercial centers in this regard are auto malls and shopping centers anchored by big-box stores such as Wal-Mart, Target, and Circuit City. However, the retail sector has relatively few high-paying jobs, and the sales tax income is mostly expended on day-to-day services. Large-scale business and industrial development, although having more permanent high-wage employment, also brings significant traffic and environmental pollution problems.

Intergovernmental Dependence The realignment has made counties and school districts dependent on the state government for funding. Other than competing with cities for the same retail developments, they have few options to generate their own income. Most of their revenues are provided by the state and federal governments and are restricted to the purposes established by those governments. Thus they "dance to the tunes" played in Washington, DC, and Sacramento. Exhibit 5-10 shows that the majority of county and school district revenue is provided by intergovernmental transfer payments.

Innovative Financing With realignment, bond financing and tax increases require a two-thirds approval of the voters—a tough sell to say the least. Cities and counties look to other financing strategies, such as certificates of participation (which were described earlier), redevelopment, and benefit assessment districts, for major purchases or infrastructure improvements. Redevelopment is an interesting financial tool. It is technically called tax increment financing. First, a city or county forms a redevelopment agency, most often with the same council or board members as the directors. They then declare a particular part of their jurisdiction to be "blighted." If this area can be improved, the property value will increase, and so will the property

TO	FROM		EXHIBIT 5-10
	Federal	*State*	**Intergovernmental Transfers: Percent and Amount of Recipient's Total Revenues**
*State**	29.0%	—	
	$42.9 billion		
Counties†	22.3%	38.0%	
	$9.1 billion	$15.6 billion	
Cities‡	4.5%	7.7%	
	$1.9 billion	$2.8 billion	
School Districts§	8.2%	54.5%	
	$3.8 billion	$25.7 billion	

*State of California, Comprehensive Annual Financial Report for the year ending June 30, 2005, controller of the state of California, 2005.
†Counties Annual Report 2003–2004, controller of the state of California, 2006.
‡Cities Annual Report 2003–2004, controller of the state of California, 2006.
§School Districts Annual Report 1999–2000, controller of the state of California, 2003.

tax receipts. The redevelopment agency borrows money for the improvements. The increased tax receipts (the tax increment) pay the debt and provide additional income to the city or county.

One type of benefit assessment is the Mello–Roos bond (named after the two legislators who carried the legislation in 1982), which can be used to fund infrastructure construction in undeveloped areas or increased community services. Two-thirds of the voters of the area, or landowners representing two-thirds of the land in the area, can vote to borrow money for the improvements. A lien is placed against the property in the area. As the property is subdivided, each individual homeowner is responsible for payment of a share of the debt (which shows up on the property tax bill).

Entrepreneurial Activity   The realignment has also stimulated imaginative, and often complicated, cooperative agreements, such as joint-power authority among public agencies and public-private development ventures. Sometimes these agreements are combined with redevelopment or tax abatement measures to entice a particular business or industrial development. The government assumes some risk in the investment. It stands to gain if the project is successful, but it can also lose. Another kind of entrepreneurship is use of money. Rather than leaving public money in low-interest bank accounts until it is spent, some governments have pooled their funds in stock market–like investments. It is a good management practice if the investments are conservative and carefully monitored. But in Orange County in 1994, a highly risky, multibillion-dollar investment portfolio soured. Scores of local governments were harmed, and the county declared bankruptcy to restructure its finances.

In sum, the realignment seems to reinforce two public finance verities. The first is the Golden Rule: "He who has the gold, rules!" or, as one writer explains, "The level of government that has the authority to generate revenues is the level that *controls* those revenues."[12] The second is that "blunt initiatives lead to the development of other (and more complicated) ways of getting things done."[13]

WHERE YOUR MONEY GOES

Budgeting

Think of everything government agencies buy: computers, office equipment, vehicles; everybody government agencies employ: police officers, clerks, professors; everything government agencies do: make benefit payments, educate, enforce the law. What exactly should government do? How much should be spent? Who should pay? These are tough questions that are asked and answered millions of times every year. The annual process of making these decisions—allocating government financial resources—among myriad needs and demands is called **budgeting**. A government budget is many things:

- It is a plan, presented as a written document, to spend money to maintain activities, accomplish program objectives, and express political and social values.

- It is a legislative act authorizing state employees to spend taxpayer dollars within a set upper limit.

---

[12]*Changes in State and Local Public Finance Since Proposition 13*. Research brief (San Francisco: Public Policy Institute of California, March 1999).

[13]Chapman, *Proposition 13*, 15.

- It is an accounting statement, providing an audit trail connecting state income to state spending.

- It is a means of transferring money from one government to another.

- It is a management mechanism for the governor and legislators to induce administrative departments to implement policies and programs in an intended way.

- It is a policy statement of the bottom line—the real priorities of government after all the political rhetoric has been swept away.

The process of developing and approving a budget is not so much a procedure as an interesting choreography involving numerous players, story lines, and scenes.

Budget Cycles   First, let's orient ourselves in time. As noted, California's *fiscal* year is from 1 July to 30 June. The present fiscal period—here and now—is the *current* year. Exhibit 5-11 shows that spending during the current year was approved up to a year earlier and planned even earlier than that. The whole sequence—planning, budgeting, and spending—is called the budget cycle. A governmental agency is always in the midst of at least three budget cycles: spending for the current year, seeking executive and legislative approval for the next fiscal year (called the budget year), and planning for the fiscal year after that.

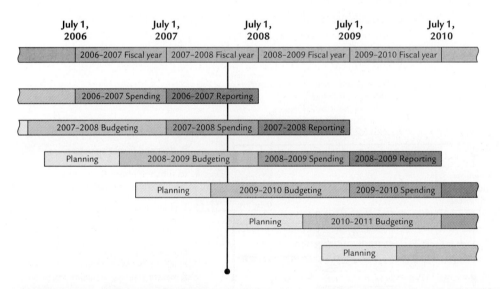

EXHIBIT 5-11   What Year Is This?

Budget cycles overlap. A department is always in the midst of at least three concurrent budget cycles.

Say the date is April 1, 2008. What is a department doing?

- The *current year* is FY 2007–2008. A department is spending funds approved in the FY 2007–2008 budget.
- Its FY 2008–2009 *budget year* request has been planned and submitted, and is now being considered by committees in the legislature.
- Meanwhile, it is submitting its FY 2009–2010 budget request to the Department of Finance and starting to plan its FY 2010–2011 budget.

What is the "lead time" between planning and spending?

FY = fiscal year.

The Budget Process   Exhibit 5-12 shows the sequence of events for the state budget. Each spring, administrative departments finalize their plans and prepare program requests. A program is a service that the department provides. For example, the Employment Development Department's (EDD) Employment and Employment-Related Services Program matches employer needs with job seekers. The California Highway Patrol (CHP) describes its basic patrol operations as its Traffic Management Program. Meanwhile, the Department of Finance (DOF) forecasts state revenue and, acting on behalf of the governor, issues policy directions. Internal review and negotiation between DOF specialists and the respective administrative agencies and

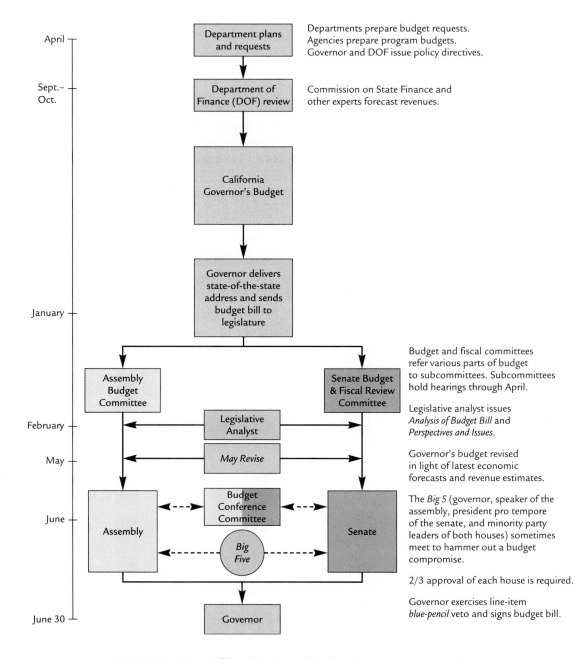

EXHIBIT 5-12   California's Annual Budget Process

departments results in the governor's budget, which is produced with great fanfare each January at the time of the governor's state-of-the-state address.

At this point, the budget is *balanced*—if spending exceeds forecasted revenues, the budget includes a combination of new taxes and fees, spending reductions, and creative accounting (such as borrowing from one fund for another) to make up the difference.

California state government is carried out by nearly 200 departments, agencies, boards, commissions, and other administrative units—by state employees, by contracts with businesses, or by transfer of funds to other units of government. "Because departments and agencies form the basic building blocks of government, the budget is organized around them as well."[14] Department by department, the budget lists all the programs, capital projects, projected costs, and funding sources (general fund or one of the special funds). These programs and projects, called **line items**, cover every aspect of a department's operation. The line-by-line dollars show the relative commitment of government to everything we expect it to do.

The legislature receives the governor's budget as the Budget Bill. The subcommittees of the assembly and senate fiscal committees begin to examine the proposal in detail. In February, the Legislative Analyst's Office issues its assessment of the revenue and expenditure plan in two key reports: *Analysis of the Budget Bill* and *Perspectives and Issues*. May and June is "crunch time." The DOF issues the *May Revise* to the budget reflecting April tax receipts and the latest economic forecasts. The legislature is working toward a constitutional deadline of 15 June to pass the budget bill. Both the assembly and the senate have to approve an identical budget bill by a two-thirds vote.[15] Invariably, this cannot be done, and budgeting brinksmanship ensues. (See the section titled "Budget Politics" below.) The governor may informally negotiate with individual legislators or the majority and minority party leaders in the assembly and the senate (the **Big Five**) to resolve an impasse.

Eventually, a budget (now the Budget Act) is approved, and the governor, with exceptions, signs it into law. The exceptions are important. The governor has the power of a line-item veto, called the **blue pencil**. If the legislature added some funding that the governor does not favor, the governor may veto just that part of the budget without vetoing the whole bill. This is a significant power that is not granted even to the president of the United States, who, for any congressional legislation, has only the options of signing, of letting a bill become law without signature, or of vetoing the bill in total.

It is midsummer, and as all this is going on, all the state departments are closing out one fiscal year; totaling their accounts, case loads, and activities; starting another fiscal year; and submitting their next-budget-year requests to the DOF.

Budget Dynamics   The budget is the scoreboard for high-stakes conflicts involving many elements:

- *Value differences*—what should or should not be done
- *Instrumental differences*—how the government should or should not pursue a given objective
- *Constituency differences*—who benefits and who pays

---

[14]*Dollars and Democracy: An Advocate's Guide to the State Budget Process*, California Budget Project, March 1999.

[15]There is no constitutional requirement for a balanced budget. The law requires only that projected expenditures not exceed projected revenues.

- *Partisanship*—which political party gains or loses power
- *Role conflicts*—which individuals and offices gain or lose influence
- *Institutional rivalry*—which departments and agencies grow, stagnate, or decline with respect to others[16]

Every year the budgeting process *works*, in the sense of reconciling the conflicting values and demands with the sheer complexity and size of California government, and allocating the state's financial resources. It does this by a combination of budgetary dynamics, constraints, and politics.

Budget Incrementalism   California budgeting is incremental. Every department and program has an inherent base that reflects its most recent level of service, personnel, and equipment. The governor's budget highlights proposed reductions and increases to this base. For example, the 2002–2003 budget augmented the Traffic Management Program for the California Highway Patrol (CHP) by $72.5 million, adding officers and aircraft to increase patrol capabilities as a means of countering the threat of terrorism.

The budget also reflects a program's or department's fair share among competing and conflicting government spending priorities. For example, the budget for the Department of Corrections and Rehabilitation is $8.6 billion, about 6.2 percent of California's general fund budget. This is equivalent to $34,150 a year to house each inmate. About half of that cost is for security; the remainder is for health care, food and clothing, facilities, inmate academic and vocational work, counseling, and administration. By contrast, the California State University system enrolls about 348,000 full-time-equivalent students, and has a general fund budget of $4.6 billion, or about $13,218 per student. Exhibit 5-13 lists key data for the two agencies.

---

[16]After James L. Gosling, *Budgetary Politics in American Governments* (New York: Garland, 1997).

EXHIBIT 5-13	California Department of Corrections and Rehabilitation (CDCR)		California State University (CSU)	
A Tale of Two Agencies: The California Department of Corrections and Rehabilitation and the California State University	Total employment	54,868	Total employment	44,000
	Correctional officers	33,428	Full-time faculty	11,069
			Part-time faculty	10,025
	CO salary	$39,732–$67,932	Faculty salary	$45,156–$97,776
	Budget 2006–2007*	$8.6 billion	Budget 2006–2007*	$4.6 billion
	Facilities	33 prisons, 40 camps	Facilities	23 campuses
	Institutional population	170,475	Institutional population†	348,000
	Cost per inmate	$34,150	Cost per FTE student	$13,218
	Commitment per 100,000 over 18	608	Enrollment per 100,000 over 18	1,243

* Proposed general fund spending.
† Estimated full-time equivalent (FTE) students, 2006–2007.

The focus on incremental change from one year to the next simplifies budgeting. Details rather than fundamental purposes are argued; fair share and trade-offs rather than needs and choices are argued. Short-range, stopgap measures easily become long-range commitments, so that over time the budget becomes a hodgepodge set of negotiated deals. This myopic, short-range, perspective is further reinforced by the recurrent budget cycles. There is really only a six-week period in May and June, between the May Revise and the June constitutional deadlines, to resolve budget disputes—precipitating an annual budget crisis. So much energy is expended on budget-year negotiations that participants are more than ready for a July-August vacation. Soon the fall brings elections and new issues. The never-ending year-to-year repetitiveness of budget cycles encourages participants to address immediate political demands. It is easy to postpone policy debates about spending because, before too long, the next budget cycle presents another opportunity to revisit the issues and reengage the budget fight. Programs and issues that failed one year can be brought up again the next.

Budget Constraints   With over $130 billion in revenue each year, you might think that there would be sufficient funds and enough discretion to adapt to changing needs and economic conditions. However, most of state spending is locked in, and there is actually very little flexibility. This uncontrollable required spending occurs in several ways:

- *Earmarking.* Certain taxes and fees have a purpose attached to the money and must be tracked and expended only for the prescribed purpose. About 17 percent of state taxes and fees go directly into some special fund. These funds can be used only for the specified purposes.

- *Matching.* Federal grants, the largest of which are for the CalWORKS and MediCal programs, require almost equal funding by the state. In addition, receipt of some federal funds requires the state to implement certain policies.

- *Mandates.* Federal or state legislation or court orders require funding for certain programs. Mandates can be explicit, requiring a specified amount of state funding, or implicit, specifying a policy or program the implementation of which requires funding but without specifying the amount of funding.

- *Entitlements.* More common with federal budgeting, entitlements specify a payment as a right to eligible beneficiaries. The budget amount equals the payment times the estimated number of people qualified to receive the benefit.

- *Funding formulas.* Funding formulas are a relatively recent budget innovation. They establish budgetary shares—guaranteed minimum percentages of state spending that must be allocated to particular purposes, programs, or projects. Under Proposition 98 (1988), the state must spend a specified minimum amount, determined by formula, on K–12 education and community colleges each year.

- *Commitments.* Sometimes California plays a "domino" game of shifting money from one fund to another. For example, revenues from the state's vehicle license fee (VLF) are allocated to city and county governments. When the VLF was reduced in the late 1990s, the legislature committed general fund money to backfill the lost revenue to local government. Similarly, in 1990, after shifting some revenues from county to state government, the legislature authorized counties to charge cities a booking fee for each arrestee the city police transported to the county jail. Later, the legislature enacted a commitment to reimburse the cities each year for the amount of the booking fees.

Although general fund (GF) spending is, by definition, discretionary, there are constraints. The first claims on the general fund are programs that must be funded at levels (by either dollar amount or formula) specified by the state constitution, state legislation, or federal matching requirements. The best example is Proposition 98 funding. Proposition 98 (1988), later amended by Proposition 111 (1990), establishes minimum formula-based funding for K–12 schools and California community colleges. The major factors are (1) general fund revenues, (2) state population, (3) personal income, (4) local property taxes, and (5) K–12 average daily attendance.

Implicit **mandates** in the form of program service levels also lay claims. For example, California's "Three Strikes" initiative (Proposition 184, 1994) increases prison terms for repeat felons, implicitly requiring additional corrections funding. These minimal definitions of budget requirements alone obligate nearly 50 percent of the GF. If we add in other fundamental state functions, such as tax collection, forest fire protection, the courts, and transportation (including the Department of Motor Vehicles), to name but a few, required GF spending approaches 75 percent. State expenditures for the university systems, housing, and environmental protection are still treated as discretionary. In good economic times, the governor and legislature find it easy to expand programs and satisfy the wants of multiple constituencies. In recessionary times, however, cutback or tax-increase decisions are hard to make. Cutbacks either are made as across-the-board fixed percentages—sharing the pain—or are focused on the programs with the weakest and least vocal political constituencies.

Budget Politics   The budget process is the perfect venue through which to pursue partisan policy agendas—to reward political friends and punish enemies. If it is in the budget, things happen. If it is not in the budget, nothing happens.

Brinksmanship. A two-thirds supermajority affirmative vote in both the assembly and the senate is needed to pass the budget bill. However, neither the Democrats nor the Republicans hold two-thirds of the seats in either house. California's constitution requires that the budget bill be passed by 15 June and signed by the governor by 30 June. Some say, "This is the only time that the minority party is important." This situation would seem to put the minority party in the proverbial "catbird seat." If the minority party members are united, they can withhold consent to the Budget Bill until the governor and majority party concede to some of their policy or program agendas. The governor might negotiate this compromise through the majority and minority party leaders in each house—the Big Five. Or the governor might try to "pick off" a few legislators in the minority by offering some additional projects for their districts or some additional funding for a favorite program in exchange for their crossover votes. Approaching or missing the June deadline, particularly in election years, provides not only negotiating leverage but also opportunities for posturing on political values—blaming the opposition party and political rivals for mismanagement and political opportunism. In 1992, Republican Governor Pete Wilson was embroiled in a standoff with a Democratic-controlled legislature. The impasse lasted until Labor Day. Republican political strategist and former Wilson aide Dan Schnur said, "Voters don't like spending cuts. They hate tax increases. But what they hate even more is the spectacle of a government that can't get its job done."[17]

Crisis. In 2002, Governor Gray Davis, facing a fall reelection campaign, encountered a budget shortfall (difference between projected revenues and expenditures) that

---

[17]Amy Chance, "Capitol Plays a Blame Game," *Sacramento Bee*, 7 July 2002.

grew during the budget cycle from an estimated $12 billion in January to $24 billion in May. He proposed closing the gap with a mix of program cuts, borrowing, and tax increases on tobacco products and motor vehicles; but when minority party Republican legislators held fast against tax increases, an impasse ensued. Who would get more of the blame, Davis or the Republicans? Given that after redistricting, Republican incumbents and most other state legislators have safe seats, who has more to lose? Late in 2002, the Legislative Analyst's Office warned that California faced another deficit exceeding $35 billion for 2002–2003:

> The deficit outstrips the entire budgets of 46 states. It is more than one-quarter of the current general fund, a percentage that rivals the shortfalls of the early 1990s, when California was mired in an economic decline that approached a depression. The shortfall approaches the annual revenues of the Walt Disney Co., Microsoft Corp. or Aetna. If the state were to halt all funding for the University of California, California State University and the MediCal program, it would still have a budget gap of several billion dollars. It breaks down to more than $700 for every man, woman and child in the state."[18]

Davis was recalled in 2003. The new Schwarzenegger administration covered the deficit by cutting program spending and borrowing from private markets, local governments, schools, transportation, and other special funds.

If the state continues its heavy reliance on capital gains income taxes, deficits of this magnitude will recur. The governor and the legislature have unpleasant choices: Cut programs, increase taxes, or borrow against the future. Should the state incur that debt? What taxes should be increased? What programs and expenditures should be cut? Who will be affected? These are important questions for you and all Californians.

Alarms and excursions. Strictly speaking, if the constitutional deadline of 30 June is not met for the Budget Act, the state cannot pay its bills. However, several court decisions over the years have ensured that a budgetary impasse will not lead to an immediate government shutdown. Nevertheless, threats and "hostage-holding" increase the pressure on the governor and legislative leadership to reach a spending compromise. During Governor Wilson's 1992 impasse, the state paid its employees and contractors with warrants (government IOUs). In the 2002 impasse, state employees were threatened with minimum wage pay, whereas vendors, school districts, and social service program recipients were threatened with no payments until the budget crisis was resolved. Without real people suffering real consequences, a budgetary impasse is just political posturing and gamesmanship. Pressure to compromise comes from political pawns—people who are visibly harmed by a shutdown of government functions. Dramatic media hardship stories and public opinion polls eventually determine political winners and losers.

Ballot box budgeting. Just as interest groups use the initiative process as a legislative bypass, they are tempted to use it as a budget bypass—locking in guaranteed state funding. The initiatives are becoming more specific. Proposition 98 (1988), later amended by Proposition 111 (1990), enacted a set of formulas to effectively allocate about 40 percent of the general fund discretionary budget to K–12 schools and community colleges. Proposition 42, approved by voters in March 2002, earmarked the SUT on gasoline to special funds for transit and highway improvements.

Backdoor policy-making. Some budget changes approved by the legislature and the governor require changes to existing law before implementation. Separate bills,

---

[18]John Hill, "Deficit Soon to Hit Where It Truly Hurts," *Sacramento Bee,* 8 December 2002.

called **trailer bills,** space out these changes. These bills mostly contain arcane language enabling budget-approved expenditures. Legislators sometimes insert policy changes to satisfy particular interests. It is a backdoor approach to policy making because these bills are considered concurrently with the Budget Bill rather than going through the normal procedure of policy hearings and legislative review. Here is an example from a 2001 trailer bill:

> After nearly six hours of successfully shaping eyebrows, pin curling and applying acrylic nails under the critical eyes of state beauty examiners, competent beauticians-to-be immediately want something to show for it: a license. But last year when the state Bureau of Barbering and Cosmetology signaled that it wanted to wait a week before mailing the licenses to save the bureau time, money and hassle, the beauticians cut the debate short. With a hand from an influential senator, they found a solution in a seemingly unlikely place: the state budget. Eight lines in a bill accompanying the budget now ensure that examinees who pass their tests will get their licenses on the spot.[19]

This seems innocuous, but such hasty, ill-considered measures can create more problems than they solve:

> The barbering and cosmetology licensing issue illustrates why opponents of trailer bills say they result in bad policy. This year [2002], the beauty practitioners lobbied intensely to protect their same-day licenses. They feared that a one-week delay could hurt stylists who wanted to get to work the minute they passed their exam. "For the student who has worked so hard, the physical piece of paper is really important," said Sam Williams, owner and director of Colleen O'Hara's Beauty Academy of Orange County in Orange. But were there public hearings in a policy committee, the people most familiar with the process could have told lawmakers why they think it is a bad idea. To license barbers and cosmetologists on the same day they took their examination means the bureau must preprint licenses—with each stylist's name—and haul them from Sacramento to Los Angeles and the Bay Area, where exams are held. But only about one-half of the 30,000 candidates per year pass the test. That means the remaining licenses must be driven back to Sacramento, counted to ensure none are stolen—the bureau says they have a street value of $3,000 each—and securely destroyed. That costs the department an extra $20,500.[20]

Budgetary vengeance. Budgeting is also a means to reward friends and settle scores with political rivals. Dan Walters describes this 2002 example:

> [Governor Gray] Davis . . . has had to contend with state Controller Kathleen Connell, who succeeded him in the controller's office and has been feuding with him for nearly eight years. She's termed out of state office this year and is using the budget crisis to settle some old scores. One example: Before agreeing to issue revenue anticipation warrants that the state is using to bridge some of the budget's deficit, Connell insisted that Davis and legislative budget writers expand the state's reserve fund. Another: Davis aides announced last week, apparently to ramp up pressure on the Legislature to act on the budget, that the state would withhold payments to counties to cover welfare checks. Within a day, Connell had undercut Davis by declaring that she would make the payments "just as they have been every other year the budget has not been enacted in a timely fashion."[21]

---

[19]Hanh Kim Quach, "Trailers Let Lawmakers Skirt Scrutiny," *Orange County Register*, 9 August 2002.
[20]Quach, *Orange County Register*.
[21]Dan Walters, "Behind Scenes of Budget Battle, Squabbling Erupts Within Parties," *Sacramento Bee*, 3 July 2002.

Seven months after ordering a statewide hiring freeze, the last thing Gov. Gray Davis needed was a headline saying, "State Government Employment Reaches Record Level of 234,505 Employees." But that's just the headline Davis got from the *Capitol Weekly*—a little (10,000 subscribers) paper that caters mostly to state employees looking for new job opportunities. And within days *Capitol Weekly* publisher Ken Mandler got something himself—word that the governor's office was pulling all the state's job listings from his paper, effective immediately. Mandler, who has been tracking government jobs for years, said even he didn't realize just how plentiful the state payroll opportunities were until November—when, a month after the governor announced the job freeze, the State Controller [Kathleen Connell] came up with the names and jobs descriptions for 4,109 new state hires. By June, seven months after the job freeze went into effect, some 22,000 new jobs had been filled—just slightly below last year's unfrozen pace. Put it all together and—freeze or no freeze—you have a state payroll still growing to record levels.[22]

The next issue of Mandler's *Capitol Weekly* included blank spaces here and there with the caption "This state agency's job advertising was ordered deleted by the governor's office."

Spending

In the end, decisions are made about public policy and program priorities. Money is appropriated, money is spent, and "next year" is always just a few calendar pages away, offering another opportunity to adjust the programs, the policies, and the funding.

"To really understand what government is doing with your money, it's important to realize that many of the public services that Californians receive are provided and/or paid for by all three levels of government, with the state passing both state and federal funds through to local governments."[23] Most public services that Californians receive and rely on every day—roads, schools, police, firefighting, building inspection, planning and zoning, water, garbage collection—are the responsibility of cities, counties, and school districts—the principal units of local government. Very few state and federal funds go directly for public services. The state of California does not educate schoolchildren or see about waste disposal. Instead, state and federal funds are transferred to local governments. It is at the local level that most of your money is actually spent to provide public services.[24]

Exhibit 5-14 shows that four areas—K–12 education, health and human services, higher education, and corrections—account for nearly 70 percent of total state government spending.

K–12 Education California has over 5.5 million schoolchildren in kindergarten through high school. The state does not educate children. Their schooling is provided by 983 local school districts that build and maintain the schools, hire the teachers, and provide the curriculum. K–12 education costs over $40 billion each year. The state, however, is the principal funding source. Two-thirds of

---

[22]Phillip Matier and Andrew Ross, "Coincidence or Revenge? Jobs Story Embarrasses Davis, Bites Publisher," *San Francisco Chronicle*, 8 July 2002.

[23]*Dollars and Democracy*.

[24]However, the state and federal governments are not loath to instruct the local governments about what to do and precisely how to do it.

EXHIBIT 5-14   California State Government Expenditures, 2004–2005

Total spending:	$152.6 billion
Total general fund spending:	$80.4 billion
Total special funds spending:	$32.0 billion
Total federal spending:	$40.2 billion

What is the largest expenditure category for state funds? For federal funds?

Source: State of California, *Comprehensive Annual Financial Report*, for the year ending June 30, 2005, controller of the state of California, December 2005.

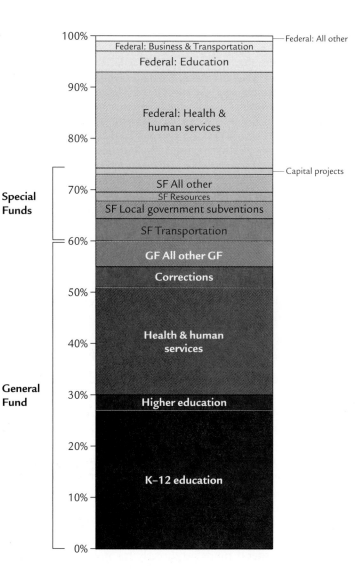

K–12 education funds are transfer payments from the state general fund to the school districts (about $29 billion, 22 percent of total state spending—including ERAF shift funds). The state passes along another $4 billion from the federal government for a variety of programs, such as child development and special education. The state lottery kicks in $900 million, less than 3 percent of state-provided K–12 funds.

Higher Education   California has three systems of higher education. The most prestigious, the University of California system, has about 185,000 students and the largest state-source general fund spending at $3.2 billion. The California State University system enrolls about 370,000 students and spends about $2.4 billion from the general fund. The California Community Colleges (CCC) is largest with about 1.6 million students. CCC general fund spending totals about $2.7 billion. Student fees (tuition) are counted as income to the state general fund, but these make up only about 17 percent of total higher education spending.

Health and Human Services CalWORKs (welfare) and MediCal (medical care) make up the bulk of health and human service spending—about equally split between the two programs, and equally split between federal and state funding.[25]

Corrections The California Department of Corrections and Rehabilitation houses about 170,000 inmates in thirty-three prisons, plus other camps and institutions.

---

[25]Health and human services also includes public health, child welfare, and in-home care for the aged and disabled programs.

Program	Policy Control	Funding*
CalWORKs	State/Federal	
Child Welfare Services	State/Federal	
General Assistance	Counties/State	
Mental Health	Counties/State/Federal	
Substance Abuse Treatment	Counties/State/Federal	
Jails	Counties/State	
Probation	Counties/State	
Sheriff	Counties/State	
Trial Courts	State	
Libraries	Counties	
Parks and Recreation	Counties	
Roads	Counties	

☐ Federal ▨ State ■ County

*All funding distributions are LAO estimates.

EXHIBIT 5-15 Major County Programs, 2004–2005

Which programs receive a majority of their funding from the federal government? State government? County government?

Source: California Legislative Analyst's Office, *Cal Facts: California's Economy and Budget in Perspective*, 2004. Used with permission.

General fund spending exceeds $8.6 billion. The California Youth Authority (CYA) operates eleven institutions for under $500 million, housing about 6,000 criminal and delinquent wards (young people age 12–24; average age 19). The CYA operates training and treatment programs that seek to educate and rehabilitate youthful offenders rather than punish them. All the rest of state government—state parks, highway patrol, the courts, employment development, transportation, and environmental protection—split up the remaining 30 percent.

The CalWORKs and Child Welfare programs administered by the counties receive a majority of their funding from the federal government. Roads and trial courts are mostly funded by the state government. County governments are principally responsible for funding general assistance, libraries, parks, sheriff's and probation departments, and the county jail.

Exhibit 5-15 lists the major county programs for 2004–2005.

WEB LINKS

Budget Analyst Guide, Department of Finance
www.dof.ca.gov/fisa/bag/bagtoc.htm

California Budget Project **www.cbp.org**

California Institute for County Government **www.cicg.org**

California Local Government Finance Almanac **californiacityfinance.com**

California Taxpayers Association **www.caltax.org**

Center on Budget and Policy Priorities **www.cbpp.org**

Center for the Continuing Study of the California Economy **www.ccsce.com**

Controller of the State of California **www.sco.ca.gov**

Department of Finance **www.dof.ca.gov**

Institute on Taxation and Economic Policy **www.itepnet.org**

Legislative Analyst's Office **www.lao.ca.gov**

Next-Ten, California Budget Challenge **www.next-ten.org**

Public Policy Institute of California **www.ppic.org**

Tax Foundation **www.taxfoundation.org**

U.S. Census Bureau, Government Finances **www.census.gov/govs/www**

PUBLICATIONS

Caiden, Naomi, and Aaron B. Wildavsky. 2001. *The New Politics of the Budgetary Process*, 4th ed. Boston: Allyn & Bacon.

Chapman, Jeffrey I. 1998. *Proposition 13: Some Unintended Consequences*. San Francisco: Public Policy Institute of California.

Doerr, David R. 2000. *California's Tax Machine*. Sacramento: California Taxpayers' Association.

Dollars and Democracy: An Advocate's Guide to the State Budget Process. California Budget Project, 1999.

Ibele, Mark A., Jennifer Borenstein, et al. 2001. *California's Tax System: A Primer*. Sacramento: Legislative Analyst's Office.

Landis, John, et al. 2001. *Pay to Play: Residential Development Fees in California Cities and Counties, 1999.* Sacramento: Department of Housing and Community Development, State of California.

Shires, Michael A. 1999. *Patterns in California Government Revenues Since Proposition 13.* San Francisco: Public Policy Institute of California. **www.ppic.org/publications/PPIC117/PPIC117.pdf/index.html**

Swenson, Jennifer. 1999. *County Services: A Tale of Eight Counties.* California Research Bureau, Report No. CRB-99-003, California State Library.

GLOSSARY

ad valorem tax   "According to the worth" (Latin); a tax levied as a percentage of the value of goods or property.

assessment (benefit assessment)   A charge levied on property to pay for facilities or services.

backfill   Replacement of revenue or other resources that have been removed or redirected (an allusion to refilling an excavation).

Big Five   The governor, speaker of the assembly, speaker pro tempore of the senate, and the minority party leaders in both houses. Although nowhere specified in the constitution or statutes, the Big Five sometimes act as a conference committee hammering out agreements and detailed spending decisions on the state budget in order to get the two-thirds vote in each house required to pass the Budget Bill.

blue pencil   A reference to the governor's exercise of the line-item veto before signing the annual state budget bill passed by the legislature.

budgeting   The process of developing and approving (1) a plan of operation expressed in terms of financial or other resources for a specific period of time and (2) legislation that implements a plan of operation and authorizes expenditures.

capital gains   Profit from the sale of assets, such as stocks, bonds, or real estate.

certificates of participation   A type of public financing instrument in which investors can purchase participation in a stream of lease, installment, or loan payments relating to the acquisition of land or equipment or the construction of facilities.

deficit   The amount by which governmental spending exceeds revenues in a given fiscal year. Projected deficit estimates can differ between financial analysts because of differences in estimating proposed government expenditures and anticipated revenues.

earmark   Direct to a specific purpose, use, or recipient (an allusion to a livestock tag used to identify ownership).

ERAF shift   The transfer of property tax revenue, previously allocated to cities and counties, to an Educational Revenue Augmentation Fund for schools.

excise tax   A tax levied on the manufacture or sale of a specific product such as liquor, cigarettes, or gasoline.

fee (user fee, charge for service)   A charge imposed on a person for a service or facility provided directly to that person.

fiscal year   A twelve-month period established for accounting purposes. California's fiscal year is 1 July–30 June.

gaming   A euphemism for gambling.

general fund   The account for revenues that are not designated for a specific purpose. The primary sources of revenue for the state's general fund are the personal income tax, sales tax, and bank and corporation taxes. The general fund is used as the major funding source for education (K–12 and higher education), health care and welfare programs, and youth and adult correctional programs.

general obligation bonds   Voter-approved indebtedness backed by the full faith, credit, and unlimited taxing power of the issuer. See *lease payment bonds*.

lease payment bonds   Indebtedness secured by the lease between the issuing authority and another agency. Payments from the agency to the authority equal the debt service. See *general obligation bonds*.

line item   A good or service that is listed as a budgeted object of expenditure. For example, the personal services budget category includes the objects of "Salaries and Wages" and "Staff Benefits." These objects may be further subdivided into items such as "State Employees' Retirement" or "Workers' Compensation." Line items do not indicate the function or purpose to be served by the expenditure.

mandate   A required action imposed on a unit of government by a higher level of government.

per capita   By or for each person. Usually used in the context of a statistical average obtained by dividing a total amount by the population.

realignment   The revolutionary change in local government financing by a succession of ballot measures and legislative acts during the 1980s and 1990s.

revenue bonds   A form of long-term borrowing in which the debt obligation is secured by a revenue stream produced by the project. Because revenue bonds are not backed by the full faith and credit of the state, they may be enacted by the legislature without voter approval.

revenue sharing   The act by which the state or federal government levies taxes and fees and then transfers funds to local governments—often with strings attached. The earmarking of vehicle license fee income to city and county governments is an example of revenue sharing in California.

shortfall   The amount by which projected government revenue is anticipated to be less than planned spending.

special funds   Accounts for revenues from taxes, licenses, and fees that are restricted by law to specific governmental functions or programs.

tax   A charge against an individual, organization, or property owner based on ownership of property, point-in-time value of property, or transactions (such as income or sales and purchases).

trailer bill   A bill changing state law in order to enable expenditures approved by the legislature and the governor in the annual budget bill. Trailer bills are considered concurrently with the Budget Bill rather than going through the normal procedure of policy hearings and legislative review.

SUGGESTED ANSWERS TO EXHIBIT QUESTIONS

Exhibit 5-2: The personal income tax is the largest source of revenue to state government.

Exhibit 5-3: For a single taxpayer with an annual income of $30,000, the California tax rate is 8 percent; the federal tax rate is 27.5 percent.

Exhibit 5-4: Over 35 percent of taxpayers have an annual income below $20,000. Altogether they account for about 1 percent of California's personal income tax receipts. Less than 5 percent of taxpayers have an annual income over $200,000. They account for over 55 percent of California's personal income tax receipts.

Exhibit 5-5: Personal income dropped sharply in 2000–2001 due to a decrease in value of stock options and capital gains investments.

Exhibit 5-7: Proposition 13 (1978) replaced the fixed-percentage tax with an acquisition-value assessment. It provided that the taxable value of property could increase by no more than 2 percent per year. This shielded property owners from rapidly skyrocketing taxes during a booming real estate market. If sold, the property was reassessed at 1 percent of the new market value, with the 2 percent yearly cap placed on this new assessment. Over time, neighbors in nearly identical houses can have significantly different tax bills.

Exhibit 5-8: The realignment of local government financing restored the allocation of property tax revenues to 1977–1978 percentages. In the 1990s, the percentage of property tax revenues allocated to counties was cut significantly.

Exhibit 5-9: Twenty propositions are listed over a 25-year period.

Exhibit 5-11: The lead time from planning to spending is about two years.

Exhibit 5-14: The largest expenditure category for state funds is education. The largest category for federal funds spent in California is health and human services.

Exhibit 5-15: The CalWORKs and Child Welfare programs administered by the counties receive a majority of their funding from the federal government. Roads and trial courts are mostly funded by the state government. County governments are principally responsible for funding general assistance, libraries, parks, sheriff's and probation departments, and the county jail.

CHAPTER SIX

PURSUIT OF JUSTICE

Justice, justice shall you pursue . . . [1]
No justice, no peace. [2]

Justice is a vital, but nevertheless elusive, concept in a representative democracy. It involves abstract principles like accountability, the righting of wrongs, redress, compensation, compromise, punishment, fairness, equality, and impartiality. But, at the same time, it also involves the drama of everyday life—people who have been injured, people who have hurt others, people in disputes, and people who need help (see Exhibit 6-1).

In a governmental setting, justice is the application of law, that is, using governmental authority to promote health, safety, and well-being—upholding policies, maintaining peace, preserving order and safety, and resolving disputes—all while adhering to civil rights and civil liberties.

What is justice in practice? This chapter (1) addresses the principles and issues in civil rights, civil liberties, and civil justice, and (2) reviews criminal justice in California.

CIVIL RIGHTS, CIVIL LIBERTIES, AND CIVIL JUSTICE

Civil rights are procedural freedoms associated with principles of fairness and equal treatment—called **due process** and **equal protection** of the law. Due process means that no person's life, liberty, or property can be taken by the government without good reason and without appropriate formal procedures, including such elements as notice, hearing, representation, evidence, witnesses, and appeal.[3] Equal protection means that everyone in like circumstances should be treated by the government in the same way and afforded the same protections and benefits. It does not mean

---

[1]Deuteronomy 16:20

[2]A protest chant.

[3]The Fifth Amendment to the U.S. Constitution says, "No *person* shall be . . . deprived of *life, liberty, or property,* without *due process* of law." The Fourteenth Amendment says, "No *State* shall . . . deprive any *person* of *life, liberty, or property,* without *due process* of law; nor deny to any person within its jurisdiction the *equal protection* of the laws" (emphasis added). These statements are repeated in the California Constitution, Article I; Declaration of Rights.

EXHIBIT 6-1 Justice

This allegorical relief by Donal Hord (1957) is located above the Hill Street entrance to Los Angeles County's Stanley Mosk Courthouse. The central female figure is dressed in judicial robes and holds a sword in her right hand. Above her are scales and an American eagle. Kneeling male figures hold symbols of Law and Truth.

What do the scales, the robes, and the sword symbolize?

What do you think is being balanced by the scales?

Source: Photo copyright © Michael Newman/Photo Edit Inc.

identical treatment for everyone. The government often treats people differently on the basis of such characteristics and attributes as age, income, education, and occupation; the poor are treated differently from the rich; children are treated differently from adults. These distinctions are permissible and need only a rational basis justification. Other criteria, such as race/ethnicity, religion, color, gender, or national origin, are impermissible (but not impossible) without strict scrutiny showing a compelling or important governmental purpose (state interest).

Civil liberties are personal conduct freedoms to which all Californians are entitled. Some of these freedoms are indirect. They exist because of constitutional limitations on the government that bar it from arbitrary and unjustified intrusions in matters such as religion, speech, press, and assembly. Some liberties are explicit, such as the right to representation in a court of law; still others are inferred, such as the right to travel freely. State constitutions can assert civil liberties beyond those provided by the U.S. Constitution. The California Constitution extends explicit civil liberties of privacy, speech, publication, and religion that are only indirectly referred to or implied in the U.S. Constitution. It even provides that Californians can "fish upon and from the public lands of the State and in the waters thereof."[4]

Even more than two hundred years after the U.S. Constitution was written, Americans and Californians are still actively debating and defining civil rights and civil liberties. This section summarizes some of the interesting principles and developments in equality, freedom of religion, freedom of speech and press, and privacy.

Equality

The Declaration of Independence states: "We hold these truths to be self-evident, that all men are created equal, that they are endowed by their Creator with certain unalienable Rights, that among these are Life, Liberty and the pursuit of Happiness.

---

[4]California Constitution, Art. I, Sec. 25, Declaration of Rights.

That to secure these rights, Governments are instituted among Men, deriving their just powers from the consent of the governed. . . ." But what is *equality*? This question will be considered in the context of employment, education, and public contracting.

Employment, Education, and Public Contracting Discrimination is unequal treatment associated with being a member of a group having certain attributes and characteristics, such as race or gender. Discrimination may be prejudicial or preferential—limiting the opportunities and rewards for one group or enhancing them for another.

One definition of equality is *equality of opportunity*. In this view, there should be no group distinctions, whether by race/ethnicity, class, religion, gender, or any other attribute or characteristic. People distinguish themselves by individual merit. Those who advocate equality of opportunity argue that any and all discrimination, whether prejudicial or preferential, is reprehensible and should be prohibited. The government should make sure that everyone is treated the same way and judged only according to relevant indicators of qualification.[5] One has an inherent right to *pursue* happiness; but happiness itself is not assured.

An alternate definition of equality is *equality of result*. In this view, certain attributes and characteristics, such as race/ethnicity, or gender, distinguish groups of people. Discrimination by group, it is argued, is inevitable. Different groups systematically experience or have experienced disparate treatment, different opportunities, and greater or lesser rewards. In an ideal society, every group would participate and share equally in employment, education, and all other aspects of life. The fundamental measure of equality is diversity. Disparities and inequalities—differences between each group's share and its proportion in the population—should be corrected. In theory, it is the government's responsibility to ensure equality, so **affirmative action** is needed to create a more equal society.[6]

California has been at the center of the equality-of-opportunity versus equality-of-result debate. The issue came to the fore in a landmark 1978 U.S. Supreme Court case, *Regents of the University of California v. Bakke*.[7] Allan Bakke applied for admission to the University of California, Davis, medical school. He was rejected even though some minority applicants with significantly lower scores on the entrance examination were admitted, because the university reserved sixteen of its one hundred places for minority and economically disadvantaged students. Bakke maintained that the university effectively discriminated against him on the basis of his race, in violation of the Equal Protection Clause of the Fourteenth Amendment. The 5-to-4 U.S. Supreme Court decision did not settle the question. It held for Bakke, ruling against quotas and allowing him to enter medical school. But it also held that race was a legitimate consideration in school admission decisions—permitting race-based affirmative action in college admissions to promote diversity.

---

[5]Phrases such as *color blind, open doors*, and *level playing field* are often heard but shed little light on the specific principles and policies being debated.

[6]The term *affirmative action* was first used in Executive Order 10925, issued by President John F. Kennedy in 1961. The order required managers of projects financed with federal funds to take affirmative action to ensure that hiring and employment practices were free of racial bias. In 1965, President Lyndon Johnson explained the goal of affirmative action: "You do not wipe away the scars of centuries by saying, 'now, you are free to go where you want, do as you desire, and choose the leaders you please.' You do not take a man who for years has been hobbled by chains, liberate him, bring him to the starting line of a race, saying, 'you are free to compete with all the others,' and still justly believe you have been completely fair. . . . This is the next and more profound stage of the battle for civil rights. We seek not just freedom but opportunity—not just legal equity but human ability—not just equality as a right and a theory but equality as a fact and as a result" (the graduation speech at Howard University, 4 June 1965).

[7]*Regents of the University of California v. Bakke*, 438 U.S. 265 (1978).

Ten years later, in another California case, the U.S. Supreme Court upheld a public agency's preferential promotion of women and minorities in order to increase the proportion of women and minorities in job classifications in which they are underrepresented.[8]

Then, in 1996, Californians passed Proposition 209, the so-called California Civil Rights Initiative. Approved by 54 percent of the voters, Proposition 209 added Section 31 to Article I (Declaration of Rights) of the California Constitution: "The state shall not discriminate against, or grant preferential treatment to, any individual or group, on the basis of race, sex, color, ethnicity, or national origin in the operation of public employment, public education, or public contracting."

The principal proponent of Proposition 209 was Ward Connerly, an African American businessman and activist. Connerly recalled his upbringing in Sacramento, being raised by relatives who were poor, worked hard, and instilled the values of education, work, self-sufficiency, and responsibility. He went on to community college and California State University, Sacramento; rose in the ranks of the state housing and urban development agencies; and befriended an up-and-coming Republican legislator, Pete Wilson. Years later, Governor Wilson appointed Connerly, then an independent businessman, to the Board of Regents of the University of California. There, he moved to end racial preferences in hiring, contracting, and admissions at the university and went on to help qualify and win passage of Proposition 209.

The opponents of Proposition 209 immediately filed suit in federal court, claiming that it violated the principle of equal protection. The Ninth U.S. Circuit Court of Appeals squarely addressed the issue of prejudicial versus preferential treatment as it dismissed the challenge to Proposition 209:

> Where a state denies someone a job, an education, or a seat on the bus because of her race or gender, the injury to that individual is clear. The person who wants to work, study, or ride but cannot because she is Black or a woman is denied equal protection. Where, as here, a state prohibits race or gender preferences at any level of government, the injury to any specific individual is utterly inscrutable. *No one contends that individuals have a constitutional right to preferential treatment solely on the basis of their race or gender.* Quite the contrary. What, then, is the personal injury that members of a group suffer when they cannot seek preferential treatment on the basis of their race or gender from local government? This question admits of no easy answer. . . . That the Constitution permits the rare race-based or gender-based preference hardly implies that the state cannot ban them altogether. . . . The Constitution permits the people to grant a narrowly tailored racial preference only if they come forward with a compelling interest to back it up. . . . To hold that a democratically enacted affirmative action program is constitutionally permissible because the people have demonstrated a compelling state interest is hardly to hold that the program is constitutionally required. The Fourteenth Amendment, lest we lose sight of the forest for the trees, does not require what it barely permits.[9] (emphasis added)

After passage of Proposition 209, the city of San Jose amended its minority business enterprise and women business enterprise (MBE/WBE) programs. The city had previously determined that minority and women entrepreneurs received disproportionately fewer public contracts and subcontracts. Attempting to "ensure that historical discrimination did not continue," the city required contractors to document outreach to and participation of minority and female subcontractors. One contractor, Hi-Voltage Wire Works, not intending to subcontract any work, failed

---

[8]*Johnson v. Transportation Agency, Santa Clara County,* 480 U.S. 616 (1987).
[9]*The Coalition for Economic Equity v. Pete Wilson,* 122 F.3d 692 (1997).

to comply. Although it was the low bidder, the bid was rejected as nonresponsive. In 2000, the California Supreme Court held that the city's program violated Proposition 209's amendment to the California Constitution:

> Because the City rejects any bid that fails to comply with one or the other requirement [outreach and participation], both of which are race and sex based, the essential structure of the Program discriminates on an impermissible basis against prime contractors that neither engage in outreach nor meet the evidentiary presumption, and it grants preferential treatment to those that do. . . . The outreach component requires contractors to treat MBE/WBE subcontractors more advantageously by providing them notice of bidding opportunities, soliciting their participation, and negotiating for their services, none of which they must do for non-MBE's/WBE's. . . . *The participation component authorizes or encourages what amounts to discriminatory quotas or set-asides, or at least race- and sex-conscious numerical goals.*[10] (emphasis added)

Research has shown that at the University of California, Davis, medical students who were admitted with affirmative action preferences graduated and completed their residencies at about the same rate, received similar evaluations from their residency supervisors, and ultimately developed practices with almost the same racial mixes of patients as did their classmates overall.[11] Undergraduate applications to the University of California dropped markedly after passage of Proposition 209 but have since recovered. The University of California system is currently considering dropping or revising the use of Scholastic Assessment Test (SAT) scores as a criterion for admission.

Freedom of Religion

Contrary to popular belief, the U.S. and California constitutions do not require a strict separation between church and state. There are many instances in which governmental and religious organizations not only interact but also cooperate. For example, many California faith-based groups, such as San Francisco's Jewish Vocational Service, Berkeley's Helping Hands of Hope (Mount Zion Missionary Baptist Church), and Upland's Foothill Family Shelter (San Bernardino County, Saint Mark's Episcopal Church), receive government grants for such things as job service and substance abuse treatment programs, food banks, homeless and family crisis shelters, and English language assistance. Religious facilities such as churches, synagogues, and mosques are subject to government regulations with respect to land use and construction.

The First Amendment to the U.S. Constitution contains two clauses about religion: (1) the Establishment Clause, "Congress shall make no law respecting an establishment of religion," . . . and (2) the Free-Exercise Clause, "or prohibiting the free exercise thereof. . . ." Article I, Section 4, of the California Constitution's Declaration of Rights has a No-Preference Clause: "Free exercise and enjoyment of religion without discrimination or preference are guaranteed. . . . The Legislature shall make no law respecting an establishment of religion." In addition, Article XVI, Section 5, of the California Constitution provides:

> Neither the legislature, nor any county, city and county, township, school district, or other municipal corporation, shall ever make an appropriation, or pay from any public fund whatever, or grant anything to or in aid of any religious sect, church, creed, or

---

[10]*Hi-Voltage Wire Works, Inc. v. City of San Jose*, 24 Cal. 4th 537 (2000).

[11]R. C. Davidson and E. L. Lewis, "Affirmative Action and Other Special Consideration Admissions at the University of California, Davis, School of Medicine," *Journal of the American Medical Association* 278 (1997), 1153–58.

sectarian purpose, or help to support or sustain any school, college, university, hospital, or other institution controlled by any religious creed, church, or sectarian denomination whatever; nor shall any grant or donation of personal property or real estate ever be made by the state, or any city, city and county, town, or other municipal corporation for any religious creed, church, or sectarian purpose whatever.

What does religious freedom mean? Does it mean religious *neutrality*—not favoring one religion over another? Or does it mean complete religious *silence*—neither promoting nor discouraging religious observance or religious organizations?

Some interesting cases develop when we try to define the *establishment* and *exercise* of religion. In 1954, the city of San Diego allowed a forty-three-foot cross to be built on Mount Soledad to honor veterans of World Wars I and II and the Korean War. In 1991, the federal district court ruled that the cross violated the state constitution's No-Preference Clause, calling it "a preeminent symbol of Christianity." The city then sold 222 square feet of land immediately under the cross to a nonprofit association. However, the court ruled that the city was still expressing a religious preference because the city sold only a small portion of its land, without considering other bidders. Trying again, the city sold one-half acre of land under the cross in an open and publicized bidding process. The nonprofit association was the high bidder. This time the district court approved the city's action. However, the Ninth U.S. Circuit Court of Appeals held that this still did not satisfy the U.S. Supreme Court's Lemon test because the sale was structured to favor the nonprofit association that wanted to preserve the cross.[12] The Lemon test principles regarding establishment are as follows:

- Government action must have a nonreligious purpose.
- The primary effect of government action must be secular (nonreligious).
- Government action must avoid excessive entanglement in religious affairs.

Another three principles apply to the consideration of free-exercise issues:

- The importance of the government interest
- The extent of interference
- Alternate means that might achieve the goal

How would you decide these examples of free-exercise cases?

- Baptized children of the Khalsa Sikh faith have a duty to wear five sacred religious symbols, including a *kirpan*, a small ceremonial knife. The Livingston Union School District (Merced County), of course, has a policy against bringing potential weapons to school. Should children be compelled to remove *kirpans* before being allowed to attend school?

The Ninth U.S. Circuit Court of Appeals ordered the school district to lift its wholesale ban on *kirpans* and to allow the children back to school under the conditions that the *kirpans* have short, dull blades and be tightly sewn into a sheath to be worn under the children's clothing.[13]

- Public school education is funded by the state—by your taxes. Families pay for their children's education in nonpublic parochial schools. The state does

---

[12]*Lemon v. Kurtzman*, 403 U.S. 602 (1971), and *Paulson v. City of San Diego*, 262 F.3d 885 (2001).
[13]*Cheema v. Thompson*, 67 F.3d 883 (1995).

not provide tuition grants or vouchers. Does this violate the Free-Exercise Clause? Can parents deduct a portion of their tuition payments to parochial schools under a tax code provision that allows deductions for solely intangible religious benefits? After all, similar payments to the Church of Scientology are deductible, despite the receipt of religious instruction.

"Both the purpose and effect of any statute appropriating tax-raised funds to assist parents in the 'free exercise of their religion' would necessarily be to support religion."[14] "If the IRS does, in fact, give preferential treatment to members of the Church of Scientology—allowing them a special right to claim deductions that are contrary to law and rightly disallowed to everybody else—then the proper course of action is a lawsuit to stop that policy. The remedy is not to require the IRS to let others claim the improper deduction, too."[15]

- California law (the Women's Contraceptive Equity Act of 1999) requires that employer-provided health insurance programs covering prescription drugs must include coverage of contraceptives. The law exempts certain religious employers, but not Catholic Charities. Does this requirement violate the Free-Exercise Clause?

The California appellate court held that the law was neutral and generally applicable, and did not target Catholicism. In 2004, the California Supreme Court upheld the decision, holding that Catholic Charities, a nonprofit public corporation operating a variety of charitable organizations around the state, served a secular purpose, was not directly involved in church activity, and employed a majority of non-Catholics.[16]

Freedom of Speech and Press

The First Amendment to the U.S. Constitution states: "Congress shall make no law . . . abridging the freedom of speech, or of the press." Article I, Section 2, of the California Constitution's Declaration of Rights states: "Every person may freely speak, write and publish his or her sentiments on all subjects, being responsible for the abuse of this right. A law may not restrain or abridge liberty of speech or press."

Freedom of speech and the press—the exchange of information and ideas—is vital to maintaining our representative democracy and political, social, economic, and cultural freedoms. California has been at the forefront of defining the meaning and limits of free speech and free press. However, "no law" does not literally mean *no law*. The time, place, manner, and sometimes even content of speech and publication may be regulated. But any such regulation must be specifically tailored to achieve a narrow and compelling government interest. Some speech and writings are more valued, and therefore more protected, than others. Political speech and participation in public debate deserves the most protection; commercial speech, somewhat less; and slander or libel, obscenity, endangerment, and incitement, even less. Speech and publication may not be preventively restricted, that is, before the fact—this constitutes prior restraint.[17] Persons may be held accountable after the fact for the consequences of their speech or writing.

---

[14]*Jackson v. State of California*, 460 F.2d 282 (1972).

[15]*Sklar v. Commissioner of Internal Revenue*, 282 F.3d 610 (2002).

[16]*Catholic Charities of Sacramento v. Superior Court of Sacramento County*, 32 Cal. 4th 527 (2004).

[17]The only possible exception would be vital national security secrets whose disclosure poses an imminent danger.

California is the scene for many speech and publication civil liberties issues. How would you decide these examples of free speech and free press cases?

- DVDs containing full-length motion pictures are protected from unauthorized use by an encryption method known as the content scramble system (CSS). In October 1999, a 15-year-old Norwegian, Jon Johansen, created a computer program titled *DeCSS* (Descramble CSS) that would allow playing a CSS-encrypted DVD on a non-CSS-equipped DVD player or computer. The program was copied and posted on the Internet, including the Website of Andrew Bunner. On 27 December 1999, the DVD Copy Control Association sued Bunner, Johansen, and others under California's Uniform Trade Secrets Act (UTSA), seeking an injunction against any further publication of *DeCSS*. Two days later, a trial court issued a preliminary **injunction**. The case was appealed to California's Sixth District Court of Appeals. Is this an attempt at prior restraint? Should the court uphold or overturn the injunction?

"DVD-CCA's statutory right to protect its economically valuable trade secret is not an interest that is 'more fundamental' than the First Amendment right to freedom of speech or even on equal footing with the national security interests and other vital governmental interests that have previously been found insufficient to justify a prior restraint. Our respect for the Legislature and its enactment of the UTSA cannot displace our duty to safeguard the rights guaranteed by the First Amendment. Accordingly, we are compelled to reverse the preliminary injunction."[18]

- In 1968 [at the height of the Vietnam War], Paul Cohen was observed in a corridor of the Los Angeles County Courthouse wearing a jacket with the words "Fuck the Draft" in large letters on the back.[19] Cohen said that he wore the jacket in order to publicly express his opposition to the Vietnam War and the draft. He was convicted of "maliciously and willfully disturbing the peace or quiet of any neighborhood or person . . . by . . . offensive conduct." Is this an example of free speech? Should Cohen's conviction be upheld by the appellate courts?

The Court of Appeals held that *offensive conduct* means "behavior that has a tendency to provoke others to acts of violence or to in turn disturb the peace" and affirmed the conviction. The U.S. Supreme Court overruled, holding that, "absent a more particularized and compelling reason for its actions, the State may not . . . make the simple public display of this single four-letter expletive a criminal offense."[20]

- Marvin Miller sent a mass mailing advertising illustrated "adult" books. When a Newport Beach restaurant manager and his mother opened the unsolicited advertisement, they complained to police. Miller was convicted of mailing sexually explicit "obscene" material in violation of California law that defined such material as "utterly without redeeming social value." What is obscene material? Is such material protected free speech or publication under the First Amendment?

---

[18]*DVD Copy Control Association v. Bunner*, 113 Cal.Rptr.2d 338 (2001).

[19]At the time, young men who were not college students or working in the defense industry faced compulsory military service—the draft.

[20]*Cohen v. California*, 403 U.S. 15 (1971).

Obscenity is not protected by the First Amendment. Speech or publication may be regulated if (1) "the average person, applying contemporary community standards," would find that the work, taken as a whole, appeals to the prurient interest; (2) the work depicts or describes, in a patently offensive way, sexual conduct specifically defined by the applicable state law; and (3) the work, taken as a whole, lacks serious literary, artistic, political, or scientific value.[21]

Advertising a product or service for profit is called commercial speech, and the government can ban commercial deception. Interestingly, under certain areas of California law, a person can act as a private attorney general representing the public as a plaintiff in a lawsuit against a business or agency for illegal or unfair practices. Marc Kasky, a consumer activist, filed such a lawsuit against Nike, Inc., the multinational marketer of athletic shoes and sports apparel—recognized by its "swoosh" logo—for "unlawful, unfair, or fraudulent" conduct. In 1996 and 1997, Nike was accused of exploitative and abusive working conditions in its Southeast Asia factories—running sweatshops with long hours, child labor, poor pay, and environmental hazards. Nike launched a public relations campaign denying the allegations and praising its labor practices. Kasky's suit accused Nike of false advertising. Nike filed a **demurrer** to the complaint, saying that the suit had no merit since Nike's presentations addressed a subject of public policy and were therefore entitled to full First Amendment speech and publication protection. In an interesting alliance, the liberal American Civil Liberties Union and the conservative Pacific Legal Foundation joined Nike's defense. What do you think? Should a company's statements about public policy in television commercials, on Websites, and in publications be protected whether or not they are true?

The trial court supported Nike's demurrer, and the state appellate court concurred. Later, in a 4-to-3 vote, the California Supreme Court, without deciding whether Nike's ads were false or misleading, overruled the lower courts, saying that Nike's speech and publication were commercial and therefore not protected by the First Amendment.[22]

- Is an Internet blogger a journalist? In December 2004, Apple Computer, Inc., filed suit against Jason O'Grady, author of the blog "O'Grady's Power-Page," and other blog writers, alleging the leak of corporate trade secrets about Apple product development. Apple sought the identity of O'Grady's sources. California has a press shield law: "A publisher, editor, reporter, or other person connected with or employed upon a newspaper, magazine, or other periodical publication . . . shall not be judged in contempt . . . for refusing to disclose the sources of any information procured while so connected or employed for publication in a newspaper, magazine, or other periodical publication, or for refusing to disclose any unpublished information obtained or prepared in gathering, receiving, or processing of information for communication to the public."[23] Apple argued that bloggers are not legitimate journalists, and the trial court agreed, issuing subpoenas. O'Grady, represented by the Electronic Frontier Foundation, appealed. What do you think? Should an Internet blogger be compelled to reveal sources?

The trial court sided with Apple. However, in May 2006, California's Sixth District Court of Appeals reversed the decision and instructed the lower court to issue a protective order, saying, "The shield law is intended to protect the gathering and

---

[21]*Miller v. California*, 413 U.S. 15 (1973).
[22]*Kasky v. Nike*, 27 Cal. 4th 939 (2002).
[23]California Constitution, Art. I, Sec. 2b.

dissemination of *news*. . . . We can think of no workable test or principle that would distinguish 'legitimate' from 'illegitimate' news. Any attempt by courts to draw such a distinction would imperil a fundamental purpose of the First Amendment, which is to identify the best, most important, and most valuable ideas not by any sociological or economic formula, rule of law, or process of government, but through the rough and tumble competition of the memetic [person-to-person] marketplace."[24]

Civil Justice

The civil justice system is important for two reasons. First, it provides a formal process for resolving disputes between two parties—litigants—either individuals or organizations. One party, the **plaintiff**, claims to have been injured by the actions of the other, the **defendant**. In some cases, the plaintiff files a **complaint**—a lawsuit—seeking monetary **damages** for the alleged wrong. Examples of alleged wrongs include car accidents, discrimination in the workplace, medical malpractice, defective products, differences over the terms of contracts, and disputes between landlords and tenants. In other cases, the plaintiff asks the court to issue an order to stop someone from doing something or to compel someone to act.

Second, the civil justice system provides a means to formally change one's status. A person or organization files a **petition** asking the court to take a certain action, such as to sever marriage ties, decide the custody of minor children, determine the mental competency of an aged or ill person, dispose of a deceased person's estate, or change a legal name.

As Exhibit 6-2 shows, more than 1.5 million civil cases are filed each year in California's superior courts. The principal types of civil cases are as follows:

- **Small claims**—cases with potential damages less than $5,000 that (as depicted on television shows such as *Judge Judy*) are argued by the plaintiff and defendant themselves rather than by lawyers
- **Civil-limited**—cases claiming damages greater than $5,000 but less than $25,000
- **Civil-unlimited**—cases claiming damages greater than $25,000
- **Family law**—cases of separation and divorce, child custody, child support, and adoption
- **Probate** and **guardianship**—cases involving settlement of a deceased person's estate and placement of someone in charge of the affairs of another
- Other **civil petitions,** covering a wide variety of matters, including restraining orders

In a two-party civil case, the defendant is issued a **summons,** along with a copy of the complaint. The defendant has thirty days to file an **answer** admitting to or denying the allegations and arguing why the plaintiff is not entitled to the judgment and damages he or she seeks.[25] Otherwise, the defendant may file a demurrer saying the plaintiff's complaint has no basis in law or has no supporting evidence. Although a civil case may ultimately be argued in a trial (before either a judge and jury or a judge alone), the process encourages settlement. One important aspect of this process is **discovery,** by which both parties obtain the relevant facts and testimony.

---

[24]*O'Grady et al. v. Superior Court (Apple)*, California Sixth Appellate District, H028579, 25 May 2006.
[25]In eviction cases, the defendant generally has only five days to answer.

EXHIBIT 6-2   Civil Cases Filed in California Superior Courts, 2004–2005 (1.5 million cases)

Small claims	Lawsuits with a value of $5,000 or less
Civil-limited	Lawsuits with a value greater than $5,000 but less than $25,000
Civil-unlimited	Lawsuits with a value greater than $25,000
Juvenile and mental health	Juvenile delinquency and dependency, and mental health matters
Probate and guardianship	Judicial certification of a will, placement of a person in charge of the affairs of another
Family law	Separation and divorce matters
Civil petitions	Including such matters as custody and visitation, child and spousal support, restraining orders, parentage, and adoption

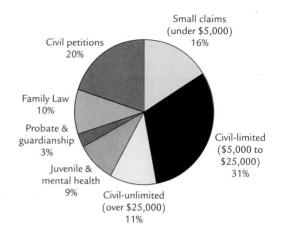

There are about 1,500 judges in California superior courts. Estimate the civil case workload.

Source: Judicial Council of California, *2006 Court Statistics Report.*

Ultimately, the case is settled, or a jury reaches a verdict, or a judge renders a decision. A party who is dissatisfied with the judgment can appeal the decision within a limited time. Few civil cases drag out for a long time—86 percent of civil-limited cases are disposed of within twelve months, and 83 percent of civil-unlimited cases are resolved within eighteen months.

Tort Reform   Tort reform is a recurring issue in California. A **tort** is action or negligence (other than breach of contract) that causes **injury**. Tort lawsuits seek damages for the injured party (the plaintiff) to compensate for such wrongs as personal injury, property damage, or wrongful death. Reformers contend that such lawsuits needlessly drive up the cost of doing business. As a result, they say, everything—from consumer products to health care—costs significantly more than it should. The tort lawyers self-righteously proclaim that they are the defenders of American democracy—ensuring that even the richest and most powerful can be held to account in a judicial venue, apart from the money-influenced forums of electoral politics and legislative lobbying. They say that such lawsuits are the only way to fairly assess and recover damages and, through possible punitive damages, deter the future marketing of dangerous products or delivery of incompetent services.

The tort reform battle peaked most recently in 1996. In March 1996, reformers pressed three initiatives: (1) Proposition 200, calling for a no-fault auto insurance system; (2) Proposition 201, limiting lawsuits by corporation shareholders; and (3) Proposition 202, capping contingent-fee contracts between plaintiffs and their attorneys at 15 percent.[26] The tort lawyers countered with two initiatives in November: (1) Proposition 207, restricting legislative interference in negotiated attorney's fees; and (2) Proposition 211, making it easier to sue for securities fraud. After millions of dollars were spent on both sides, the outcome was a draw. All five propositions lost,

[26]Plaintiffs pay their attorneys a percentage of any settlement or damage judgment. The attorney pays all costs of the litigation. If the plaintiff loses, the attorney is paid nothing.

and the tort reform debate continues today. Meanwhile, more important reforms such as legal aid—to assist the poor in areas of housing, food, health care, domestic situations, employment, education, consumer finance, and individual rights—are diminishing, underfunded, and regarded as superfluous charity.

Alternative Dispute Resolution   **Alternative dispute resolution (ADR),** such as **arbitration** or **mediation,** is intended to resolve disputes without lawsuits or without going to trial, thus saving the parties (and the courts) time and money.

If you have a credit card, a bank account, telephone service, health insurance, automobile insurance, or a product warranty, or have purchased a car or other major item with a loan, rented an apartment, been to a sporting event or concert, or parked in a public garage, you probably have seen a "contract of adhesion." This is a legal agreement written entirely by (and mostly for the benefit of) the employer, lender, merchant or provider of a good or service. Few, if any, of the terms are negotiable. You, as a consumer or employee, have a choice—take it or leave it! One of the fine-print terms in many of these contracts is the requirement that any dispute between you and the party who wrote the contract be submitted to binding arbitration.

Called a system of "private justice," binding arbitration has been criticized on several grounds, including exorbitant filing fees for someone who wants to pursue a complaint, inexpert arbitrators who do not necessarily have to be lawyers, unfair rules and procedures, loser-pays-winner's-costs rules, confidentiality breaches and a lack of written opinions to make the dispute and resolution secret, conflicts of interest between companies and arbitration firms, and awards limited only to direct damages. Being binding, the result is final and not subject to appeal. What do you think? Should consumers have a choice between submitting to arbitration and going to court?

Workplace Rights   You do not have a right to a job. Employment is not a civil liberty—nor is housing, food, or health care.

Employees in California are divided into two classes: (1) *at-will* employees and (2) *just-cause* employees. Most employees in the private sector are at-will employees. Their employer can terminate them at any time, for any reason—or even no reason at all. "An employment, having no specified term, may be terminated at the will of either party on notice to the other. Employment for a specified term means an employment for a period greater than one month."[27]

However, you do have rights *in* employment. A combination of state and federal laws prohibit discrimination on the basis of race, color, religion, national origin, ancestry, gender, pregnancy, marital status, sexual orientation, or medical condition (and to some extent, age and disability). Workers have a right to minimum wages, safe working conditions, and freedom from sexual harassment. Other laws prohibit retaliation for whistle blowing—reporting an employer for unlawful employment practices or illegal conduct.

Just-cause employees can be dismissed from employment only for a good reason, such as poor job performance. These employees have contracts with their employers. They may be civil service government employees, and they are usually members of a union that negotiates terms and conditions of employment on their behalf and represents them in any employment dispute. Public employees may refer to "Skelly rights." This 1975 California Supreme Court decision held that a public employee has a property interest in employment and cannot be fired without adhering to due process.[28] Ironically, labor unions will often seek binding arbitration

---

[27]California Labor Code, Sec. 2922.
[28]*Skelly v. State Personnel Board,* 15 Cal.3d 194 (1975).

of employee grievances in order to speed resolution of personnel problems—but in this forum, the employee, with union-provided representation, is on an equal footing with management.[29]

CRIMINAL JUSTICE

The criminal justice system is the process by which anyone who is accused of committing a crime can be punished—sometimes by losing his or her liberty. This function, to say the least, makes the system critically important to Californians. A **crime** is any act prohibited by law for which there is a formally sanctioned punishment. This definition can include the failure of a person to perform an act specifically required by the law. The law recognizes three broad categories of crimes based on the seriousness of the offense and potential penalties: **felonies, misdemeanors,** and **infractions**. In addition, crimes can be classified as violent, property, or drug-related.

There are three main parts of the criminal justice system as shown in Exhibit 6-3.

- *Investigation and arrest.* City, county, and state police agencies investigate crimes; seek out and arrest criminals and other malefactors; and otherwise maintain civil order. They are entrusted with extraordinary power and discretion to remove people's liberty and property, using force if necessary. They are constantly called upon to exercise judgment—balancing public order and safety against the rights of people in a free society. They are our guardians, but sometimes their actions can threaten the very principles they are sworn to uphold.

- *Prosecution and **adjudication**.* County district attorneys prosecute cases, and for most indigent persons, county public defenders provide legal representation. Juvenile authorities (sometimes a unit of the probation department) are involved with youthful offenders. The cases are filed in California's trial courts—the county superior courts.

- *Sentencing and corrections.* Superior court judges in each county decide the disposition of each case and determine **sentences** and sanctions.[30] Administration of sentences is carried out by county probation departments, county sheriff departments (which operate the county jails), or the state Department of Corrections (which operates the state prisons).

California's crime rate has dropped significantly in recent decades. Exhibit 6-4 shows that three of every one hundred Californians were victimized by property crime in 1980. The current rate is about half that. Violent crime peaked in 1992. That year, one of every one hundred Californians was a victim. The rate is now half that—the lowest level since 1975. Nevertheless, all parts of the criminal justice system have been the subject of controversies during the 1990s and early 2000s. The issues start with the role of the police. California's population is diverse and very segregated. African Americans, Latinos, and whites differ not only by residential neighborhood and cultural/racial interactions but also by perceptions of and experiences with legal authority. Nowhere is this more evident than in Los Angeles.

---

[29]For example, SB 402 (Burton, 2000) allows binding arbitration of labor issues by unions representing local government public safety personnel.

[30]Juries decide sentences in death penalty cases.

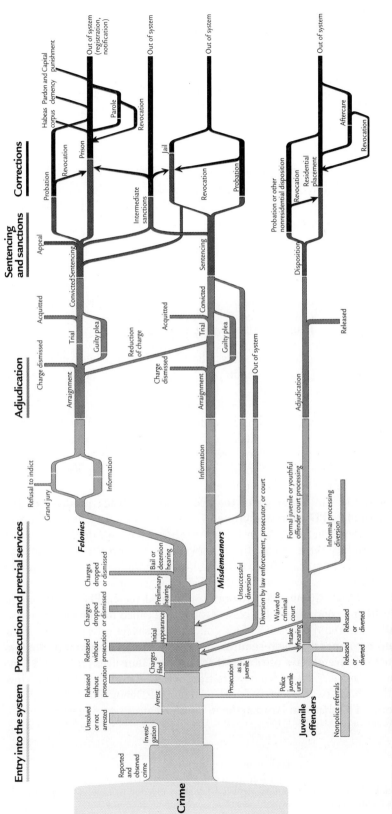

EXHIBIT 6-3   The Criminal Justice System

What is the sequence of events in the criminal justice system?

Note: This chart gives a simplified view of caseflow through the criminal justice system. Procedures vary among jurisdictions. The weights of the lines are not intended to show actual size of caseloads.

Source: Adapted from *The Challenge of Crime in a Free Society,* President's Commission on Law Enforcement and Administration of Justice, 1967. This revision, a result of the Symposium on the 30th Anniversary of the President's Commission, was prepared by the Bureau of Justice Statistics in 1997.

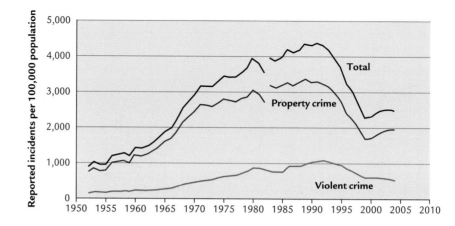

EXHIBIT 6-4   California Crime Index

In what previous year was the crime rate as low as it was in 2000?

Note: Larceny-theft over $400 not included in property crime rates before 1983.

Investigation and Arrest

Often featured in movies and television shows, the 13,000-member Los Angeles Police Department (LAPD) had a vaunted reputation as a by-the-book police force—the epitome of impartial professionalism, who live by their motto "To Protect and to Serve" and who are the ideal model for police officers and police departments.

The reality is that police behavior varies. Most are heroic, a few are racist; most are problem solvers, a few are bureaucratic rule enforcers; most render compassionate assistance, a few are brutal; most are intelligent, a few are not. A succession of dramatic events, televised to the world, tore at the LAPD during the 1990s and challenged our view of the role of the police.

The perception at the beginning of the decade among black residents of Los Angeles was that the LAPD addressed crime by racist and brutal tactics. These perceptions were reinforced in 1991, when four LAPD officers were videotaped beating Rodney King as twenty-three other officers looked on. Excerpts of the tape were widely and repeatedly broadcast. Mayor Tom Bradley appointed a special commission headed by former U.S. Secretary of State Warren Christopher to investigate the LAPD. The Christopher Commission Report condemned the LAPD for systematic racial harassment and routine use of excessive force, and called for the resignation of Police Commissioner Daryl Gates. The four police officers were arrested and tried in Simi Valley, a predominantly Anglo suburb. In 1992, the jury's acquittal of the four officers touched off several days of rioting that cost fifty-four lives and over $1 billion in property damage.[31] News helicopters transmitted disturbing images of fires, looting, and the brutal assaults on truck driver Reginald Denny and Fidel Lopez at the intersection of Florence and Normandie in South Central Los Angeles.[32]

---

[31]Some still insist on calling the riot a rebellion or civil disturbance.

[32]The four officers were later convicted on federal civil rights charges. People still debate whether the Rodney King incident involved excessive force or was a necessary reaction by officers to a person who would not comply with orders to stop his vehicle and passively submit to arrest.

In January 1994, another aspect of police responsibility was seen in the aftermath of the Northridge earthquake, as the entire LAPD force was mobilized for rescue and relief efforts.

Later in 1994, O.J. Simpson, a former star football player and media celebrity, was arrested for the murders of his estranged wife, Nicole Brown Simpson, and Ron Goldman. The televised "trial of the century" (120 witnesses, 45,000 pages of evidence, and 1,100 exhibits) in 1995–1996 took almost nine months, revealed perjury and racism on the part of an investigating detective, and hinted at the planting of evidence by police. The jury's not-guilty verdict (by ten women and two men—nine blacks, two Anglos, and one Latino) was generally applauded by blacks as a rare successful challenge to the perceived racially biased criminal justice system. Anglos just shook their heads in dismay.[33]

In 1997, the courage and heroism of LAPD officers—men and women, black, Latino, Asian, and Anglo—was dramatically televised as they confronted bank robbers armed with automatic weapons in a North Hollywood street shootout.

Then in May 1998, the Ramparts scandal broke. Officer Rafael Perez, a member of a special anti–gang enforcement unit in the Ramparts division, confessed and implicated scores of other officers in police corruption—everything from drinking while on duty to robbery, stealing impounded drugs, lying in court, planting evidence to frame suspects, to shooting unarmed suspects. Dozens of convictions that involved arrests by the accused officers were overturned by the courts.

Recently, police statewide have been accused of **racial profiling**—race-biased actions that range from extra attention to and visual surveillance to people based on ethnic background; to doing traffic and field stops, identity checks, and vehicle searches on pretexts; to using excessive force and even making racially motivated arrests. Several studies of vehicle stops in California show that the percentage of African Americans and Latinos among motorists pulled over by the police greatly exceeds the proportion of African Americans and Latinos in the population at large. Also, after being stopped, blacks and Latinos are more likely to be subjected to vehicle searches.[34] Police deny stopping motorists solely on the basis of the person's color or apparent ethnicity.[35] They claim to act on suspicious cues including location, time of day, recent crime reports, erratic behavior, and the appearance of the vehicle, as well as traffic violations. Searches may be prompted by missing driver's licenses, vehicle registrations, or insurance documents and by the dress, demeanor, and statements of the driver or passengers.

Comparisons with population data can be misleading. Certain roads or neighborhoods having a higher proportion of blacks and Latinos may draw law enforcement attention because of a pattern of criminal incidents or traffic problems. In social science terms, race may be a coincident rather than a causal factor. The police feel caught in the middle of conflicting public demands. Proactive crime prevention enforcement may draw criticism, but so will an increase in the crime rate.

Almost everyone, sooner or later, encounters the criminal justice system. You may be a victim (hopefully of nothing more serious than theft of your property). Rarely, you might witness a crime. And sometimes you might be a suspect, contacted by the police regarding a crime (hopefully nothing more serious than a traffic infraction).

---

[33]Simpson was later found liable for the murders in a civil wrongful-death lawsuit.

[34]Erin McCormick and Jim Herron Zamora, "Racial Bias in CHP Searches: Latinos, Blacks More Likely to Have Vehicles Examined After Being Pulled Over," *San Francisco Chronicle*, 15 July 2001.

[35]These stops have been dubbed DWB—"driving while black" (or brown).

The criminal justice process starts with police stops, searches, and seizures (arrests or the taking of items as evidence). The police are supposed to have probable cause for a traffic stop or an arrest. Probable cause exists when the facts and circumstances known to the police (objective information that can be articulated) would lead a "prudent person to believe that a suspect has committed, is committing, or is about to commit a crime."[36] The police need only reasonable suspicion to stop and frisk a pedestrian.[37] Reasonable suspicion is more than an intuitive hunch but less than probable cause. In practice, these principles are so loosely defined that police have wide discretion in whom they stop and why. Searches, which may elicit evidence against suspects, are an even more complicated matter. The Fourth Amendment to the U.S. Constitution and Article I, Section 13, of the California Constitution require the police to obtain a search warrant—written permission from a judge—before making a search.[38] A person may waive this constitutional right and grant permission for a search of possessions, car, or home. In addition, warrantless searches are legal in many circumstances, such as at crime and arrest scenes, airports, or international border crossings or in emergencies.

What should you do if you are stopped by the police? Basically, cooperate, but be aware of your rights. Remain polite and respectful. Keep your words, behavior, and emotions in check. Keep your hands where the police can see them. Don't run. Follow directions. Don't touch or resist any officer. Don't protest or argue. Don't lie (better to say nothing). Remember the officer's name and patrol car number, and write everything down—exactly what happened, word for word and moment to moment, as soon as you can. If you are stopped in your car, you must show the police your driver's license, registration, and proof of insurance. Your basic rights at this point are (1) the right to remain silent[39] and (2) the right to refuse consent if asked by the police for permission to search your car.[40] The dilemma for a suspect is how far to go in cooperating with police. A layperson, with only basic knowledge of rights and law, and usually ignorant of police intentions and of the circumstances that prompted the stop, is now confronted by assertive governmental authority—trained professionals. Should you answer questions and consent to a search, or should you assert your constitutional rights? No one answer covers all situations. Sometimes explanation and agreement to a search will lead to a quick "You're free to go." But anything you say (or anything the police find in a search) can be used as evidence against you. Other times, merely answering basic identification questions and saying, "I do not consent to a search" will end the matter.[41] But it may also heighten police suspicion and scrutiny. The police are not obligated to truthfully explain the situation, their intentions, the law, or your rights, other than to provide the *Miranda* warnings before further questioning after an arrest.[42] The general

---

[36]*United States v. Hoyos,* 892 F.2d 1387, 1392 (Ninth Cir. 1989), cert. denied; 489 U.S. 825 (1990) (citing *United States v. Greene,* 783 F.2d 1364, 1367 (Ninth Cir. 1986), cert. denied; 476 U.S. 1185 (1986).

[37]A "frisk" is a superficial patting of a person's outer clothing to check for weapons.

[38]The U.S. and California constitutions state: "The right of the people to be secure in their persons, houses, papers, and effects against unreasonable searches and seizures shall not be violated; and a warrant may not issue except on probable cause, supported by oath or affirmation, particularly describing the place to be searched and the persons and things to be seized."

[39]The U.S. and California constitutions state: "No person . . . shall be compelled in any criminal case to be a witness against himself."

[40]If the police are satisfied that they have probable cause, they will proceed with a search. If they do not have probable cause, they will ask you to waive your constitutional rights and voluntarily consent to a search.

[41]If you are a U.S. citizen not driving a vehicle, you are not required to carry identification papers.

[42]"Prior to any questioning, the person [in custody] must be warned that he has a right to remain silent, that any statement he does make may be used as evidence against him, and that he has the right to the presence of an attorney"; *Miranda v. Arizona,* 384 U.S. 436 (1966).

advice of defense attorneys seems to be that if you are arrested rather than released, you need the help of your own trained professional advisor and representative—a lawyer—and probably ought to sit quietly (in jail) until you get one.

Prosecution and Adjudication

Well over 6 million criminal cases—felonies, misdemeanors, and infractions—are filed in California's superior courts each year. Exhibit 6-5 shows that three-fourths of these cases are relatively minor traffic infractions such as speeding; but there are about 750,000 cases of more serious traffic misdemeanors such as driving recklessly, engaging in speed contests and exhibitions, ignoring previous tickets and fines, driving with a suspended license, and driving under the influence of alcohol or drugs. Felonies such as robbery, murder, rape, burglary, or drug dealing (crimes punishable by a year or more in state prison); nontraffic misdemeanors such as petty theft, assault, or drug possession (crimes punishable by a fine or imprisonment for up to a year in county jail); and nontraffic infractions such as disorderly conduct, trespassing, or possession of illegal fireworks (generally punishable by a fine) altogether make up nearly 1 million criminal cases each year—about 283,000 felonies, 540,000 misdemeanors, and 291,000 infractions.

A criminal case begins when a prosecutor **charges** a person—the defendant—with one or more crimes, usually following a police arrest. The prosecutor (most often a county assistant district attorney) represents the People of the State of California because a crime is considered an act against society. A prosecutorial charge is an information. A grand jury charge is an indictment.

The first court appearance is an **arraignment,** held within forty-eight hours of the arrest.[43] Several things happen at this hearing. The defendant is presented with the charges and informed about his or her constitutional rights. If a defendant has been charged with a felony or a misdemeanor and says that he or she cannot afford to hire an attorney, the court will appoint one from the public defender's office. (The court does not appoint a public defender in infraction cases because these cases cannot result in jail or prison terms.) **Bail** will be set. In some cases, defendants may be released on their promise to appear, called **OR,** short for "own recognizance." The defendant will also be asked to enter an initial plea—"not guilty," "guilty," or "**nolo contendere**" (no contest). If a defendant pleads not guilty to a misdemeanor, the

---

[43]Weekends are not counted. The arraignment may occur in two or more sessions several days apart.

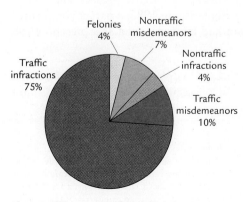

Traffic infractions 75%

Felonies 4%

Nontraffic misdemeanors 7%

Nontraffic infractions 4%

Traffic misdemeanors 10%

About 1 million cases are nontraffic infractions, misdemeanors, and felonies.

EXHIBIT 6-5 Criminal Cases Filed in California Superior Courts, 2004–2005 (7.4 million cases)

What percentage of all criminal cases are nontraffic misdemeanors or felonies?

Source: Judicial Council of California, *2006 Court Statistics Report.*

judge will set the date for a trial. The trial will be held within thirty days if the defendant is in custody or within forty-five days if the defendant is not in custody—unless the defendant waives the right to a speedy trial. If a defendant pleads not guilty to a felony, a **preliminary hearing** is scheduled. At this hearing, the district attorney must show evidence establishing probable cause that the defendant committed a felony and should be brought to trial. This step (or the alternative, a grand jury indictment) is necessary to make sure that only defendants against whom there is significant evidence will undergo a felony trial. A guilty or nolo contendere plea will lead to sentencing.

The next formal step is a trial at which, as portrayed on television and in movies, witnesses testify, evidence is presented to a judge and jury, and the prosecutor must prove the charges *beyond a reasonable doubt*. But this drama rarely happens. Less than 3 percent of felony cases and 0.4 percent of misdemeanor cases go to trial. Cases are not adjudicated so much as they are settled by **plea bargaining**. Plea bargaining is just that: *bargaining*—negotiation between the defendant, represented by defense counsel, and the prosecutor to reach a mutually acceptable disposition of the case subject to court approval. It usually involves the defendant's pleading guilty or nolo contendere to a lesser offense or to only one or some of the charges in return for a lighter sentence than would be possible if convicted of the most serious charges. The principal issue is not guilt or innocence. Most arrests are valid; nearly all defendants are indeed guilty of a crime. The questions are: What crimes should the defendant be found guilty of? and What is the appropriate sentence? Plea bargaining is sometimes falsely regarded as letting criminals off in the interests of expediency. Certainly, plea bargaining is efficient, saving significant time and money for the criminal justice system, but it is also a fair and just way to resolve cases.[44] The prosecuting and defense attorneys review the events, weigh the strengths and weaknesses of the evidence, and consider the seriousness of the charge, mitigating circumstances, and the potential sentence. Most of the time, they work out a compromise charge and plea that satisfies the government's burden-of-proof obligation and criminal punishment interest, and the punishment-is-proportional-to-the-crime interest of the defendant.

Prosecutors have two responsibilities. First, they are obliged to uphold the law—to obtain convictions and seek punishment. Second, they are obliged to investigate the case, present evidence to the court, and determine the best way to serve the overall interests of the people. Sometimes justice is served by not filing a case, by diverting a case to another part of the system, by reducing the charges, or by dismissing a case for lack of evidence or improperly obtained evidence.[45] Prosecutors' power to decide what crimes to prosecute and how to charge cases is called "prosecutorial discretion."

There have been instances of abusive, excessive, or selective prosecution in California.[46] Most famous is the McMartin preschool case. In 1983, a parent complained to the Manhattan Beach police that her son had been molested at a preschool run

---

[44]From first court appearance to final disposition, 81 percent of felony cases and 87 percent of misdemeanor cases are resolved within ninety days; Judicial Council of California, *2002 Court Statistics Report*, **www.courtinfo.ca.gov/reference**

[45]Diversion programs assign a defendant to medical treatment or counseling or to community service work in lieu of a fine or jail sentence.

[46]Selective prosecution is the pursuit of charges against some persons, but not others, for seemingly the same offense—possibly on the basis of race, or to set an example or send a message. For example, blacks and Latinos are more likely than whites to be charged with a felony rather than a misdemeanor if they are caught with a concealed or loaded firearm; Criminal Justice Statistics Center, California Department of Justice, *Concealable Firearms Charges in California, 2000–2003*, **ag.ca.gov/cjsc/publications/misc/CWSS03/rpt03.pdf**

by Peggy McMartin Buckey and her mother, Virginia McMartin. Peggy Buckey's son, Ray Buckey, who worked part-time at the preschool, was arrested. At first, the district attorney refused to prosecute because there was no physical evidence or corroboration. Nevertheless, the incident quickly escalated, fueled by continuing police inquiries, sensationalist television news reports, pressure from panicky parents, and rumors of satanic rituals and child pornography. Repeatedly pressuring the children, parents and social workers elicited several outlandish and unproven stories about animal slayings and secret tunnels that nevertheless were believed. In 1984, McMartin, the Buckeys, and four schoolteachers were charged with 208 counts of child abuse involving forty children. The preliminary hearing lasted eighteen months. The ensuing trial took six years and cost the county over $13 million.[47] Eventually, a new district attorney was elected, and most of the charges were dropped. The remaining charges resulted in not-guilty verdicts or a hung jury in favor of acquittal.

Nobody was convicted of anything in the McMartin case, but it set the stage for a rash of similar prosecutions and wrongful convictions across the country. Whether influenced by public outrage, media attention, or prosecutorial "get-tough-on-crime" zeal and zero tolerance for criminal behavior, wrongful convictions take place. Many are described by Edward Humes in his book *Mean Justice*, which focuses on such a case in Kern County.[48] Rights and liberties are in the prosecutor's hands, so it is vital that the prosecutor be an objective, fair-minded advocate.

Sentencing and Corrections

Exhibit 6-6 shows that while arrest and conviction rates have remained virtually unchanged since 1980 and the crime rate has dropped by 40 percent, the **incarceration** rate in California has increased 450 percent.

On a typical day in California, about 164,000 people are in one of the thirty-three state prisons and thirty-eight camps administered by the California Department of Corrections and Rehabilitation (CDCR), including 634 men and 15 women on death row.[49] About 4,000 persons are in state youth prisons administered by the Division of Juvenile Justice (formerly known as the California Youth Authority). About 6,900 other youths are in a county juvenile hall, and another 4,000 or so are in a county juvenile probation camp. And about 764,000 adults are in county jail. Altogether, about 255,000 people—one out of every 140 Californians, or 675 per 100,000 population. This is among the highest state incarceration rates in the United States—the country that has the highest rate of incarceration among its population in the world. Four public policies account for this increase.

"Lock-'em-up-and-throw-away-the-key" sentencing. Law-and-order policies call for long mandatory—determinate—sentences for felony convictions and a virtually total abandonment of corrections and rehabilitation as system goals. The mission of

---

[47]The McMartin case was the longest and most expensive criminal trial in U.S. history. By contrast, the O.J. Simpson trial cost $8 million. Ray Buckey did not make bail and consequently spent several years in pretrial detention.

[48]Edward Humes, *Mean Justice* (New York: Simon & Schuster, 1999). See **www.edwardhumes.com/mean.htm** However, an "innocence project," in which Orange County prosecutors and public defenders reviewed the cases of twenty-seven inmates who claimed to have been wrongly convicted, found that none deserved new trials; Monte Morin, "Panel Says No Retrials for O.C. Prison Inmates," *Los Angeles Times*, 15 June 2002.

[49]Thirty-three "special circumstances" make almost every first-degree murderer eligible for capital punishment. However, California courts apply the death sentence in less than 12 percent of eligible cases. The courts are considering whether allowing the death sentence in so many cases, but imposing it in so few, is unconstitutional.

EXHIBIT 6-6 California Crimes, Arrests, Convictions, and Incarcerations (indexed to 1980)

Between 1980 and 2004, California's crime rate dropped nearly 40 percent while the rates of arrests and convictions remained relatively constant. Why was there a fourfold increase in the adult state institution incarceration rate?

1980 crime rate = 3,922 violent & property crimes per 100,000 population

1980 arrest rate = 8,035 felony & misdemeanor arrests per 100,000 population 10–69

1980 felony conviction rate = 55.8 percent of arrests

1980 incarceration rate = 176.9 inmates in state institutions per 100,000 population 10–69

Source: California Department of Justice, *Crime in California*, 2004.

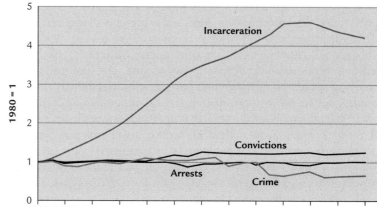

prisons is to warehouse inmates—remove them from society—for the purposes of deterrence and incapacitation. The principal example of tough-on-crime sentencing policy is Proposition 184, California's "Three-Strikes-and-You're-Out" initiative. Passed in 1994, at the height of public outrage about the home-abduction kidnapping and murder of 12-year-old Polly Klass by a criminal with prior violent crime convictions, "Three Strikes" continued a pattern of legislation and judicial rulings in California that attempted to combat crime by more frequently imposing, and increasing the length of, jail and prison sentences. It provided for doubling the prison sentence of someone convicted a second time for any felony and tripling the sentence (or twenty-five years to life, whichever was greater) of criminals convicted of a third felony "strike." More than a quarter of the inmates in state prison are serving second- or third-strike sentences. Forty states have lengthened the prison sentences of repeat criminals; twenty-six of the forty (and the federal government) have a third-strike provision allowing a life sentence after a third felony conviction. Under "Three Strikes," a felony is a felony, regardless of whether it is a property crime or a crime against a person, or whether it is a violent or nonviolent offense. In California, crimes that are misdemeanors on the first offense become felonies on the second offense.[50] Thus seemingly minor crimes, such as shoplifting, can be charged as felonies and trigger the third-strike sentence. California's law was challenged in the courts as being unconstitutional as cruel and unusual punishment, because it makes no distinction with respect to third-strike offenses, but the sentences were upheld by the U.S. Supreme Court.[51]

---

[50]Prosecutors have discretion as to whether to charge an offense as a second or third strike.

[51]The Eighth Amendment to the U.S. Constitution states: "Excessive bail shall not be required, nor excessive fines imposed, nor cruel and unusual punishments inflicted." The California Constitution, Art. I, Sec. 17, states: "Cruel or unusual punishment may not be inflicted or excessive fines imposed." Leandro Andrade, a heroin addict with a record of burglary and shoplifting, was sentenced to twenty-five years to life after conviction for shoplifting $153 worth of videotapes from a Kmart store; *Lockyer v. Andrade*, 538 U.S. 63 (2003). Gary Ewing, with four prior robbery and burglary convictions, was sentenced to twenty-five years to life after shoving three golf clubs down his pants leg and trying to walk out of a pro shop; *Ewing v. California*, 538 U.S. 11 (2003).

Proponents of deterrence and incapacitation say that this policy will reduce crime because stiff penalties will dissuade persons from criminal conduct and because increased incarceration will remove career criminals from society. They regard the reduction in California's crime rate as confirming this policy approach. However, crime rates are down in all parts of the nation, even those without such stringent imprisonment policies as "Three Strikes."

Prisons are dangerous, overcrowded, dungeonlike warehouses. There is little emphasis on education, rehabilitation, and reintegration into society. California's prison system costs more than $7 billion per year—more than $1 billion for prisoner health care alone. Even at that level of expenditure, a U.S. district court has found the level of health care so poor that it violated the constitutional cruel-and-unusual-punishment provision. Beginning in 2006, the CDCR's medical program has been administered by a federal receiver with authority to determine the program budget, make medical staff personnel decisions, and contract for health care provider services.

Zero tolerance of parole violations. Increased incarceration means an increasing ex-felon population—people who have done little else but serve their time and are released with no treatment, no training, no education, and no opportunities. Ninety percent of those who enter prisons eventually return to the community. In any given year, about 40 percent of California's prisoners are released. Of the 500,000 parolees who leave U.S. prisons annually, 17.2 percent—or nearly 1 in 5—live in California.[52] California's convicts have lengthy parole periods. Reimprisonment for several months is the principal penalty for violating any parole condition, whether major or minor. Sixty percent of parolees return to prison—the highest rate in the nation, so many that at any one time they comprise one-third of California state prison inmates.

Increased use of incarceration as a penalty for drug crimes. In November 2000, Californians passed Proposition 36, the Substance Abuse and Crime Prevention Act, providing alternative treatment for simple drug possession. Until then, California led the nation in using incarceration as the primary response to illicit drug use and drug-related crime. About 20 percent of California imprisonments are due to drug offenses, close to the national average. Proposition 36 is a departure from the get-tough, deterrence-and-incapacitation policy. It provides for sentencing first- and second-time nonviolent offenders on low-level charges of possession-for-personal-use only to a substance abuse treatment program instead of prison. Since passage, more than 10,000 people a year have been diverted to treatment rather than jail, and California's steadily increasing rate of adult incarceration has stopped and even declined slightly.

Increased use of incarceration as a response to mental illness. At least 16 percent of the inmates in California jails and prisons are severely mentally ill. Over thirty years ago, a revolution in the treatment of mental illness called for the deinstitutionalization of the mentally ill in favor of community-based outpatient treatment. State psychiatric facilities were closed, but community treatment programs were never established. Today, thousands of Californians with serious mental illnesses eke out an existence between hospitalization, homelessness, and jail. Why don't they receive treatment? In part, the reason is the nature of such diseases as schizophrenia and bipolar disorder. Individuals with these disorders lack the capacity to objectively evaluate hallucinations, delusions, depression, and paranoia as symptoms of an illness that needs medication

---

[52]Joan Petersilia, "Challenges of Prisoner Reentry and Parole in California" (Berkeley: University of California, California Policy Research Center, CPRC Brief, vol. 12, no. 3, June 2000), **www.ucop.edu/ cprc/parole.html**

and treatment services, and not as reality. The applicable law—the Lanterman-Petris-Short (LPS) Act (1967)—essentially provides that a person cannot be involuntarily committed to a psychiatric facility unless he or she is shown to be a danger to him- or herself or to others. They are most often arrested for such misdemeanor charges as trespassing, disorderly conduct, threats, and assault. Alcohol and drug charges are also common. The Los Angeles County Jail is one of America's largest mental institutions. In San Diego, an average of 750 of the 5,500 inmates in the county jail system have documented mental illnesses. There are more beds in the San Diego jail's psychiatric unit than in the county's mental health hospital. Despite the frequency with which they deal with the mentally ill, sheriff's deputies, correctional officers, and police receive only a few hours of training in psychiatric problems. The general approach is detention, control, and medication, rather than treatment.[53]

WEB LINKS

Affirmative Action and Diversity Project: A Web Page for Research
aad.english.ucsb.edu

American Civil Liberties Union–Northern California **www.aclunc.org**

American Civil Liberties Union–Southern California **www.aclu-sc.org**

American Civil Rights Coalition **www.acrc1.org**

American Civil Rights Institute **www.acri.org**

California District Attorneys Association **www.cdaa.org**

California Drunk Driving Law Guide **www.california-drunkdriving.org**

California First Amendment Coalition **www.cfac.org**

California Judges Association **www.calcourts.org**

California Prisons **www.californiaprisons.org**

Center for Juvenile and Criminal Justice **www.cjcj.org**

Civil Justice Association of California **www.cjac.org**

Death Penalty Information Center **www.deathpenaltyinfo.org**

Debt to Society **www.motherjones.com/prisons/atlas.html**

Drug Policy Alliance **www.drugpolicy.org**

FindLaw **www.findlaw.com**

Freedom Forum **www.freedomforum.org**

Hieros Gamos[54] **www.hg.org**

---

[53]Greg Moran, "Jails Face Challenge in Dealing with Mentally Ill," *San Diego Union-Tribune*, 2 June 2002. Carla Jacobs and E. Fuller Torrey, "It's Time We Help California's Helpless," *San Diego Union-Tribune*, 16 February 2000. "Fact Sheet: Criminalization of Americans with Severe Mental Illnesses," Treatment Advocacy Center, **www.psychlaws.org.** In an effort to reform the LPS law, the legislature passed the Outpatient Treatment Demonstration Act of 2002 (AB 1421, Thomson, D-Davis). Named "Laura's Law" after a Nevada County mental health worker, Laura Wilcox, who was shot to death by a person who had refused treatment for a mental illness, AB 1421 gives counties the authority to compel a court-ordered 180-day outpatient treatment program for individuals suffering from severe mental illness who refuse voluntary treatment. Participating counties must assure an intensive 10-to-1 patient–staff ratio and fund the program without reducing the budget of existing voluntary-treatment mental health services. Eve Bender, "Law Gives California Counties Commitment Authority," *Psychiatric News* 22 (4), 15 November 2002.

[54]Greek meaning the "synthesis of seeming contradictions"—in this case, using the Internet to facilitate access to information in electronic and written forms.

Judicial Council of California **www.courtinfo.ca.gov**

Law.com California **www.law.com/california**

'Lectric Law Library **www.lectlaw.com**

Mean Justice **www.edwardhumes.com/mean.htm**

National Center for State Courts **www.ncsconline.org**

National Freedom of Information Coalition **www.nfoic.org**

Prison Activist Resource Center **www.prisonactivist.org**

Privacy Clearinghouse **www.privacyrights.org**

Reporters Committee for Freedom of the Press **www.rcfp.org**

Web-Law **www.web-law.com**

PUBLICATIONS

Ball, Howard. 2000. *The Bakke Case: Race, Education, and Affirmative Action.* Lawrence: University Press of Kansas.

Bedau, Hugo Adam, and Paul G. Cassell. 2004. *Debating the Death Penalty: Should America Have Capital Punishment? The Experts on Both Sides Make Their Best Case.* New York: Oxford University Press.

Cannon, Lou. 1999. *Official Negligence: How Rodney King and the Riots Changed Los Angeles and the LAPD.* New York: Basic Books.

Connerly, Ward. 2000. *Creating Equal: My Fight Against Race Preferences.* San Francisco: Encounter Books.

Delsohn, Gary. 2003. *The Prosecutors: A Year in the Life of a District Attorney's Office.* New York: E. P. Dutton.

Dershowitz, Alan M. 1996. *Reasonable Doubts: The O.J. Simpson Case and the Criminal Justice System.* New York: Simon & Schuster.

Eberle, Paul, and Shirley Eberle. 1993. *The Abuse of Innocence: The McMartin Preschool Trial.* Amherst, NY: Prometheus Books.

Geller, Laurence H., and Peter Hemenway. 1997. *Last Chance for Justice: The Juror's Lonely Quest.* Dallas: NCDS Press.

Glantz, Stanton A., and Edith D. Balbach. 2000. *The Tobacco War: Inside the California Battles.* Berkeley: University of California Press.

Grodin, Joseph R. 1989. *In Pursuit of Justice: Reflections of a State Supreme Court Justice.* Berkeley: University of California Press.

Holbert, Steve, and Lisa Rose. 2004. *The Color of Guilt and Innocence: Racial Profiling and Police Practices in America.* San Ramon, CA: Page Marque Press.

Humes, Edward. 1999. *Mean Justice: A Town's Terror, a Prosecutor's Power, a Betrayal of Innocence.* New York: Simon & Schuster.

Humes, Edward. 1996. *No Matter How Loud I Shout: A Year in the Life of Juvenile Court.* New York: Simon & Schuster.

McCoy, Candace. 1993. *Politics and Plea Bargaining: Victims' Rights in California.* Philadelphia: University of Pennsylvania Press.

Morris, James McGrath. 2001. *Jailhouse Journalism: The Fourth Estate Behind Bars.* Somerset, NJ: Transaction.

Olsen, Jack. 2000. *Last Man Standing: The Tragedy and Triumph of Geronimo Pratt*. New York: Doubleday.

Unlawful Discrimination: Your Rights and Remedies, Civil Rights Handbook, 3rd ed. Sacramento: Office of the Attorney General, Public Rights Division, Civil Rights Enforcement Section, 2001. **ag.ca.gov/civilrights/pdf/01cr_handbook.pdf**

When You Become 18: A Survival Guide for Teenagers. Sacramento: State Bar of California, 2005.

Zimring, Franklin E., Gordon Hawkins, and Sam Kamin. 2001. *Punishment and Democracy: Three Strikes and You're Out in California*. New York: Oxford University Press.

GLOSSARY

adjudication   The process of hearing and deciding a criminal or civil case.

affirmative action   Preferential treatment in such matters as admissions, hiring, and contracting that can range from race- or gender-conscious efforts to provide information and encouragement to priorities, incentives, set-asides, and quotas.

alternative dispute resolution (ADR)   Referral of a civil lawsuit to arbitration or mediation as a means of speeding resolution of the case and reducing costs.

answer   In a civil case, the formal written statement by a defendant responding to a complaint setting forth the grounds for his or her defense.

arbitration   The process by which a neutral party conducts a hearing, reviews evidence, and decides the outcome of a dispute.

arraignment   The initial appearance before a judge in a criminal case for the purposes of informing the defendant of the charges, appointing a lawyer if the defendant cannot afford one (in the case of misdemeanor or felony charges), entering the defendant's plea, and setting bail.

bail   Money deposited with a court to obtain the temporary release of an arrested person and to ensure that the person will comply with court orders and appear for trial at a later date. In a minor infraction, the prepayment of the fine (refunded if the person is not convicted).

charge(s) (counts)   In a criminal case, a formal statement by the prosecution specifying the alleged crimes of the defendant.

civil liberties   Fundamental freedoms from arbitrary governmental interference in personal conduct that are guaranteed by the Constitution of the United States (Bill of Rights) and the constitution of the state of California. Civil liberties include freedom of speech and press and freedom to practice religion.

civil-limited (lawsuit)   A civil dispute with a damage claim greater than $5,000 but not exceeding $25,000.

civil-unlimited (lawsuit)   A civil dispute with a damage claim greater than $25,000.

civil petitions   Cases that deal with such matters as custody and visitation, child and spousal support, restraining orders, parentage, and adoption.

civil rights   Procedural freedoms associated with principles of fairness and equal treatment. See *due process* and *equal protection*.

complaint   A written statement filed by the plaintiff that initiates a civil case, stating the wrongs allegedly committed by the defendant and the relief sought from the court.

crime   Any act prohibited by law for which there is a formally sanctioned punishment. This can include the failure of a person to perform an act specifically required by the law. The law recognizes three broad categories of crimes based on the seriousness of the offense and potential penalties: felonies, misdemeanors, and infractions. In addition, nontraffic crimes can be classified as violent, property, or drug-related crimes.

damages   The monetary sum awarded by a judge in a civil action in satisfaction for the wrong suffered by the plaintiff. Damages may be *compensatory*, reimbursing the plaintiff for costs, or *punitive*, punishing the defendant for actions or negligence that resulted in injury to the plaintiff.

defendant   In a civil case, the person or organization against whom the plaintiff brings suit. In a criminal case, the person accused of the crime.

demurrer   A response by the defendant in a civil case stating that, even if the facts alleged by the plaintiff are true, the case should be dismissed either because no law was violated or because the evidence is insufficient.

discovery   The gathering of information (facts, documents, testimony, or other potential evidence) before a case goes to trial.

discrimination   A prejudicial or preferential treatment process such that opportunities and rewards are limited for some and enhanced for others on the basis of group attributes or characteristics.

due process   Procedural fairness. Government will not take a person's life, liberty, or property without following formal procedures (procedural due process) and having good reason (substantive due process).

equal protection   The principle that everyone in like circumstances should be treated the same way and afforded the same protections, opportunities, and benefits.

family law   Cases that deal with separation and divorce.

felony   A serious crime punishable by a sentence of one or more years in state prison.

guardianship   A person legally placed in charge of the affairs of another (such as a child or someone who is mentally ill).

incarceration   Imprisonment.

infraction   A minor crime punishable by a fine.

injunction   A court order to cease an activity.

injury   Harm done to a person's body, property, reputation, or rights.

justice   The process of using authority and power to promote the health, safety, and well-being of the people—upholding lawful principles and policies, maintaining peace, preserving order and safety, and resolving disputes—while respecting the fundamental civil rights and civil liberties of the people.

mediation   The process by which a neutral party helps the parties in a civil case negotiate a settlement.

misdemeanor   A crime punishable by a sentence of less than one year in county jail.

nolo contendere   Latin for "I will not defend it" or "no contest." The plea of a defendant in a criminal case in which the defendant declines to refute the evidence of the prosecution; has the same effect as a plea of guilty, as far as the criminal sentence is concerned, but may not be considered as an admission of guilt for any other purpose.

OR (own recognizance)   The release of an arrested person without bail on the promise of that person to comply with court orders and appear in court at a later date.

petition   A formal written request presented to the court requesting specific judicial action.

plaintiff   In a civil case, the person or organization who brings a lawsuit. Sometimes called the *complainant* or *petitioner* depending on the type of case.

plea bargaining   The process whereby the defendant, represented by defense counsel, and the prosecutor in a criminal case negotiate a mutually acceptable disposition of the case subject to court approval. It usually involves the defendant's pleading guilty or nolo contendere to a lesser offense or to only one or some of the counts of a multicount indictment in return for a lighter sentence than would be possible if convicted of the most serious charge.

preliminary hearing   In felony cases, a judicial hearing at which the prosecution presents evidence establishing probable cause that the defendant committed the alleged crime and should be held to answer for it.

probate   Judicial certification of a will.

racial profiling   The practice of suspecting a person of a crime for no reason other than the color of that person's skin or apparent nationality or ethnicity.

sentence   The punishment for a crime including imprisonment, probation, or a fine.

small claim (lawsuit)   A civil dispute having a damage claim of $5,000 or less.

summons   Formal notification of a lawsuit informing the recipient of the place and time to appear in court.

tort   An action or negligence (other than breach of contract) that causes injury.

SUGGESTED ANSWERS TO EXHIBIT QUESTIONS

Exhibit 6-1: The Lady of Justice symbolizes the impartial administration of the law by a powerful government. The scales might indicate that justice balances the government's interest to uphold public policy, maintain peace, preserve order and safety, and resolve disputes, on the one side, and fundamental civil rights and civil liberties, on the other. The sword might symbolize the power of the government to right wrongs by accountability, redress, compensation, and punishment. The robes may suggest formality and judicial proceedings.

Exhibit 6-2: The workload average is about 1,000 civil cases per year per judge.

Exhibit 6-3: The sequence of events in the criminal justice system is investigation and arrest, prosecution and adjudication, and sentencing and corrections.

Exhibit 6-4: The last time the total crime and property crime indexes were as low as they were in 2000 was 1965. The violent crime index is at the 1975 level.

Exhibit 6-5: Eleven percent of criminal cases are nontraffic misdemeanors or felonies. That is still 825,000 cases each year. Another 10 percent are traffic misdemeanors.

Exhibit 6-6: There are three basic reasons for the increase in the incarceration rate: (1) state laws that define new crimes with jail or prison penalties, (2) increasing use of jail or prison sentences as criminal penalties rather than probation or other alternatives, and (3) increasing length of jail or prison sentences. Research has not resolved the extent to which the decreasing crime rate is due to increasing incarceration.

CHAPTER SEVEN

EMPLOYMENT, EDUCATION, AND SOCIAL SERVICES

Think of it! The biggest, richest, most powerful country cannot keep its full job force working. It cannot tend all its sick people. It cannot feed all its hungry people or decently house its poor people. It cannot educate everyone who needs an education.[1]

California is a paradox—a land of contrasts and contradictions. In employment, education, housing, and health care, there are haves and have-nots. In a state with one of the largest economies in the world, there is significant poverty. In a state with world-class universities and research institutions, there is educational failure. There is upscale living for some and paycheck-to-paycheck lives centered around work and commuting for others. There is a booming housing market in some areas and significant homelessness in others. There are fine medical schools and hospitals, yet inadequate access to health care.

Employment, education, housing, and health care are necessities. Although various social services supposedly provide a societal safety net, for many Californians, access to these necessities is problematic—unaffordable, unavailable, or inadequate. Access is contingent on one's economic well-being in matters such as housing and health care and on governmental policies and programs—especially budgetary funding—with respect to education and social services. This chapter reviews several indicators of economic well-being in California: unemployment, income, education, housing, and health care.

---

[1]Excerpt from a speech by fictional California politician Bill McKay, portrayed by Robert Redford, in the motion picture *The Candidate*, prod. Walter Coblenz, dir. Michael Ritchie, screenwriter Jeremy Larner, 110 min., Warner Brothers, 1972, DVD.

EMPLOYMENT AND INCOME

California's civilian labor force numbers about 18 million people, but nearly 1 million—5 percent—do not have jobs. Another 1 million underemployed people reportedly desire more work hours.

The **unemployment rate** is a key indicator of the health of an economy. The statistic is based on a monthly federal government estimate, called the *Current Population Survey,* of the number of people not working but who are able, available, and actively looking for work. Persons working at least one hour for a wage or salary during the second week of the month are counted as employed.

Exhibit 7-1 shows unemployment rates for California's most populous regions. Unemployment in the metropolitan Los Angeles region, where most of the state's population resides and where most of the jobs are, closely matches the state average. The region with the lowest unemployment rate is San Diego, which, along with the San Francisco Bay Area, enjoyed the 1990s economic boom. But the 2001–2003 economic **recession** hit the West Coast states hard. Centered on the high-tech industries, the Bay

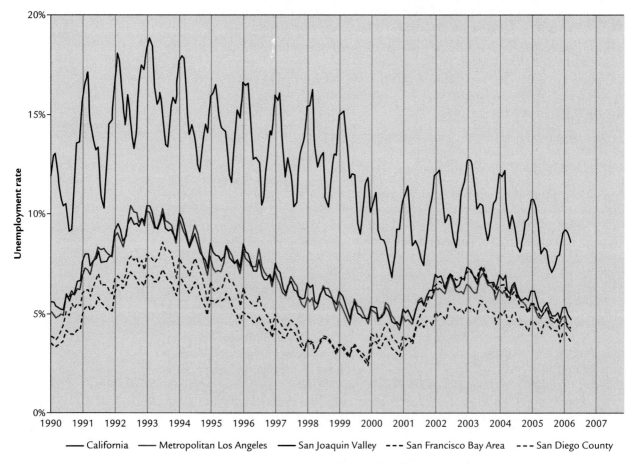

EXHIBIT 7-1   Unemployment Rates in California

Which regions currently have the lowest and highest unemployment rates? Are unemployment rates predictable? Why?

Source: California Labor Market Information System, **www.labormarketinfo.edd.ca.gov**

Area unemployment rate climbed sharply. The most dramatic part of Exhibit 7-1 is the top line describing the San Joaquin Valley. Here we see a significant disparity—chronically high **structural unemployment**. Month after month, year after year, the San Joaquin Valley's unemployment rate is double the state average. In addition, we observe volatile **seasonal unemployment**. Through the spring and summer months, the unemployment rate drops four to six percentage points, only to quickly return to its previous level in September through December. This oscillation closely follows the seasonal nature of the agriculture and food-processing industries. The long, wavelike swell, rising and falling over about a ten-year period, indicates that California's economy is integrally connected to the national economy, which exhibits the same periodic increase and decrease in employment. It may be that California, because of its size, influences the national economy more than the other way around.

California has two economies. The economy in the Los Angeles and San Diego regions and the Bay Area has mixed manufacturing, white-collar professions, technology, government, finance, retail trade, and service industries. Here, unemployment steadily dropped during most of the 1990s, reaching less than 5 percent by December 2000 and returning again to that level in 2006. The dominant industries in the other economy, the San Joaquin Valley, are agriculture, retail trade, and services. The San Joaquin Valley's unemployment rate stayed consistently between 10 and 15 percent in the 1990s and remains about 10 percent in the 2000s. Although the economy is depressed, the valley is growing in population and housing, as a destination for immigrants, and in sprawl, as urban workers seek lower-cost housing. However, jobs do not necessarily follow people. Manufacturing, technology, and white-collar employers regard the San Joaquin Valley workforce as largely undereducated and untrained. Investments in transportation and public works infrastructure have also lagged. It is a perverse catch-22. Population growth increases the demand for services, but there is inadequate capital to fund these services or provide for public infrastructure investment—especially highway, rail, and air transport improvements. Private investment will continue to be directed toward the coastal regions, and the two-tier economic disparity is thus reinforced rather than alleviated.

If you are an educated professional or technician in California, you are doing relatively well. Jobs in high-wage industries such as computer hardware and software design, motion picture production, brokerage services, professional consulting, and education pay more than $50,000 per year.

The number of lower-skilled jobs—child care, food service, retail trade, landscaping, housecleaning—has increased, reflecting economic affluence and a larger demand for personal services. However, there is a big difference in income between a professional job that requires education or training and lower-skilled jobs. These jobs pay less than $31,200 per year ($15 per hour). Jobs in the middle-income range actually declined as aerospace, banking, and telecommunications industries cut back or consolidated.[2]

Exhibit 7-2 shows the employment and wage disparities. Nearly two-thirds of all workers are in occupations in which the entry-level wage is less than $10 per hour. Economists attribute this increasing income disparity to such factors as (1) an increasing number of younger workers, in part due to immigration, who have less experience, education, and skills; (2) globalization, which increases the market in high-tech industries while also increasing international competition in labor-intensive low-wage industries; and (3) technology, which increases productivity and automation in most fields other than retail trade or personal services.

---

[2]*California's Changing Income Distribution* (Sacramento, Calif.: Legislative Analyst's Office, 2000), **www.lao.ca.gov/0800_inc_dist/0800_income_distribution.html**

EXHIBIT 7-2

Work and Pay:
Wages by
Occupation in
California, Third
Quarter 2005

What is the entry-level hourly wage for a school teacher?

Which occupations have close-to-minimum-wage entry-level pay?

Occupational Category	WAGES		
	Entry-Level Hourly Wage	50th Percentile (Median) Hourly Wage	Percentage of Employment
State Average	$8.88	$15.91	—
Over $10/hour (38% of all workers)			
Management	$23.99	$43.28	5.2%
Architecture and engineering	21.71	34.18	2.2
Computer and mathematical	21.59	35.31	2.6
Legal	20.20	38.60	0.7
Health care practitioners and technical	17.79	30.08	4.1
Business and financial operations	17.71	27.13	4.3
Life, physical, and social science	16.92	28.22	1.0
Education, training, and library	12.27	22.17	6.2
Community and social services	11.97	18.92	1.3
Construction and extraction	11.94	19.96	5.1
Installation, maintenance, and repair	11.68	19.23	3.4
Arts, design, entertainment, sports, and media	10.31	19.18	2.0
Under $10/hour (62% of all workers)			
Office and administrative support	$9.78	$14.72	18.3%
Protective service	9.08	17.79	2.4
Health care support	8.99	12.02	2.1
Sales and related	8.18	12.18	10.4
Production	8.16	11.49	6.8
Transportation and material moving	8.02	11.57	7.1
Building and grounds cleaning and maintenance	7.81	10.19	3.3
Personal care and service	7.72	9.55	2.2
Farming, fishing, and forestry	7.71	8.19	1.2
Food preparation and serving-related	7.68	8.36	7.9

Note: The mean of the first third of the wage distribution is provided as a proxy for entry-level wage. Estimated 2004 employment = 14,598,240.

Source: California Labor Market Information System, **www.labormarketinfo.edd.ca.gov/cgi/career/?PageID=3&SubID=152**

But what is an adequate wage in California? Exhibit 7-3 summarizes the financial status of Californians. The California Budget Project (CBP) has calculated basic bare-bones family cost-of-living budgets for Californians. These budgets range from just over $25,000 per year for single adults, to about $54,000 per year for families with one working adult and two children, to $64,000 for families with two working

	Hourly Wage	Annual Income*	Estimated Percent Below[†]
Basic family budget for a two-working-adult, two-child family (2005)[‡]	$15.37	$63,921	56% of joint-return taxpayers
Basic family budget for a two-adult, two-child family with one adult working (2005)[‡]	21.22	44,130	39% of joint-return taxpayers
Basic family budget for a one-adult, two-child family (2005)[‡]	25.96	53,987	87% of head-of-household taxpayers
Basic budget for a single adult*	12.44	25,867	60% of single taxpayers
California median hourly wage (2004)[§]	15.06	31,325	50% of employees
California median family income (2004)		58,327	50% of joint-return taxpayers
California minimum wage (2005)	6.75	14,040	9% of all taxable returns
Federal poverty level for a one-adult, two-child family (2004)	7.32	15,219	26% of head-of-household taxpayers
Low income: 2 × federal poverty level for a one-adult, two-child family (2004)	14.64	30,438	61% of head-of-household taxpayers
Federal poverty level for a two-adult, two-child family (2004)	9.21	19,157	12% of joint-return taxpayers
Low income: 2 × federal poverty level for a two-adult, two-child family (2004)	18.42	38,314	32% of joint-return taxpayers

*California Budget Project estimates. Assume forty hours per week, fifty-two weeks per year of work; families include two children; and both parents in two-working-parent families are employed full time.

[†]In 2003, California had 14.6 million employees; 13.6 million taxpayers (5.5 million joint-return taxpayers, 6.0 million single-return taxpayers, 1.9 million head-of-household taxpayers).

[‡]A two-adult, two-child family can live on less than a one-adult, two-child family because one adult can stay home with the children.

[§]All occupations

Sources: *Making Ends Meet: How Much Does It Cost to Raise a Family in California?* California Budget Project, 2005; *Annual Report 2004* (Sacramento: State of California, Franchise Tax Board), **www.ftb.ca.gov/aboutftb/annrpt/2004/2004ar.pdf**

EXHIBIT 7-3

Family Budgets, Wages, and Poverty Levels

How would you define the working poor in California?

adults and two children with significant child day care costs. Sixty percent of all single adults; 87 percent of one-adult, two-child families; and over 40 percent of two-adult, two-child families report incomes below these levels. The median hourly wage for California workers is about $15 per hour ($31,000 annually), and the median family income is $58,000 (half earn less and half earn more).

Poverty is also a key indicator of the health of an economy. The operational definition of poverty is insufficient income to meet basic family needs, including food, clothing, housing, child care, health care, and transportation. The **federal poverty level (FPL)** is the official statistical reference. For a one-adult, two-child family, the 2006 FPL is $16,600, about one-third of the income required by the CBP estimate for a basic family budget. Currently, 26 percent of one-adult, two-child families fall below the FPL. Nearly one-fifth of all children in California live in households with

EXHIBIT 7-4

Poverty in California: Percent Below Federal Poverty Level, 2003–2004

What regions of California have the highest concentrations of poverty?

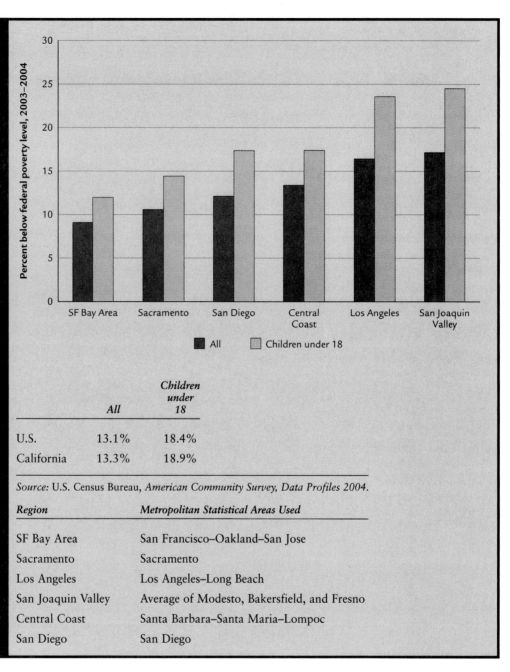

	All	Children under 18
U.S.	13.1%	18.4%
California	13.3%	18.9%

Source: U.S. Census Bureau, *American Community Survey, Data Profiles 2004.*

Region	Metropolitan Statistical Areas Used
SF Bay Area	San Francisco–Oakland–San Jose
Sacramento	Sacramento
Los Angeles	Los Angeles–Long Beach
San Joaquin Valley	Average of Modesto, Bakersfield, and Fresno
Central Coast	Santa Barbara–Santa Maria–Lompoc
San Diego	San Diego

income below the FPL. Further, many social scientists think that the FPL seriously understates the extent of poverty and use a relative poverty level—double the FPL—to define the working poor. Sixty-one percent of one-adult, two-child families and 32 percent of two-adult, two-child families in California meet this **low-income** criterion.

Although poverty rates declined in California during the 1990s, they remain above the national average. Exhibit 7-4 shows significant regional disparities in California. Poverty is concentrated in Los Angeles and the San Joaquin Valley. The poverty rate in these areas exceeds 15 percent, and the child poverty rate approaches 25 percent. Ethnic disparities are correlated with region, and even though three-fourths of Latino parents and over 80 percent of African American and Anglo parents work, the poverty rate among African American and Latino families is double (at over 20 percent) the rate among Anglo families. Thirty-four percent of foreign-born Californians (predominantly Latino) fall below the FPL.

THE SAFETY NET

Some think that poverty is a personal failing of those too lazy, irresponsible, or inept to hold a job. However, poverty much more often is a matter of circumstance. In any event, 30 percent of those in poverty are children. Federal, state, and local government have a number of policies and programs, the so-called social safety net, to provide basic subsistence and ease the worst effects. They fall in three general categories: (1) income and tax measures, (2) social insurance, and (3) public assistance.

Income and Tax Measures

Two of the most important antipoverty measures are relatively simple income and tax policies: the minimum wage and the federal Earned Income Tax Credit (EITC).

One seemingly simple way to resolve the low-income poverty problem is to mandate a **minimum wage.** Minimum wage laws were first passed in the 1930s in order to provide a "minimum standard of living necessary for health, efficiency and general well-being of workers." The national minimum wage is currently $5.15 per hour—unchanged by Congress since 1997. California set a minimum wage of $6.75 per hour in 2002. In 2006, Democrats worked out a bipartisan compromise with Governor Arnold Schwarzenegger to increase the minimum wage in two steps—75¢ an hour in January 2007 and an additional 50¢ in January 2008. Schwarzenegger, who had vetoed previous minimum wage bills, agreed when Democrats dropped demands to build in an automatic cost-of-living inflation adjustment. At $8.00 an hour, California's minimum wage will be the highest in the nation.

Adjusted for inflation, California's minimum wage is no higher today than it was fifty years ago. Totaling only about $14,000 per year for full-time work, the minimum wage is often called a "poverty-level wage." Several California communities have adopted "living wage" ordinances mandating a higher minimum wage for workers in companies that do business with the city or county. Hourly living wages (without employment benefits) range from $8.82 in San Francisco to $9.00 in Sacramento, $10.00 in Los Angeles, $12.00 in Santa Cruz County, and $12.50 in Ventura County. Living wage proponents argue that businesses can easily afford to pay living wages after raking in profits during the post-2003 economic recovery. Wage increases, they say, would also help the economy by increasing consumer purchasing power and help move some people off the welfare roles. Critics say that most of any increase in the minimum wage goes to single youths working part-time, whose families are not even near poverty levels. Further, they argue, any increase in labor costs leads to job losses—unemployment, especially in entry-level, low-skill jobs, that causes some families to fall into poverty. Research has not settled these issues, and lawmakers need to balance these arguments against the pros and cons of several other antipoverty policies and programs.

The federal **Earned Income Tax Credit (EITC)** is a *reverse* income tax—a direct cash supplement in the form of a federal income tax refund to low-income working families. The EITC is a form of income redistribution called a **transfer payment,** which funnels some income tax revenue—most of which comes from well-to-do taxpayers— to lower-income workers with children. The EITC is simple to administer—application and eligibility are established with the annual federal personal income tax return.

Although averaging less than $2,000 per year per family, the EITC is credited with being the most significant program to bring family incomes above the poverty line. Several states, though not California, have their own supplemental EITC. This measure has been considered in California, but the policy question is whether to redistribute government revenue to aid low-income workers generally or to direct assistance more specifically to the needy.

Social Insurance

Another set of antipoverty measures is called "social insurance." These include unemployment insurance (UI), Social Security insurance, Medicare, and Medi-Cal. *Insurance* is a misnomer in the sense that accounts are not funded by individual contributions. The programs are funded by taxes on employers and current employees. These **entitlement programs** provide benefits—in the form of either cash income (UI and Social Security) or payment for health care services (Medicare and Medi-Cal)—to persons who meet the eligibility requirements.

Unemployment Insurance   We often think that **unemployment insurance** alleviates the distress of unemployment. However, not every unemployed person is eligible for unemployment insurance compensation, and even for those who are eligible, the benefits are less than half of prior wages. The regulations are complicated and intimidating. For example, to be eligible for unemployment, a worker must have earned at least $1,400 in one quarter of a base period and have base period wages equal to 1.5 times high-quarter wages or wages in two quarters equal to 1.5 times the maximum taxable wage base.

Social Security and Medicare   **Social Security** and **Medicare** are federal programs, based on payroll taxes (the Federal Insurance Contributions Act or FICA, and Medicare deductions on employee pay stubs), that provide financial payments and health care to retired persons and the elderly.

Medi-Cal and Healthy Families   Medical insurance for the poor is provided by two programs. **Medi-Cal** is California's implementation of the federal **Medicaid** program—providing health insurance to low-income persons (primarily families with children and the aged, blind, or disabled). The Healthy Families Program extends health coverage to children in families with incomes up to 250 percent of the FPL. Together these jointly federal- and state-funded programs (nearly $30 billion) insure about one-fifth of all Californians (7.3 million people). Nevertheless, the programs miss many eligible children and adults who may enroll for medical insurance without necessarily participating in other public assistance programs. In addition, participants often face difficulty finding available and accessible primary-care physicians and specialists. Almost two-thirds of Medi-Cal spending is for the elderly and disabled, although they account for only about one-fourth of the total enrollment. Costs are rising rapidly for both programs, driven by double-digit increases in drug spending and growing enrollment.

Public Assistance

A third set of antipoverty measures is called "public assistance" or "welfare." The principal cash assistance programs are CalWORKs and SSI/SSP (Supplemental Security Income/State Supplementary Payment). Other programs provide **in-kind benefits**—services rather than cash.

CalWORKs   CalWORKs (California Work Opportunity and Responsibility to Kids) is California's implementation of the federal Temporary Aid to Needy Families (TANF) program—the major welfare policy change of the 1990s—intended to "end welfare as we know it" and alleviate child poverty by encouraging people to work rather than rely on welfare. It targets about 500,000 poor families—*needy* (very poor) children and the relatives who care for them. The most common family unit receiving CalWORKs assistance is a single mother with young children. A CalWORKs family cannot have more than $2,000 in countable property, and in most California counties, its income must be less than $754 per month for a family of three. In addition to this income **means test**, there are rules concerning age, residence, citizenship, criminal record, immunization, school attendance, child support collection, and time limits. Counties, which administer the program, also impose "welfare-to-work" training, education, or employment requirements.

SSI/SSP Supplemental Security Income/State Supplementary Payment Program   The SSI/SSP program provides cash payments to poor persons who are elderly, blind, or disabled. In California and other states, the federal SSI payment is augmented with a State Supplementary Payment (SSP), which may vary from year to year depending on state budget appropriations. The federal Social Security Administration administers the SSI/SSP program, making eligibility determinations and grant computations, and issuing combined monthly checks to recipients. The SSI/SSP grant (about $750 per month for an individual) provides an income close to the FPL.

Food Stamps   The federal food stamp program provides low-income persons with **vouchers** that can be used to purchase food at most grocery stores. Basic eligibility requirements include income less than 130 percent of FPL, less than $2,000 in financial resources, twenty hours of work per week for adults without dependents, and citizenship or legal immigration status. Eligible households are issued a monthly allotment based on household size minus 20 percent of household net income. The average monthly allotment was about $245 per household in 2006.

General Assistance   Counties are responsible for all other public assistance, including emergency assistance, cases that "slip through the cracks," and the treatment of medically indigent adults—people without health insurance who rely on a hospital emergency room for their occasional health care needs. In 1991, the state legislature resolved a budget crisis through enactment of realignment legislation. Under realignment, the state shifted billions in tax revenues to the counties, including vehicle license fees and state sales taxes. In return, the counties assumed full financial responsibility for a range of social service programs, including mental health and substance abuse services, foster child care, and indigent health care.

Housing   The single-family home is part of the California (and American) dream. Homeowners currently make up 59 percent of California households—the second lowest rate among the fifty states. To keep pace with population growth, California homebuilders would have to construct more than 220,000 additional housing units every year for the next twenty years. However, since 1990, annual production has been about half that, averaging just over 100,000 units per year. California also has the most expensive housing markets in the country. Exhibit 7-5 shows that eighteen of the twenty least affordable **metropolitan areas** are in California. The median price of a California home in 2006 exceeded $550,000, ranging from well over $600,000

EXHIBIT 7-5

Least Affordable
Metropolitan
Areas in the
United States,
First Quarter
2006

*How many
Californians live
in these least
affordable areas?*

Metropolitan Area	Percent Homes Affordable for Median Income	Median Family Income (thousands)	Q1 2006 Median Sales Price (thousands)
Santa Rosa–Petaluma, CA	10.7%	$75.1	$532
Oakland–Fremont–Hayward, CA	9.4	83.8	555
Fresno, CA	9.2	47.0	297
Riverside–San Bernardino–Ontario, CA	8.4	57.5	385
Madera, CA	8.1	48.0	308
Sacramento–Arden-Arcade–Roseville, CA	7.9	65.4	400
San Francisco–San Mateo–Redwood City, CA	7.8	91.2	745
San Luis Obispo–Paso Robles, CA	7.8	63.8	533
Stockton, CA	6.5	57.1	430
Nassau–Suffolk, NY	6.1	91.0	475
New York–White Plains–Wayne, NY-NJ	6.1	59.2	472
Santa Cruz–Watsonville, CA	5.9	75.1	672
Napa, CA	5.8	75.0	600
Merced, CA	5.5	46.4	365
San Diego–Carlsbad–San Marcos, CA	5.2	64.9	491
Salinas, CA	5.0	62.2	600
Modesto, CA	3.9	54.4	380
Santa Barbara–Santa Maria, CA	3.2	65.8	580
Santa Ana–Anaheim–Irvine, CA	2.5	78.3	608
Los Angeles–Long Beach–Glendale, CA	1.9	56.2	500
National	41.3	59.6	250

Source: *Housing Opportunity Index 2006* (Washington, DC: National Association of Homebuilders),
www.nahb.org

along the coast to about $100,000 less inland. In most regions, less than one-third of homes sell for a price affordable by a family with a median income. High prices (fueled by population growth and good financing deals), low interest rates, and longer mortgage periods (and, of course, the continuing incentive of tax-deductible mortgage interest) have stimulated housing construction inland—which translates into suburban sprawl and long commutes. This development is not generally welcomed by local cities because property and development taxes do not completely cover the cost of additional government services (schools, roads, police, parks, and so on), and the only job growth housing brings is in the relatively low-paying retail trade and service sectors.

The construction of multifamily apartment units is lagging, at only one-fourth of what is needed. Analysts think that this is due to a combination of developer disincentives: high land costs and municipal discouragement because of increased public service needs. The average rent for a two-bedroom unit exceeds $1,000 per month, and availability in many areas is very low. Exhibit 7-6 shows the "housing wages" for

EXHIBIT 7-6

Fair Market Rents (FMR) in California, 2005

What is the housing wage in California— the amount a 40-hours-per-week worker must earn in order to afford a two-bedroom unit at the fair market rent?

| Metropolitan Area | FMR BY NUMBER OF BEDROOMS | | | | | HOURLY WAGE (AT 40 HOURS PER WEEK) NEEDED TO AFFORD FMR | | | | |
	Zero	One	Two	Three	Four	Zero	One	Two	Three	Four
California	*$ 805*	*$ 942*	*$1,149*	*$1,598*	*$1,864*	*$15.48*	*$18.11*	*$22.09*	*$30.72*	*$35.85*
Bakersfield	485	524	624	902	1,081	9.33	10.08	12.00	17.35	20.79
Chico	473	562	678	956	1,141	9.10	10.81	13.04	18.38	21.94
El Centro	471	533	657	904	1,152	9.06	10.25	12.63	17.38	22.15
Fresno	540	595	702	1,021	1,100	10.38	11.44	13.50	19.63	21.15
Hanford–Corcoran	495	527	612	892	1,075	9.52	10.13	11.77	17.15	20.67
Los Angeles–Long Beach	789	952	1,189	1,597	1,921	15.17	18.31	22.87	30.71	36.94
Madera	496	521	664	965	995	9.54	10.02	12.77	18.56	19.13
Merced	458	523	635	906	1,057	8.81	10.06	12.21	17.42	20.33
Modesto	564	623	734	1,053	1,216	10.85	11.98	14.12	20.25	23.38
Napa	754	845	1,098	1,519	1,725	14.50	16.25	21.12	29.21	33.17
Oakland–Fremont	943	1,130	1,339	1,865	2,288	18.13	21.73	25.75	35.87	44.00
Orange County	1,034	1,161	1,392	1,992	2,288	19.88	22.33	26.77	38.31	44.00
Oxnard–Thousand Oaks–Ventura	1,042	1,156	1,462	2,127	2,453	20.04	22.23	28.12	40.90	47.17
Redding	464	540	657	959	1,155	8.92	10.38	12.63	18.44	22.21
Riverside–San Bernardino–Ontario	715	781	911	1,294	1,512	13.75	15.02	17.52	24.88	29.08
Sacramento–Roseville	742	846	1,008	1,469	1,712	14.27	16.27	19.38	28.25	32.92
Salinas	827	931	1,069	1,510	1,582	15.90	17.90	20.56	29.04	30.42
San Benito County	588	796	885	1,254	1,552	11.31	15.31	17.02	24.12	29.85
San Diego–Carlsbad–San Marcos	836	954	1,158	1,688	2,036	16.08	18.35	22.27	32.46	39.15

(continued)

159

EXHIBIT 7-6

Fair Market Rents (FMR) in California, 2005 (continued)

Metropolitan Area	FMR BY NUMBER OF BEDROOMS					HOURLY WAGE (AT 40 HOURS PER WEEK) NEEDED TO AFFORD FMR				
	Zero	One	Two	Three	Four	Zero	One	Two	Three	Four
California	$805	$942	$1,149	$1,598	$1,864	$15.48	$18.11	$22.09	$30.72	$35.85
San Francisco	998	1,227	1,536	2,051	2,167	19.19	23.60	29.54	39.44	41.67
San Jose–Sunnyvale–Santa Clara	939	1,103	1,302	1,870	2,051	18.06	21.21	25.04	35.96	39.44
San Luis Obispo–Paso Robles	641	758	923	1,345	1,384	12.33	14.58	17.75	25.87	26.62
Santa Barbara–Santa Maria–Goleta	828	924	1,037	1,366	1,559	15.92	17.77	19.94	26.27	29.98
Santa Cruz–Watsonville	873	1,030	1,343	1,933	1,992	16.79	19.81	25.83	37.17	38.31
Santa Rosa–Petaluma	749	912	1,151	1,633	1,910	14.40	17.54	22.13	31.40	36.73
Stockton	602	686	846	1,162	1,463	11.58	13.19	16.27	22.35	28.13
Vallejo–Fairfield	796	857	983	1,378	1,698	15.31	16.48	18.90	26.50	32.65
Visalia–Porterville	481	538	625	894	918	9.25	10.35	12.02	17.19	17.65
Yolo	679	719	879	1,281	1,362	13.06	13.83	16.90	24.63	26.19
Yuba City	437	493	606	882	944	8.40	9.48	11.65	16.96	18.15

Note: A unit is considered affordable if it costs no more than 30 percent of the renter's income.

Source: National Low-Income Housing Coalition, *Out of Reach 2005: America's Growing Wage-Rent Disparity,* **www.nlihc.org**

rents around California—the amount a 40-hour-per-week worker must earn to afford a two-bedroom unit. The state average is $22.00 per hour—well above a minimum wage income and far exceeding the poverty-level income of SSI/SSP and CalWORKs. Californians have adapted to the housing collapse by scrimping in other areas of the family budget to, in many cases, pay over half their household income for housing. Reduced housing demolition keeps very old housing in the market, and doubling-up increases the average household size per housing unit.[3]

The principal low-income housing assistance program is the Housing Choice Voucher (Section 8) Program. Funded by the U.S. Department of Housing and Urban Development (HUD) and administered by local county housing authorities, Section 8 pays part of a low-income family's monthly rent directly to the landlord. However, landlords do not have to accept Section 8 vouchers. Although Section 8 vouchers provide a landlord with a dependable income, high rental rates in a local market and various Section 8 rules may make the participation unattractive. Section 8 waiting lists can run to years.

The tight, high-cost housing market exacerbates the problem of homelessness in California. It is estimated that on any given day there are approximately 300,000 homeless men, women, and children in California. The problem is not as simple as providing low-cost shelter. Many cities and counties, frustrated by the multiple problems of substance abuse, mental illness, poorly funded governmental services, and recurring public complaints about panhandling and antisocial behaviors, have defined homelessness as a law enforcement problem—occasionally rousting the homeless from one place to another.

EDUCATION

The largest government benefit program of all is public education—and it's huge. Large state bureaucracies, a complex Education Code, more than $60 billion in annual expenditures largely funded by the state rather than local government, and 983 locally elected school boards employing more than 300,000 teachers provide 6.4 million California children thirteen years of compulsory K–12 education. In addition, California heavily subsidizes postsecondary college educational opportunities in the California Community College (109 colleges, 2.8 million students, $5 billion), California State University (23 universities, 405,000 students, $2.6 billion), and University of California (10 universities, 208,000 students, $3 billion) systems.

K–12 education is a significant state issue. Exhibit 7-7 shows that the National Assessment of Educational Progress (NAEP) scores for eighth-grade students are lower in California than in most other states for mathematics, science, and reading. Although showing slight improvement in recent years, fewer than 60 percent of eighth graders scored at or above a *basic* level, and no more than 22 percent scored at the *proficient* level, in these subjects. While 70 percent of California's ninth-grade students go on to graduate high school (comparable to the national average), only 23 percent have a "C" or better in the courses required to qualify for the University of California and California State University systems.[4]

[3]Dowell Myers and Julie Park, *The Great Housing Collapse in California* (Washington, DC: Fannie Mae Foundation, 2002), **www.usc.edu/schools/sppd/futures/pdf/fmf_0426_myers_park.pdf**

[4]U.S. Department of Education, Institute of Education Sciences, National Center for Education Statistics, National Assessment of Educational Progress (NAEP), and Education Trust–West.

EXHIBIT 7-7
Nation's Report Card

How does California compare with
other states in mathematics, reading,
and science?

_____

Source: U.S. Department of Education,
Institute for Education Sciences, National
Center for Educational Statistics, National
Assessment of Educational Progress (NAEP),
nces.ed.gov/nationsreportcard

National Assessment of Educational Progress—
Mathematics Grade 8
2005

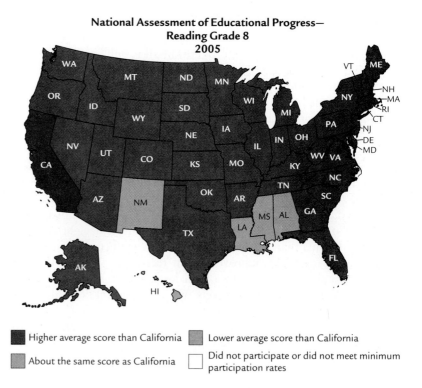

National Assessment of Educational Progress—
Reading Grade 8
2005

(continued)

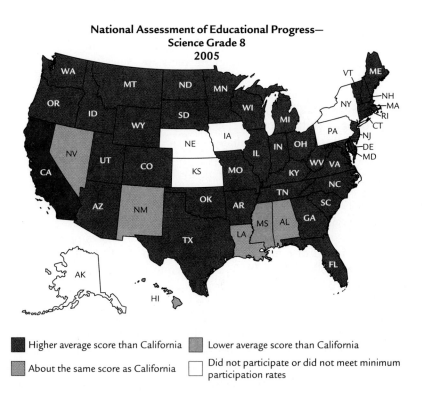

**National Assessment of Educational Progress—
Science Grade 8
2005**

EXHIBIT 7-7
Nation's Report Card
(continued)

■ Higher average score than California   ▨ Lower average score than California

▨ About the same score as California   ☐ Did not participate or did not meet minimum
participation rates

Analysts cite two sets of reasons for this educational lag:

- The children and their family circumstances
- School funding, facilities, and teachers

Educational performance is associated with poverty, immigration, and ethnicity. Socioeconomic, have-and-have-not, two-tier disparities are reflected in marked differences in Academic Performance Index (API) scores, even within the same school district, throughout the state. The percentage of students who qualify for the school free/reduced-price lunch program—meaning that their family income is less than 185 percent of the FPL—is an indicator of poverty, and nearly 50 percent of California schoolchildren qualify. In California schools, a 10-point increase in the percentage of free/reduced-price lunch students is correlated with a 10-percent-lower API score. One of every four students is in an English-language learning (ELL) program (and of these, 84 percent have Spanish as their primary language). A 10-point increase in the percentage of ELL students at a California school is correlated with 10-percent-lower API score. The proportion of African American and Latino students who score below the basic level on the NAEP math, reading, and science tests is double that of Anglo and Asian students.[5]

Educational performance is also associated with per-pupil spending, class size, school facilities, and teacher qualifications. As recently as the 1970s, school finance and management was the primary responsibility of locally elected school boards and

---

[5]NAEP and *Teacher Qualification Index*, June 2006, **www.edfordemocracy.org/tqi**

local public officials. The principal source of funding was the property tax, and the relative wealth of the city and county created significant differences in per-pupil expenditures from one place to another throughout the state. Since then, a series of court decisions, laws, regulations, and ballot measures highlighted by the *Serrano v. Priest* opinion equalizing per-pupil spending, Proposition 13 (1978) curtailing reliance on the property tax, and Proposition 98 (1988) formulating a minimum funding level for schools has shifted school finance and policy-making to the state government.[6] In 2001–2002, after more than twenty years of low per-capita K–12 school expenditures, California's per-capita expenditures of $1,520 ranked twelfth among the states, exceeding the national average by $100. However, because California has more children in proportion to adults than other states, California's $7,580 per-pupil K–12 expenditure ranks twenty-sixth among the states, $500 below the national average.[7]

California's relentless population growth requires a constant supply of new classrooms. The Department of Education estimates that the K–12 student population will increase by 850,000 before 2010. That is equivalent to needing to open twenty new classrooms, or one new elementary school, *every day* for the next five years—and not even considering the ongoing needs of modernization and maintenance. School facilities are funded roughly 50-50 by voter-approved state bond measures totaling about $28 billion since 1998 and by revenues from local bond measures and development fees. In November 2000, voters reduced the two-thirds approval requirement for local school bond measures to 55 percent. Nevertheless, enrollment planning and school construction to state standards take time, and many school facilities are overcrowded as the state struggles to meet the need.

California's teachers are relatively well paid. California ranks third among the states in average annual teacher salary. However, there are not enough fully credentialed, state-certified teachers, and class sizes are large. Class size is a function of funding, enrollment growth, facilities, and the number of teachers. Despite a state-mandated class-size-reduction program implemented in the late 1990s that limited class sizes in the early elementary grades to twenty students, California's overall K–12 student–teacher ratio is 21, the second highest rate among the states (see Exhibit 7-8). Underqualified teachers, newly employed and lacking formal training and state certification, make up about 17 percent of the teacher workforce—a proportion that has been increasing in recent years. Teacher training and qualifications affect academic achievement. Students in high-poverty schools, where 90 percent of the students qualify for the free/reduced-price lunch program, are 2.2 times more likely to have an underqualified teacher. Students in schools where 75 percent or more of the students are classified as English language learners are 2.3 times more likely to have an underqualified teacher. And students in schools with low API scores are 4.1 times more likely to have an underqualified teacher.[8]

California has responded to educational shortcomings with a three-pronged approach: standards, assessment, and accountability. The state has developed comprehensive academic content standards for K–12 education. The Thomas B.

---

[6]School Finance Overview, EdSource Online, **www.edsource.org/edu_fin.cfm**. *Serrano v. Priest* consisted of three California Supreme Court opinions: 5 Cal.3d 584 (1971), 18 Cal.3d 728 (1976), and 20 Cal.3d 25 (1977).

[7]Among the five most populous states, California's per-pupil K–12 spending exceeds that of Texas and Florida but is less than that of New York and Illinois. In order to match New York's $11,841 per pupil K–12 spending, California's education budget would have to increase by $27 billion annually. National Education Association, *Rankings and Estimates: Rankings of the States 2004 and Estimates of School Statistics 2005*, **www.nea.org/edstats/images/05rankings.pdf**

[8]Teacher Qualification Index.

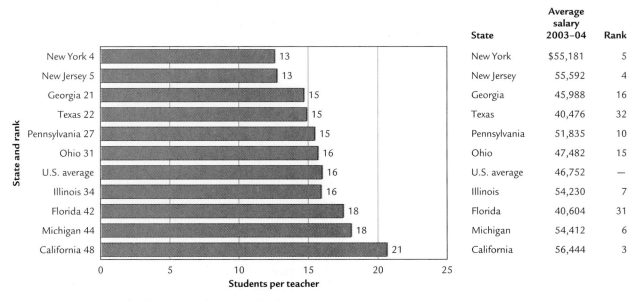

State	Average salary 2003–04	Rank
New York	$55,181	5
New Jersey	55,592	4
Georgia	45,988	16
Texas	40,476	32
Pennsylvania	51,835	10
Ohio	47,482	15
U.S. average	46,752	—
Illinois	54,230	7
Florida	40,604	31
Michigan	54,412	6
California	56,444	3

EXHIBIT 7-8 Student–Teacher Ratio: Comparing the Largest States—Students Enrolled per Teacher in Public K–12 Schools, Fall 2003

Where does California rank with respect to average K–12 class sizes?

Source: National Education Association, *Rankings and Estimates: 2004,* **www.nea.org**

Fordham Foundation rates California as the best state in the country for developing English, history, mathematics, and science standards that are specific, measurable, and demanding.[9]

Assessment is accomplished by an alphabet soup of acronymic tests, called the "Standardized Testing and Reporting" (STAR) program, to assess student learning proficiency. It includes the following:

- California Standards Tests (CSTs) cover the English, mathematics, history/social science, and science academic content standards—what teachers are supposed to be teaching and students are supposed to be learning.

- Achievement tests compare the basic skills of California students with those of other students nationwide. In 2003, the California Achievement Tests, sixth edition, (CAT/6) replaced the Stanford-9 Test.

- California High School Exit Examination (CAHSEE) is a pass/fail test of reading, writing, and mathematics skills required of all students to receive a high school diploma beginning with the class of 2004. In 2006, an Alameda County superior court judge issued a temporary injunction against the exam. This was quickly overturned by a California court-of-appeal decision. The three-judge appellate court acknowledged that students don't have access to equal education throughout the state, but reasoned that stopping the test as a graduation requirement would harm disadvantaged students more than it would help them.

---

[9]Chester E. Finn, Jr. and Michael J. Petrilli, eds., *State of the State Standards: 2000* (The Thomas B. Fordham Foundation, January 2000), **www.edexcellence.net/library/soss2000/2000soss.html**

The principal indicator for accountability is the API—a number between 200 and 1,000 that is computed for every school. Nominally, the State Board of Education expects an API score of 800 or above. Schools that show API improvements receive financial rewards, while underperforming schools receive attention from special assistance teams and could ultimately be taken over by the state. The API calculation is a weighted average of CST and CAT/6 scores for elementary schools and of these tests plus CAHSEE results for high schools. Accountability also extends to individual teachers, who must earn their teaching credential by passing the California Basic Educational Skills Test (CBEST), as well as tests to certify competency in other areas, including:

- The Bilingual, Crosscultural, Language and Academic Development (CLAD/BCLAD) examinations to teach limited-English-proficient students
- The Reading Instruction Competence Assessment (RICA)
- The California Subject Examinations for Teachers (CSET)

The tests have become all-important, and schools are increasingly being criticized for "teaching to the test." The tests define the expectations, curricula, lessons, and books and, ultimately, the substance of teaching. Acknowledgment and rewards are defined by test results, and teaching is increasingly characterized by continuous test preparation and test-taking training.

The bottom line, in education and elsewhere, is that we are a long way from realizing the California dream for everyone.

WEB LINKS

California Association of Realtors **www.car.org**

California Budget Project **www.cbp.org**

California Building Industry Association **www.cbia.org**

California Economic Indicators
www.dof.ca.gov/HTML/FS_DATA/indicatr/ei_home.htm

California Health Care Foundation **www.chcf.org**

California Health Interview Survey, UCLA Center for Health Policy Research **www.chis.ucla.edu**

California Housing Law Project **www.housingadvocates.org**

CalWORKs, California Department of Social Services
www.dss.cahwnet.gov/cdssweb/California_169.htm

Children Now: California Focus **www.childrennow.org/california**

County Welfare Directors of California **cwda.org**

Ed-Data: fiscal, demographic, and performance data on California's K–12 public schools **www.ed-data.k12.ca.us**

Education for Democracy: a teacher qualification index for California's schools, 2002–2003 **www.edfordemocracy.org**

Education Trust–West **www.edtrustwest.org**

Learning First Alliance **www.learningfirst.org**

Medi-Cal Policy Institute **www.medi-cal.org**

National Association of Home Builders **www.nahb.org**

National Center for Educational Statistics, Nation's Report Card, state profiles **nces.ed.gov/nationsreportcard**

National Center for Homeless Education: California Resources **www.serve.org/nche/stateres/res-CA.htm**

National Education Association, Education Statistics **www.nea.org/edstats**

National Health Law Program (NHeLP): California **www.healthlaw.org/california.shtml**

National Low Income Housing Coalition **www.nlihc.org**

Policy Analysis for California Education, Graduate School of Education, University of California, Berkeley **www-gse.berkeley.edu/research/PACE**

Public Policy Institute of California **www.ppic.org**

Social Security Online **www.ssa.gov**

State Health Facts Online **www.statehealthfacts.kff.org/cgi-bin/healthfacts.cgi?**

State of California, California Commission on Teacher Credentialing **www.ctc.ca.gov**

State of California, Department of Education **www.cde.ca.gov**

State of California, Office of the Patient Advocate **www.opa.ca.gov**

Thomas B. Fordham Foundation **www.edexcellence.net**

PUBLICATIONS

California: The State of Our Children. Children Now. 2005. **www.childrennow.org**

Carroll, Stephen J., et al. 2005. *California's K–12 Public Schools: How Are They Doing?* Santa Monica, CA: Rand Corporation.

Clayton, Serena, et al. 2000. *Investing in Adolescent Health: A Social Imperative for California's Future*. School of Medicine, University of California, San Francisco. **youth.ucsf.edu/nahic/img/sp.pdf**

A Growing Divide: The State of Working California. California Budget Project. 2005. **www.cbp.org**

Hohm, Charles F., and James A. Glynn. 2001. *California's Social Problems*, 2nd ed. Thousand Oaks, CA: Pine Forge Press.

Making Ends Meet: How Much Does It Cost to Raise a Family in California? California Budget Project. 2005. **www.cbp.org**

Rankings and Estimates: Rankings of the States 2004 and Estimates of School Statistics 2005. National Education Association. 2005. **www.nea.org/edstats**

Reed, Deborah, and Amanda Bailey. "California's Young Children: Demographic, Social, and Economic Conditions." *California Counts* 4 (2). Public Policy Institute of California, November 2002.

GLOSSARY

CalWORKs   California Work Opportunity and Responsibility to Kids: California's implementation of the federal Temporary Aid to Needy Families (TANF) program—the major welfare policy change of the 1990s—intended to alleviate child poverty and encourage people to work rather than rely on welfare.

Earned Income Tax Credit (EITC)   A form of income redistribution providing cash payments to low-income working families. See *transfer payment*.

entitlement program   A benefit available to everyone who meets the eligibility criteria.

federal poverty level (FPL)   Also called "federal poverty guidelines" or "threshold"; the annual family unit income that is used by the federal government to define poverty. The amount varies by family size and is changed every year to reflect changing costs of essential goods and services. Many public assistance programs, such as Medicaid and Supplemental Security Income (SSI), calculate eligibility by comparing income to the FPL. Often the programs provide different levels of benefits to people based on some percentage of the FPL, such as 175 percent of FPL. The FPL has been criticized because it does not include the cost of child care or the geographic differences in cost of living. However, there is no widely accepted alternative, so it continues to be the standard definition for statistical and administrative purposes.

in-kind benefits   Aid provided in the form of goods and services rather than cash.

low income   An income less than 200 percent of FPL. See *federal poverty level*.

means test   An assessment of an individual's or family's income (means) and potential eligibility (entitlement) for public assistance.

Medicaid (Medi-Cal)   A federal program—called "Medi-Cal" in California—providing health care to the poor.

Medicare   A federal program to provide health benefits for people age 65 and older, and for adults younger than 65 with disabilities.

metropolitan area   A core area containing a large population nucleus, together with adjacent communities having a high degree of economic and social integration with that core.

minimum wage   A government antipoverty policy to provide everyone with a basic hourly rate of pay.

poverty   The condition of having little or no income or means of support and therefore having inadequate food, shelter, health care, and other basic needs. See *federal poverty level*.

recession   A period of general economic decline; specifically, a decline in gross domestic product for two or more consecutive quarters.

seasonal unemployment   A regular and predictable yearly cycle in the number of workers having jobs correlated with the season of the year.

Social Security Insurance   A federal program providing payments to retired or disabled workers.

SSI/SSP   Supplemental Security Income/State Supplementary Payment (SSI/SSP) Program. The federally funded SSI Program provides income support to the aged (65 or older), blind, or disabled. SSI benefits are also available to qualified blind or disabled children. The SSP Program is the state program that augments SSI. Both SSI and SSP benefits are administered by the Social Security Administration (SSA). Eligibility for both programs is determined by the SSA using federal criteria. If you qualify for SSI, you qualify for SSP. Benefits are in the form of cash assistance.

structural unemployment   An ongoing mismatch between the number and general skill level of people looking for work and the number and skill requirements of available jobs.

transfer payment   A program that redistributes revenue from higher-income to lower-income groups.

unemployment insurance   A joint federal–state program, funded by payroll taxes, that provides partial income replacement for a limited period (usually about three months) in the event of a person losing a job.

unemployment rate   The number of unemployed as a percentage of the labor force.

voucher   A document authorizing the delivery of a good or service.

SUGGESTED ANSWERS TO EXHIBIT QUESTIONS

Exhibit 7-1: The San Diego region currently has the lowest unemployment rate, and the San Joaquin Valley the highest. The average unemployment rate in a region is predictable on the basis of the long-term trend because basic economic structures usually remain relatively stable over time. However, this does not always hold true as evidenced by the increase in the San Francisco Bay Area unemployment rate in 2001 and 2002.

Exhibit 7-2: The entry-level wage for school teachers is about $13 per hour. Food preparation and service, farming, personal care, and grounds maintenance occupations have close-to-minimum-wage entry-level pay.

Exhibit 7-3: A one-adult, two-child family can be considered among the working poor with an income less than $30,438.

Exhibit 7-4: Los Angeles and the San Joaquin Valley are the most impoverished regions listed in the exhibit.

Exhibit 7-5: At least two-thirds of Californians live in the state's least affordable metropolitan areas.

Exhibit 7-6: The housing wage in California is $22.09. This is the amount a full-time (40 hours per week) worker must earn per hour in order to afford a two-bedroom unit at the area's fair market rent.

Exhibit 7-7: California eighth-grade students score lower than students in most other states for mathematics, science, and reading.

Exhibit 7-8: California has the second-highest K–12 student–teacher ratio.

CHAPTER EIGHT

ENERGY AND THE ENVIRONMENT

The stereotypes are true. Californians are a bunch of bottled-water-guzzling, aluminum-can-recycling, organic-food-eating SUV drivers who love national parks and hate offshore oil drilling.[1]

Energy, the environment, the economy, lifestyle, and quality of life are linked. Energy is the lifeblood of the economy. Although Americans make up only 5 percent of the world's population, the United States has the largest economy (one-fourth of the world economy) and accounts for one-fourth of global energy consumption. China, Russia, Japan, and Germany together account for another 25 percent of global energy consumption. California's economy, the fifth largest in the world, ranks eighth in global energy consumption (3 percent of the world total—just ahead of France).

The greater the production of goods and services, the greater the energy consumption. The more energy is consumed, the more **emissions** are produced—all the solid, liquid, and gaseous products and by-products of manufacturing, fuel combustion, and the California lifestyle that are sooner or later discharged and discarded to the air, water, and land.

This chapter is about California's energy–environment system. It addresses the supply and use of our energy, air, water, and land resources—reviewing many of the important concepts about California politics and government that have been introduced in the preceding chapters.

ENERGY

Sources of Energy

Oil and natural gas are the largest primary energy sources for California (see Exhibit 8-1). Oil accounts for over 40 percent of California's energy consumption. Most of it is converted to gasoline and other liquid fuels for personal and commercial transportation. Thirty-seven percent of the oil is produced in-state—from oil wells in Southern California and off the coast of Santa Barbara. Oil companies use techniques such as thermally enhanced recovery to extract the maximum amount from this gradually diminishing supply. Twenty-one percent of the state's oil imports

---

[1]Paul Rogers, "California Residents See Little Environmental Progress, Survey Finds," *San Jose Mercury News*, 27 June 2002.

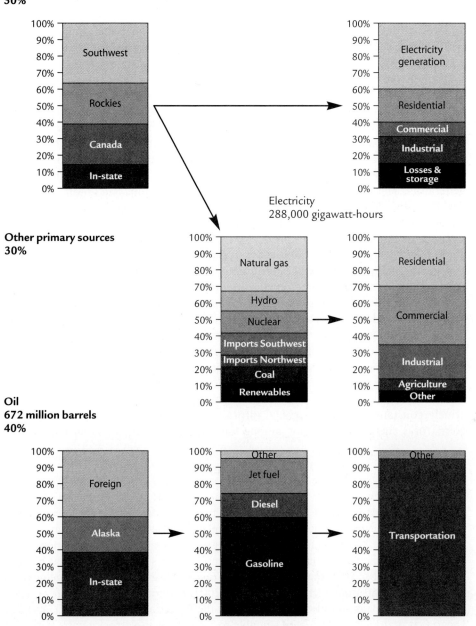

Natural gas
7.0 trillion cubic feet per day
30%

100% ┐
90% │
80% │ Southwest
70% │
60% ┤
50% │ Rockies
40% ┤
30% │ Canada
20% │
10% │ In-state
0% ┘

Other primary sources
30%

Electricity
288,000 gigawatt-hours

100% ┐
90% │ Natural gas
80% │
70% ┤
60% │ Hydro
50% │ Nuclear
40% ┤ Imports Southwest
30% │ Imports Northwest
20% │ Coal
10% │ Renewables
0% ┘

Oil
672 million barrels
40%

100% ┐
90% │ Foreign
80% │
70% ┤
60% ┤
50% │ Alaska
40% ┤
30% │
20% │ In-state
10% │
0% ┘

100% ┐ Other
90% │ Jet fuel
80% │
70% ┤ Diesel
60% ┤
50% │
40% │ Gasoline
30% │
20% │
10% │
0% ┘

EXHIBIT 8-1
California's Energy Supply and Use

Where is oil obtained? How is it used?

Where is natural gas obtained? How is it used?

How important is nuclear electric and hydroelectric power generation in California?

How important is geothermal, wind, solar, and other renewable power generation in California?

Source: California Energy Commission, **www.energy .ca.gov**

come from Alaska, transported to California by seagoing oil tankers after being pumped from the far north through the Alaskan pipeline. But this source is rapidly diminishing—down from 50 percent of California's supply in 1994, it will make up less than 10 percent of the supply by 2015. The remaining amount, 42 percent, is imported from overseas—principally from Saudi Arabia and Ecuador, with lesser amounts from Iraq and several Central and South American countries. As domestic supplies decrease in the face of continued population and economic growth, foreign imports are projected to steadily increase to over 50 percent of the state's oil needs.

Natural gas accounts for more than 30 percent of California's energy requirements. This is projected to increase to 38 percent by 2009. Eighty-four percent of California's natural gas supplies are obtained from sources outside the state—36 percent from the American Southwest (principally Texas), 24 percent from Canada, and 24 percent from the Rocky Mountain area—delivered via long-range pipelines. Natural gas is burned to provide heat. One-third is consumed by residential and commercial kitchen stoves and by hot water and space heating; another one-third fuels industrial furnaces and other processes; the remaining third is used to produce electricity.

Electricity is a secondary, intermediate source of energy. Imported natural gas—burned to boil water in large power plants to produce high-pressure steam that in turn drives turbine generators—produces 30–40 percent of California's total electricity. (A smaller amount is used in "peaker" gas-turbine electric power plants—something like jet engines.) Other primary heat sources also power steam turbine generators. The state's two commercial nuclear power plants, San Onofre (north of San Diego) and Diablo Canyon (near San Luis Obispo), provide about 13 percent of the state's electricity. Ten percent is provided by out-of-state coal-fired plants dedicated to California electricity production. Renewable primary energy sources include hydroelectric facilities (about 8 percent of electricity), solar cells, windmills, and geothermal plants (together accounting for about 11 percent).[2] The remaining electricity needed (about 22 percent) is imported to California over interstate transmission lines from southwestern and northwestern states. Electricity demand, to be met by increased natural gas consumption, is projected to increase by up to 25 percent within ten years. The residential, commercial, and industrial sectors each account for about one-third of electricity consumption.

California uses more energy than any state but one (Texas). Despite population growth and an economic boom toward the end of the 1990s, California's energy consumption in the transportation, commercial, and residential sectors has remained relatively constant, and per capita, Californians maintain the second-lowest (after New York) energy consumption among the states with over 5 million population.

The 2000–2001 Electricity Crisis

In January, March, and May 2001, hundreds of thousands of Californians experienced "rolling blackouts"—one- or two-hour electricity outages that rotated through much of the state. For the most part, it was merely an inconvenience: Lights and appliances turned off; traffic lights went out; some businesses temporarily closed; and clocks had to be reset. At the same time, wholesale electricity prices skyrocketed—eleven times higher in December 2000 than they had been one year earlier, while the state government limited retail price increases. By April 2001, California's three investor-owned utilities—Pacific Gas and Electric (PG&E), Southern California Edison (SCE), and San Diego Gas and Electric (SDG&E)—unable to balance their electricity costs with rate increases, were in serious financial trouble, with enormous debts. PG&E even declared bankruptcy. There may have been a power shortage, but there was no shortage of explanations, excuses, and blame. The litany included the following:

- Excessive government regulation
- Insufficient government regulation

---

[2]California now has 40 percent of the world's geothermal power plants, 20 percent of the installed windmill capacity, and 70–80 percent of the world's solar electricity generation.

- Flawed deregulation
- Old, overworked power plants that had to be taken out of service for maintenance at critical times
- Inadequate transmission lines, with bottlenecks in key places
- Drought in the Northwest, reducing hydroelectric generation
- Growing demand due to population and economic expansion with no growth in new generating capacity
- Increase in energy costs and fixing of retail prices
- Conspiracy and greed by private sector corporations

Electricity   Unlike oil and natural gas, electricity is not a commodity. It is not extracted, pumped, shipped, and stored before being consumed. Electricity moves at the speed of light and flows instantaneously to consumption once it is generated. In order to get electricity to flow through a transmission system, generation is set at one end (power plants) to exceed loads at the other end (consumer locations). The system is operated on the basis of a schedule of forecasted demand (see Exhibit 8-2). Generation is scheduled in advance and revised weekly, daily, and hourly up to the real-time moment in order to match generation with transmission capacity and consumer demand. If everything works, electricity is delivered within the rated capacity of the system. No lines overheat and no equipment fails. If demand approaches generating and transmission capacity, operators order temporary blackouts to protect the system.

The electric industry used to be vertically integrated. That is, within a region, one company built and operated the generating plants and transmission lines, and sold its electricity to the customers in the region. Each customer was hardwired to the utility; there was no question whose electricity they bought. Today, electric utilities

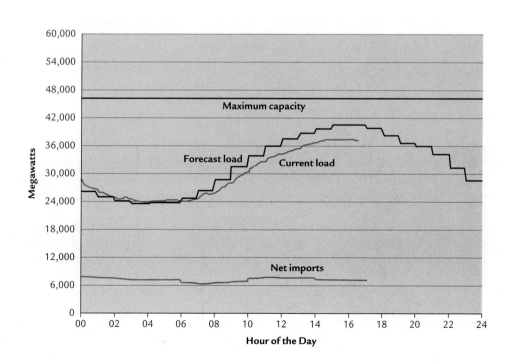

**EXHIBIT 8-2
California's
Electrical System on
a Hot Summer Day**

How much electricity does California need on a hot summer day (June 24, 2006)?

What would happen if load approached capacity?

Source: Current Energy, Lawrence Berkeley Laboratory, **currentenergy.lbl.gov**

are part of intrastate and interstate grids.[3] Electric utilities input energy to the grid and draw energy from the grid as needed. Electricity use and generation are independent concepts. Electricity flow is an abstract reference to the location of customer demand relative to the generation facilities.

Restructuring   In the early 1990s, electricity prices in California were nearly double the national average. The regulated market ensured that electric utility companies would recover their investment costs in building new generating capacity—even in the face of huge cost overruns such as at the Diablo Canyon nuclear plant. California's reserve capacity (the difference between generating capacity and anticipated peak demand) approached 30 percent. This high reserve margin assured everyone—producers, regulators, policy makers, and consumers—of reliable service. However, it was very expensive.

It seemed logical that the electric grid system could be used to deregulate the electric industry, somewhat like the deregulation of long-distance telephone services, instilling competition and lowering consumer prices. Because all the electricity generated goes into the same grid, the utility would buy electricity wholesale from the cheapest provider. Individual residential, commercial, and industrial customers could contract with competing utility companies for the lowest electric rates. Ideally, a competitive free market would prevail. Anyway, that was the way it was *supposed* to work.

The basic idea was that the state's three large investor-owned utilities—PG&E, SCE, and SDG&E—would sell their nonhydro and nonnuclear power plants to other companies—independent power producers—while maintaining their distribution systems. In order to guarantee open access to transmission lines, a new nonprofit corporation, the California Independent System Operator (CAISO), was created to control electricity transmission. Another nonprofit corporation, the California Power Exchange (PX), would run wholesale auctions of electricity. In order to break the utility monopolies and encourage price competition, long-term supply contracts between the utilities and independent producers were initially restricted and eventually prohibited. The utilities would acquire electricity at the PX "spot" wholesale auctions for power needed that day or the next. Occasionally, CAISO would buy electricity at the last minute to maintain reserve margins (see Exhibit 8-3).

The plan's jurisdiction covered the PG&E, SCE, and SDG&E service areas—affecting about 70 percent of the population. Other power producers and distributors—notably municipal utilities run by city, county, and special district governments—were not covered by the plan and were affected only to the extent of their reliance on the electricity grid.

The Crisis   With competition, excess generating capacity became a liability, called "stranded costs." The restructuring plan froze retail electricity prices (residential prices were reduced 10 percent) in order to give the utilities time to pay off their stranded costs and to reassure consumers that restructuring would not force them to pay even higher prices.

Things began to come apart in 2000. Electricity consumption, which closely tracks personal income, steadily increased during the economic expansion of the late 1990s. Meanwhile, no significant new generating or transmission capacity was added, and peak load reserve margins closed to about 10 percent. Several other things were happening, too. Natural gas prices, which had been relatively stable for

---

[3]There are three major electricity grids in the United States. California is part of an eleven-state grid called the Western Interconnect. The others are the Texas Interconnect and the Eastern Interconnect.

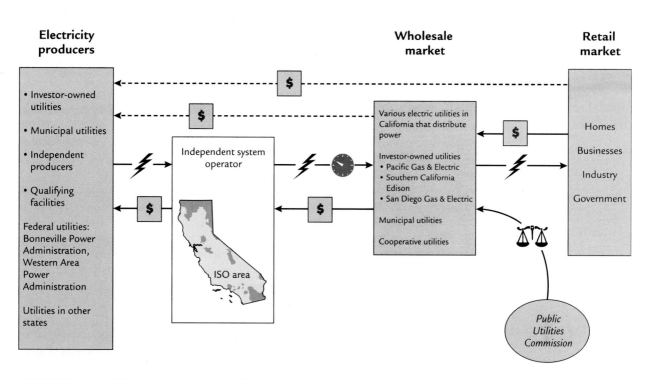

EXHIBIT 8-3   California's Restructured Electrical System

As a consumer, where does your money go, and where does your electricity come from?

a long time, suddenly increased—doubling, then skyrocketing—likely due to a near-monopoly control over pipeline capacity and supply from the Southwest held by El Paso Energy.[4] Drought in the Northwest and increased demand in other western states limited import reserve capacity.

SDG&E was the first to begin to charge its customers market prices for electricity. Instead of the rates lowering as anticipated by the restructuring plan, rates quickly increased—for some, up to 300 percent. Electricity prices on the wholesale market exceeded the frozen retail rates. Fixed prices, which had seemed to provide a safe floor income base for the utilities, now were a ceiling, forcing the utilities to operate at a loss. By the end of the year, the crisis was in full sway. The legislature passed a law rolling back SDG&E rates. Decorative holiday lighting, far from the peak summer air-conditioning months, was curtailed. In early 2001, CAISO declared power emergencies and then ordered widespread rolling blackouts. Rate hikes were approved for PG&E and SCE, the PX was closed as the state took over purchasing wholesale electricity on behalf of the utilities, and PG&E declared bankruptcy.

The Aftermath   In retrospect, although generating capacity was tight, there was no overall shortfall of electricity supply relative to demand in 2000–2001 The electricity crisis was a confluence of several factors, including a decade of disincentives and inadequate planning for the construction of electrical plants and transmission lines, convoluted restructuring in the name of deregulation, and scams and gaming by energy companies and energy brokers in the wholesale market—seeking to profit from every regulatory loophole, regardless of consequences for the public. The private sector

---

[4]Kevin Fagan and Bernadette Tansey, "How Texas Firm Outfoxed State, PG&E," *San Francisco Chronicle*, 13 May 2001.

machinations played on the noncommodity, instantaneous generation–consumption nature of electricity—capacity and electricity purchases being scheduled on the basis of forecasted load. Energy brokers such as Enron concocted a dozen or more schemes, with code names such as "Deathstar," "Perpetual Loop," and "Black Widow," that manipulated or exploited the electricity market. For example, generation–load relationships might be scheduled to threaten congestion at key transmission points. Enron would then receive a bonus payment to reschedule and alleviate the forecasted conflict that it created in the first place. Or the energy load would be overestimated. Enron would schedule the promised amount but then be paid extra to remove the unnecessary generation from the system. Or, with short reserves, sporadic unscheduled outages in California's largest electricity plants would create sudden shortages that could not be quickly offset. The result was rolling blackouts or spot purchases from independent producers, such as Duke Energy and Reliant Energy, at premium prices.

The crisis eventually passed, leaving in its wake failed public policy, large corporate bankruptcies, investment losses by ordinary citizens, increasing public debt, and high electricity rates. New generating capacity has come online from independent producers as the early-2000s economic recession constrained demand growth. Rather than having a deregulated competitive market, the state is now more involved than ever in managing the energy system.

In 2006, Enron executives Kenneth Lay and Jeffrey Skilling were convicted in federal court on a combined twenty-five counts of securities and wire fraud, conspiracy, insider trading, and making false statements. Lawsuits filed by California's attorney general against electrical and natural gas energy companies have so far netted over $5 billion in judgments, including $1.5 billion against Enron. However, given Enron's bankruptcy, the actual return to the state may be no more than one-fifth of that—a fraction of the losses.

AIR, WATER, AND LAND

Californians care about their environment. Environmental problems, especially air and water quality, and land use are among their top concerns. A review of selected environmental issues shows three aspects of American federalism. California sometimes takes the lead over Washington, DC, in developing environmental policy in the United States, particularly in the policy issue area of air pollution. Water problems involve multiple federal, state, and local governmental agencies and also private sector, interstate, and international organizations, with overlapping, competing, and conflicting interests and jurisdictions. In certain land use issues, such as preservation of wilderness and habitat for endangered species, the federal government dominates policy-making.

Air Resources

California has the worst air quality in the country. The good news is that California has the nation's most stringent air quality regulations and that air quality is gradually improving. The air we breathe at ground level is not free flowing. Mountains define "air basins" that limit circulation and allow the gaseous, liquid, and solid byproducts of combustion and industrial processes to accumulate. Exhibit 8-4, for example, depicts the San Joaquin Valley air basin. Air flows from the San Francisco Bay Area and forms a slow-moving eddy over several counties.

There are two principal components of air pollution in California: (1) ground-level **ozone** and (2) **particulate matter** (**PM**) (see Exhibit 8-5). Ground-level ozone

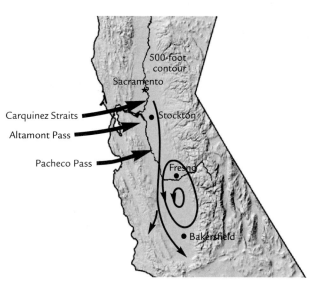

EXHIBIT 8-4   Smog—The Fresno Eddy

Air flows into the San Joaquin Valley from the Bay Area. Due to temperature inversions and mountainous terrain, the air tends to be trapped, moving in a circular pattern called an "eddy." Pollution is concentrated as the air is heated by the sun to produce ozone and smog.

Why is the San Joaquin Valley called an "air basin"?

Source: Photo courtesy of NASA/JPL/NIMA/USGS

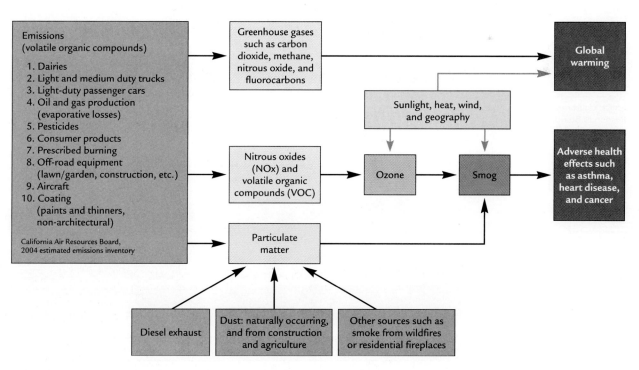

EXHIBIT 8-5   Air Pollution

What is smog? How is it formed?

is a three-atom oxygen molecule created by the chemical reaction of heat and sunlight with two types of precursor emissions: (1) **nitrogen oxides (NOx)** and (2) **volatile organic compounds (VOC)**. NOx and VOC (also called "ROG," reactive organic gases) are waste by-products of our industrial economy, especially our automotive-dependent transportation system. Nitrogen oxides are produced by burning fuel—whether that fuel is gasoline, diesel, oil, or natural gas (methane), or organic fuels (such as wood). Volatile organic compounds are a variety of gaseous and aerosol chemicals containing carbon and other elements such as hydrogen, oxygen, fluorine, chlorine, bromine, sulfur, and nitrogen. The most ozone-polluted areas are Metropolitan Los Angeles and the southern San Joaquin Valley (Fresno, Visalia, and Bakersfield). On hot summer days, ozone plumes blossom and envelop these areas.

Exhibit 8-6 shows that the number of high-ozone days has been declining in the air basins with the greatest air quality problems—the South Coast Basin (Metropolitan Los Angeles) and San Diego—whereas the ozone problem has remained relatively constant in the San Joaquin Valley, Sacramento, and San Francisco Bay Area regions.

EXHIBIT 8-6   High Ozone and High Particulate Days in California

What regions have had the greatest decline in the number of high-ozone days?

What regions show little change?

What regions exceed the state PM10 standard for 100 days or more each year?

Source: California Air Resources Board, *California Almanac of Emissions and Air Quality*, 2006.

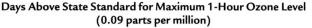

**Days Above State Standard for Maximum 1-Hour Ozone Level
(0.09 parts per million)**

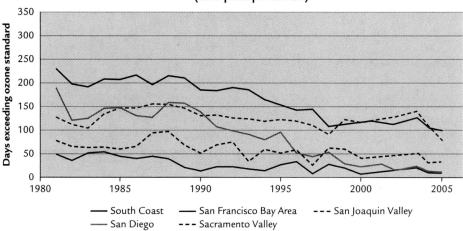

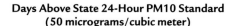

**Days Above State 24-Hour PM10 Standard
(50 micrograms/cubic meter)**

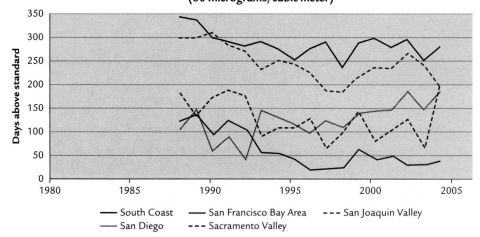

PM is various dust, smoke, mists, or fumes whose constituent parts are so small—less than 10 microns (called "PM10"—about one-tenth the diameter of a human hair)—that they can be inhaled. Exhibit 8-7 shows that recent PM levels exceed the state standard over 250 days per year in the Metropolitan Los Angeles (South Coast) region, about 200 days in the San Joaquin Valley, and over 150 days in the San Diego and Sacramento regions.

Thirty miles high in the atmosphere, ozone protects the Earth from harmful radiation, but ground-level ozone and PM are serious respiratory irritants. Immediate effects range from the nasal and eye irritation that you might feel on a hot, smoggy day to chest pain and shortness of breath. Repeated exposure, over a long term, can reduce lung function and worsen preexisting health problems such as asthma, bronchitis, and emphysema. Chemical reactions of ozone with PM, stimulated by heat and sunlight, create photochemical **smog**, the palpable dull-brown haze that all too often obscures California's urban centers and the San Joaquin Valley.

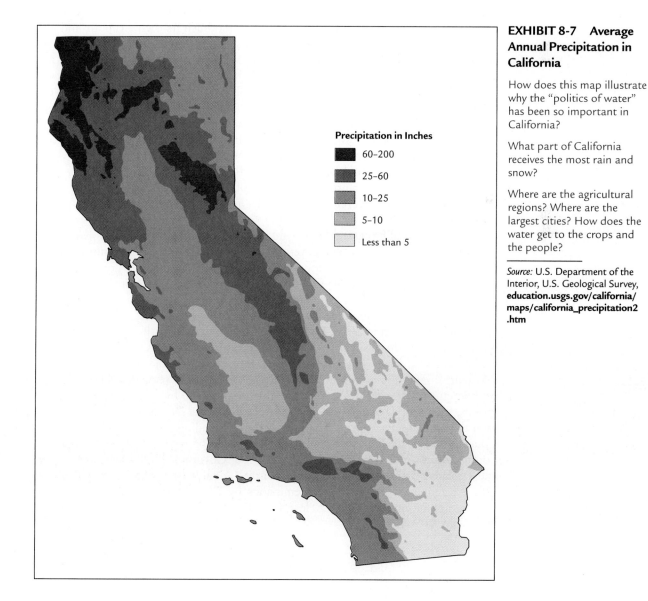

Precipitation in Inches

- 60–200
- 25–60
- 10–25
- 5–10
- Less than 5

EXHIBIT 8-7   Average Annual Precipitation in California

How does this map illustrate why the "politics of water" has been so important in California?

What part of California receives the most rain and snow?

Where are the agricultural regions? Where are the largest cities? How does the water get to the crops and the people?

Source: U.S. Department of the Interior, U.S. Geological Survey, **education.usgs.gov/california/ maps/california_precipitation2 .htm**

Emissions also contribute to **global warming,** the increase in the average temperature of Earth's atmosphere. Global warming is caused by **greenhouse gas** emissions, principally carbon dioxide and NOx, both products of combustion from gasoline- and diesel-powered engines. Carbon dioxide is a greenhouse gas pollutant rather than a local health hazard. It naturally makes up less than 1 percent of Earth's atmosphere. However, with worldwide industrialization, its atmospheric concentration is rapidly increasing. NOx, in addition to being a precursor of ground-level ozone, is 300 times more effective by weight at blocking infrared radiation than is carbon dioxide. When sunlight strikes the Earth's surface, some of it is reflected back toward space as infrared radiation (heat). Greenhouse gases block this energy from being radiated to the vastness of outer space, trapping the heat in the atmosphere. Corresponding to its economic size and energy consumption, the United States accounts for about one-fourth of worldwide greenhouse gas emissions. California alone is the twelfth-largest producer of greenhouse gases worldwide.

California government has responded to air pollution and global warming with increasingly stringent regulations. California has special status under the federal Clean Air Act amendments of 1970 to establish its own clean air and automotive emission regulations—and has consistently led the country in the enactment of air quality standards. California vehicles are regularly inspected for air pollution. In a program called "Smog Check II," cars are tested every two years on dynamometers—treadmill-like machines that simulate driving conditions and test for several kinds of emissions. The regulations have been effective. Since 1975, yearly NOx and VOC emissions have been cut in half, with emissions from stationary "point" sources being cut by 50 percent and emissions from gasoline vehicles by 75 percent. Regulations are gradually being extended to reduce NOx and VOC emissions from so-called areawide sources (such as the wide variety of consumer products) and "mobile" sources besides gasoline vehicles, such as diesel-powered vehicles and equipment used in construction and agriculture.

In 2002, the California legislature—taking the lead on the problem of global warming over the unresponsive federal government—passed a bill requiring California's Air Resources Board (ARB) to develop regulations limiting automotive greenhouse gas emissions.[5] The ARB issued the first such regulations in the country in 2004—calling for an average reduction in greenhouse gases from new passenger cars, SUVs and pickup trucks, starting in model year 2009, amounting to about 22 percent in 2012 and about 30 percent in 2016. Eleven other states followed with similar regulations on the basis that the gases should be classified as air pollutants endangering public health. The U.S. Environmental Protection Agency (EPA) objected on the grounds that federal law does not authorize the agency or states to regulate carbon dioxide or other greenhouse gas discharges, and the states, joined by various environmental groups, sued. The U.S. Circuit Court of Appeals for the District of Columbia sided with the federal government. The matter is now pending before the U.S. Supreme Court in what is likely to be a landmark policy decision regarding governmental action to address global warming. Then, in 2006, Governor Arnold Schwarzenegger and legislative Democrats enacted the California Global Warming Solutions Act, which calls for reducing greenhouse gas emissions by 25 percent over the next fifteen years—capping emissions at 1990 levels—so far the toughest legislation on this issue in the United States.

---

[5]AB 1493, Vehicular Emissions: Greenhouse Gases, 2002, Assemblywoman Fran Pavley (D-Agoura Hills).

Water is the most essential commodity for Californians. It is vital to urban life, industrial development, and agriculture. As the precipitation map in Exhibit 8-7 shows, 75 percent of the rain and snow falls in Northern California and the Sierras. However, 75 percent of the state's demand is in the agricultural Central Valley and dry but populous Southern California.

The largest reservoir in the state is actually the yearly snowpack in the Sierra Nevada. The average annual supply is about 80 million acre-feet. As illustrated in Exhibit 8-8, 46 percent of the annual runoff is "environmental"—flowing through the rivers to the Pacific Ocean. The other half is captured and redistributed by the largest water storage and transfer system in the world. Water is the subject of conflict between competing and conflicting interests—cities, big agriculture, flood control agencies, electric utilities, industry, environmentalists, landowners adjacent to surface water (riparian rights) and above underground aquifers, and interstate and international claimants—to name only a few.

East of San Francisco, between Sacramento and Stockton, the Sacramento–San Joaquin Delta—a fertile, 1,000-square-mile maze of islands and channels—is formed by the Sacramento and San Joaquin rivers as the waters merge before flowing into San Francisco Bay and out to the Pacific. The delta is the major collection point and water source for two-thirds of the state's population. As much as 60 percent of the potential freshwater inflow into San Francisco Bay is diverted to the agricultural San Joaquin Valley and Southern California. It is the confluence not only of two large rivers but also of many complex, water-related issues of statewide significance.

State and federal pumps near Tracy suck freshwater from the delta into the California Aqueduct, the 444-mile-long central feature of the massive California Water Project, and the federal Delta-Mendota Canal. Water is shipped south, irrigating the farms on the west side of the San Joaquin Valley and Tulare Basin, and then on to Southern California cities for drinking and other uses. The pumping allows saltwater intrusion into the delta. Drainage from the valley farms, carrying salt, boron, selenium, and agricultural chemicals, flows into the marshes and lowlands east of the aqueduct and eventually into the San Joaquin River, which carries it north back to the delta. The drainage water and saltwater pulled inland from San Francisco Bay are picked up by the Tracy pumps—establishing a large "salt loop" that jeopardizes not only the ecological health of the Bay and the delta estuary but also farmlands and urban water supplies.

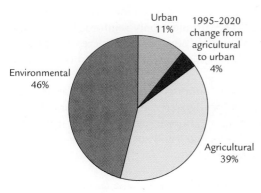

Urban
11%

1995–2020 change from agricultural to urban
4%

Environmental
46%

Agricultural
39%

Average annual supply = 80.5 million acre-feet

EXHIBIT 8-8   Water Use in California

What proportion of California's annual water supply is captured and redistributed for urban or agricultural uses?

Does the urban population use more water than agriculture?

What is the greater hazard for Californians: earthquakes or floods? Actually, it's floods. Millions of Californians live in high-risk flood plains. However, earthquake dangers and water supplies are interrelated. The levees in the San Joaquin Delta are particularly important and vulnerable. They maintain a careful interface between freshwater and saltwater. Levee breaches caused by an earthquake could affect freshwater intake for the California Aqueduct, threatening not only agricultural water but also drinking water for much of the state's population.

In Southern California, Los Angeles's water needs continue to grow as its population increases. In the early 1900s, Los Angeles met its needs by draining the Owens Valley on the east side of the Sierras and laying claim to a large share of the Colorado River. Now there is a $1-billion, fifty-year project proposal to bank Colorado River water in wet years by pumping surplus water into the extensive underground aquifer under the Mojave Desert for withdrawal in dry years. The Cadiz Corporation, which has substantial land holdings above the aquifer, would be paid for each acre-foot pumped. Once again, Californians question whether water is a commodity subject to ownership and marketing or a collective good to be administered by the government for the general benefit of the people, near and far.

Land Resources

It may seem that California has lots of space—and it does. It's the third-largest state in land area (after Alaska and Texas). But California is also among the most urbanized states. More than 90 percent of Californians live in cities (about 28 percent in Los Angeles County alone). Five of the nation's ten most crowded metropolitan areas are in California.[6] The median price of a California home in 2006 was over $550,000—and substantially more in these major urban areas. As a consequence, major urban areas—Los Angeles County, Orange County, and the San Francisco Bay Area—are actually seeing a population *decrease*—outmigration— as Californians seek more affordable homes in new tracts of single-family housing 20, 50, and even 100 miles or more from metropolitan centers. Small towns are expanding into bedroom suburbs, and new housing is crowding into formerly agricultural and open-space areas.

Can California sustain its urban and suburban development? This development pattern—called **sprawl**—is a fundamental policy issue for California. Political, water, air, employment, education, and social service issues all seem to be concentrated at the suburban–rural interface. On the one hand, growth is necessary. It fuels the California economy and helps families realize the California dream of suburban home ownership and lifestyle. On the other hand, the development is not accompanied by jobs, infrastructure, and services. The distances only reinforce California's automobile-dependent culture. While California's population is increasing at just over 1 percent per year, its cumulative vehicle-miles-traveled (cars and trucks) has been increasing at twice the rate—just over 2 percent per year. Land use decisions are principally the province of local, city, and county government, and housing developers are the strongest financial force in local government politics. Sprawl may be good for the new homebuyer on the distant suburban perimeter, and it may be politically practical in the near term, but Californians will encounter long-range political, social, economic, and environmental problems.

---

[6]William Fulton et al., *Who Sprawls Most? How Growth Patterns Differ Across the U.S.* (Washington, DC: Brookings Institution, 2001).

AirNow, U.S. Environmental Protection Agency air quality forecast and ozone maps **www.epa.gov/airnow**

CalFed Bay-Delta Program **calwater.ca.gov**

California Energy Commission **www.energy.ca.gov**

California Environmental Resources Evaluation System (CERES) **ceres.ca.gov**

California League of Conservation Voters **www.ecovote.org**

Californians Against Waste **www.cawrecycles.org**

California Public Interest Research Group **www.calpirg.org**

Center on Race, Poverty, and the Environment, California Rural Legal Assistance Foundation **www.crlaf.org/crpe.htm**

CEQA summary **ceres.ca.gov/topic/env_law/ceqa/summary.html**

Environmental Defense **www.environmentaldefense.org**

Environmental Working Group, California **www.ewg.org/california**

Foundation for Taxpayer and Consumer Rights **www.consumerwatchdog.org/**

Nature Conservancy, California **www.tnccalifornia.org**

Pacific Research Institute, Center for Environmental Studies **www.pacificresearch.org/centers/ces/index.html**

Panoramic photo of sprawl **www.exuberance.com/photos/panos/Sprawl-Clayton-CA.html**

Planning and Conservation League **www.pcl.org**

Reason Public Policy Institute **www.rppi.org**

Scorecard: Online information about pollution and environmental issues. Type in a zip code to obtain environmental data in your community. Scorecard ranks and compares the pollution situation in areas across the United States. **www.scorecard.org**

Sierra Club **www.sierraclub.org**

U.S. Energy Information Administration, California data **www.eia.doe.gov/emeu/states/main_ca.html**

Arax, Mark, and Rick Wartzman. 2005. *The King of California: J. G. Boswell and the Making of a Secret American Empire.* New York: Public Affairs.

Beyond Sprawl: New Patterns of Growth to Fit the New California. Bank of America, 1996. **www.rut.com/misc/beyondSprawl.html**

Beyond "Beyond Sprawl." California Planning Roundtable, 2005. **www.cproundtable.org/cprwww/docs/bbs/bbs.htm**

Eichenwald, Kurt. 2005. *Conspiracy of Fools.* New York: Broadway Books.

Environmental Protection Indicators for California. Sacramento: Office of Environmental Health Hazard Assessment, State of California, 2005. **www.oehha.ca.gov/multimedia/epic/**

Erie, Steven P. 2006. *Beyond Chinatown: The Metropolitan Water District, Growth, and the Environment in Southern California.* Palo Alto, CA: Stanford University Press.

Flood Warnings: Responding to California's Flood Crisis. Resources Agency, Department of Water Resources, State of California, 2005. **www.publicaffairs.water .ca.gov/newsreleases/2005/01-10-05flood_warnings.pdf**

Fulton, William. 1999. *Guide to California Planning.* Point Arena, CA: Solano Press.

Landis, John D., Lan Deng, and Michael Reilly. 2002. *Growth Management Revisited: A Reassessment of Its Efficacy, Price Effects and Impacts on Metropolitan Growth Patterns.* Berkeley: University of California, Institute of Urban and Regional Development. **www-iurd.ced.berkeley.edu/pub/WP-2002-02.PDF**

Sharp, Renee, and Bill Walker. 2002. *Particle Civics: How Cleaner Air in California Will Save Lives and Save Money.* Oakland: Environmental Working Group. **www.ewg.org/reports/particlecivics/particlecivics_report.pdf**

State of the Air: 2006. New York: American Lung Association, 2006. **lungaction.org/reports/stateoftheair2006.html**

Sweeney, James L. 2002. *The California Electricity Crisis.* Stanford, CA: Hoover Institution Press.

GLOSSARY

emissions   The solid, liquid, or gaseous by-products of manufacturing, fuel combustion, and, to a lesser extent, natural processes that are discharged to the environment.

global warming   An increase in the near-surface temperature of the Earth. Global warming has occurred in the distant past as the result of natural influences, but the term is most often used to refer to the warming predicted to occur, and actually occurring, as a result of increased emissions of greenhouse gases. Scientists generally agree that the Earth's surface has warmed by about 1 degree Fahrenheit in the past 140 years.

greenhouse gases   Emissions that contribute to global warming—chiefly carbon dioxide—but also including methane, nitrous oxide, and fluorocarbons.

nitrogen oxides (NOx)   A general term pertaining to compounds of nitric oxide (NO), nitrogen dioxide (NO_2), and other oxides of nitrogen. Nitrogen oxides are typically created during combustion processes and react with volatile organic compounds in the presence of heat and sunlight to form ground-level ozone and smog. Nitrogen oxides are also greenhouse gases, contributing to global warming.

ozone   A molecule of three oxygen atoms formed by the interaction of sunlight on nitrous oxides and volatile organic compounds. At ground level, ozone is a significant component of air pollution.

particulate matter (PM)   Material so fine that it can be inhaled into a person's lungs—usually classified as *coarse* PM10 (10 microns—about one-seventh the diameter of human hair) and *fine* PM2.5 (2.5 microns); a significant component of air pollution.

smog   A brownish atmospheric haze caused by the interaction of sunlight and heat with ozone and particulate matter pollutants.

sprawl A pattern of urban growth characterized by expansion of urban boundaries and extensive residential development into open space and agricultural areas.

volatile organic compounds (VOC) Carbon-containing compounds (such as gasoline, alcohol, and solvents) that evaporate into the air. VOCs contribute to the formation of smog. Also called "reactive organic gases" (ROG).

SUGGESTED ANSWERS TO EXHIBIT QUESTIONS

Exhibit 8-1: Oil is obtained from in-state, Alaskan, and foreign sources (principally Saudi Arabia and Ecuador). Almost all of it is used as fuel for transportation. Natural gas is imported to California from the American Southwest (Texas) and from Canada. One-third is burned in electricity-generating plants; one-third is used by industry; and the remaining third is used by the residential and commercial sectors. Nuclear and hydroelectric primary energy sources each account for about 15 percent of the electricity production for California. Renewable sources, such as solar, wind, and geothermal, altogether provide about 11 percent of California's electricity demand.

Exhibit 8-2: California's peak electricity demand is about 42,000 megawatts on a hot summer day. Emergency alerts begin when electricity reserves drop below 7 percent of capacity. Rolling blackouts are ordered if reserves fall below 1.5 percent of capacity.

Exhibit 8-3: As a consumer, you pay the local electric utility. The utility, in turn, buys electricity either directly from electricity producers or indirectly through the California Power Authority. California's Independent System Operator schedules electricity production and distribution to the local utilities that deliver electricity to the consumer.

Exhibit 8-4: The San Joaquin Valley is called an "air basin" because air is trapped by surrounding mountains, allowing pollutants to accumulate.

Exhibit 8-5: Chemical reactions of ozone with PM, stimulated by heat and sunlight, create photochemical smog.

Exhibit 8-6: The South Coast (Metropolitan Los Angeles) and San Diego regions have shown the greatest decline in the number of high-ozone days, whereas the San Francisco Bay Area and the Sacramento and San Joaquin Valley regions show less change over time. All regions except the San Francisco Bay Area exceed the state PM10 standard for 100 days or more each year.

Exhibit 8-7: The precipitation map shows that California's water resources are in the Northern California Sierra, whereas the state's thirsts are in the agricultural Central Valley and in dry but populous Southern California.

Exhibit 8-8: Fifty percent of the average annual runoff is redistributed for urban or agricultural uses. Projected water use by 2020 will be 15 percent urban and 39 percent agricultural.

CALIFORNIA CONGRESSIONAL DELEGATION

U.S. Senate

Dianne Feinstein
Barbara Boxer

U.S. House of Representatives

District	Representative (Party)	District	Representative (Party)
1	Thompson, Mike (D)	28	Berman, Howard L. (D)
2	Herger, Wally (R)	29	Schiff, Adam B. (D)
3	Lungren, Daniel E. (R)	30	Waxman, Henry A. (D)
4	Doolittle, John T. (R)	31	Becerra, Xavier (D)
5	Matsui, Doris (D)	32	Solis, Hilda L. (D)
6	Woolsey, Lynn C. (D)	33	Watson, Diane E. (D)
7	Miller, George (D)	34	Roybal-Allard, Lucille (D)
8	Pelosi, Nancy (D)	35	Waters, Maxine (D)
9	Lee, Barbara (D)	36	Harman, Jane (D)
10	Tauscher, Ellen O. (D)	37	Millender-McDonald, Juanita (D)
11	McNerney, Jerry (D)	38	Napolitano, Grace F. (D)
12	Lantos, Tom (D)	39	Sanchez, Linda T. (D)
13	Stark, Fortney Pete (D)	40	Royce, Edward R. (R)
14	Eshoo, Anna G. (D)	41	Lewis, Jerry (R)
15	Honda, Michael M. (D)	42	Miller, Gary G. (R)
16	Lofgren, Zoe (D)	43	Baca, Joe (D)
17	Farr, Sam (D)	44	Calvert, Ken (R)
18	Cardoza, Dennis A. (D)	45	Bono, Mary (R)
19	Radanovich, George (R)	46	Rohrabacher, Dana (R)
20	Costa, Jim (D)	47	Sanchez, Loretta (D)
21	Nunes, Devin (R)	48	Campbell, John (R)
22	McCarthy, Kevin	49	Issa, Darrell E. (R)
23	Capps, Lois (D)	50	Bilbray, Brian (R)
24	Gallegly, Elton (R)	51	Filner, Bob (D)
25	McKeon, Howard P. "Buck" (R)	52	Hunter, Duncan (R)
26	Dreier, David (R)	53	Davis, Susan A. (D)
27	Sherman, Brad (D)		

California State Assembly

District	Representative (Party)	District	Representative (Party)
1	Patty Berg (D)	37	Audra Strickland (R)
2	Doug La Malfa (R)	38	Cameron Smyth (R)
3	Rick Keene (R)	39	Richard Alarcon (D)
4	Ted Gaines (R)	40	Lloyd E. Levine (D)
5	Roger Niello (R)	41	Julia Brownley (D)
6	Jared W. Huffman (D)	42	Mike Feuer (D)
7	Noreen Evans (D)	43	Paul Krekorian (D)
8	Lois Wolk (D)	44	Anthony Portantino (D)
9	Dave Jones (D)	45	Kevin De Leon (D)
10	Alan Nakanishi (R)	46	Fabian Nuñez (Speaker) (D)
11	Mark J. DeSaulnier (D)	47	Karen Bass (D)
12	Fiona Ma (D)	48	Mike Davis (D)
13	Mark Leno (D)	49	Mike Eng (D)
14	Loni Hancock (D)	50	Hector De La Torre (D)
15	Guy S. Houston (R)	51	Curren D. Price (D)
16	Sandre Swanson (D)	52	Mervyn M. Dymally (D)
17	Cathleen Galgiani (D)	53	Ted Lieu (D)
18	May Hayashi (D)	54	Betty Karnette (D)
19	Gene Mullin (D)	55	Laura Richardson (D)
20	Alberto Torrico (D)	56	Tony Mendoza (D)
21	Ira Ruskin (D)	57	Ed Hernandez (D)
22	Sally J. Lieber (D)	58	Charles M. Calderon (D)
23	Joe Coto (D)	59	Anthony Adams (R)
24	Jim Beall (D)	60	Bob Huff (R)
25	Tom Berryhill (R)	61	Nell Soto (D)
26	Greg Aghazarian (R)	62	Wilma D. Carter (D)
27	John Laird (D)	63	Bill Emmerson (R)
28	Anna Marie Caballero (D)	64	John J. Benoit (R)
29	Michael N. Villines (R)	65	Paul J. Cook (R)
30	Nicole Parra (D)	66	Kevin D. Jeffries (R)
31	Juan Arambula (D)	67	Jim Silva (R)
32	Jean Fuller (R)	68	Van Tran (R)
33	Sam Blakeslee (R)	69	Jose Solorio (D)
34	Bill Maze (R)	70	Charles S. DeVore (R)
35	Pedro Nava (D)	71	Todd Spitzer (R)
36	Sharon Runner (R)	72	Mike Duvall (R)

District	Representative (Party)
73	Mimi Walters (R)
74	Martin Garrick (R)
75	George A. Plescia (R)
76	Lori Saldaña (D)

District	Representative (Party)
77	Joel Anderson (R)
78	Shirley Horton (R)
79	Mary Salas (D)
80	Bonnie Garcia (R)

APPENDIX C

California State Senate

District	Representative (Party)
1	Cox, Dave (R)
2	Wiggins, Patricia "Pat" (D)
3	Migden, Carole (D)
4	Aanestad, Samuel (R)
5	Machado, Michael (D)
6	Steinberg, Darrell S. (D)
7	Torlakson, Tom (D)
8	Yee, Leland (D)
9	Perata, Don (President Pro Tempore) (D)
10	Corbett, Ellen (D)
11	Simitian, S. Joseph (D)
12	Denham, Jeff (R)
13	Alquist, Elaine (D)
14	Cogdill, Dave (R)
15	Maldonado, Abel (R)
16	Florez, Dean (D)
17	Runner, George C. (R)
18	Ashburn, Roy (R)
19	McClintock, Tom (R)
20	Padilla, Alex (D)
21	Scott, Jack (D)

District	Representative (Party)
22	Cedillo, Gilbert (D)
23	Kuehl, Sheila (D)
24	Romero, Gloria (Majority Leader) (D)
25	Vincent, Edward (D)
26	Ridley-Thomas, Mark (D)
27	Lowenthal, Alan S. (D)
28	Oropeza, Jenny (D)
29	Margett, Bob (R)
30	Calderon, Ron (D)
31	Dutton, Robert (R)
32	McLeod, Gloria Negrete (D)
33	Ackerman, Dick (Minority Leader) (R)
34	Daucher, Lynn (D)
35	Tom Harman (R)
36	Hollingsworth, Dennis (R)
37	Battin, James (R)
38	Wyland, Mark (R)
39	Kehoe, Christine (D)
40	Ducheny, Denise Moreno (D)

CALIFORNIA CONSTITUTION

PREAMBLE

We, the People of the State of California, grateful to Almighty God for our freedom, in order to secure and perpetuate its blessings, do establish this Constitution.

ARTICLE 1 DECLARATION OF RIGHTS

SECTION 1. All people are by nature free and independent and have inalienable rights. Among these are enjoying and defending life and liberty, acquiring, possessing, and protecting property, and pursuing and obtaining safety, happiness, and privacy.

SECTION 2.
(a) Every person may freely speak, write and publish his or her sentiments on all subjects, being responsible for the abuse of this right. A law may not restrain or abridge liberty of speech or press.
(b) A publisher, editor, reporter, or other person connected with or employed upon a newspaper, magazine, or other periodical publication, or by a press association or wire service, or any person who has been so connected or employed, shall not be adjudged in contempt by a judicial, legislative, or administrative body, or any other body having the power to issue subpoenas, for refusing to disclose the source of any information procured while so connected or employed for publication in a newspaper, magazine or other periodical publication, or for refusing to disclose any unpublished information obtained or prepared in gathering, receiving or processing of information for communication to the public. Nor shall a radio or television news reporter or other person connected with or employed by a radio or television station, or any person who has been so connected or employed, be so adjudged in contempt for refusing to disclose the source of any information procured while so connected or employed for news or news commentary purposes on radio or television, or for refusing to disclose any unpublished information obtained or prepared in gathering, receiving or processing of information for communication to the public. As used in this subdivision, "unpublished information" includes information not disseminated to the public by the person from whom disclosure is sought, whether or not related information has been disseminated, and includes, but is not limited to, all notes, outtakes, photographs, tapes or other data of whatever sort not itself disseminated to the public through a medium of communication, whether or not published information based upon or related to such material has been disseminated.

(a) The people have the right to instruct their representatives, petition government for redress of grievances, and assemble freely to consult for the common good.

(b) (1) The people have the right of access to information concerning the conduct of the people's business, and, therefore, the meetings of public bodies and the writings of public officials and agencies shall be open to public scrutiny.

(2) A statute, court rule, or other authority, including those in effect on the effective date of this subdivision, shall be broadly construed if it furthers the people's right of access, and narrowly construed if it limits the right of access. A statute, court rule, or other authority adopted after the effective date of this subdivision that limits the right of access shall be adopted with findings demonstrating the interest protected by the limitation and the need for protecting that interest.

(3) Nothing in this subdivision supersedes or modifies the right of privacy guaranteed by Section 1 or affects the construction of any statute, court rule, or other authority to the extent that it protects that right to privacy, including any statutory procedures governing discovery or disclosure of information concerning the official performance or professional qualifications of a peace officer.

(4) Nothing in this subdivision supersedes or modifies any provision of this Constitution, including the guarantees that a person may not be deprived of life, liberty, or property without due process of law, or denied equal protection of the laws, as provided in Section 7.

(5) This subdivision does not repeal or nullify, expressly or by implication, any constitutional or statutory exception to the right of access to public records or meetings of public bodies that is in effect on the effective date of this subdivision, including, but not limited to, any statute protecting the confidentiality of law enforcement and prosecution records.

(6) Nothing in this subdivision repeals, nullifies, supersedes, or modifies protections for the confidentiality of proceedings and records of the Legislature, the Members of the Legislature, and its employees, committees, and caucuses provided by Section 7 of Article IV, state law, or legislative rules adopted in furtherance of those provisions; nor does it affect the scope of permitted discovery in judicial or administrative proceedings regarding deliberations of the Legislature, the Members of the Legislature, and its employees, committees, and caucuses.

SECTION 4. Free exercise and enjoyment of religion without discrimination or preference are guaranteed. This liberty of conscience does not excuse acts that are licentious or inconsistent with the peace or safety of the State. The Legislature shall make no law respecting an establishment of religion. A person is not incompetent to be a witness or juror because of his or her opinions on religious beliefs.

SECTION 5. The military is subordinate to civil power. A standing army may not be maintained in peacetime. Soldiers may not be quartered in any house in wartime except as prescribed by law, or in peacetime without the owner's consent.

SECTION 6. Slavery is prohibited. Involuntary servitude is prohibited except to punish crime.

SECTION 7.

(a) A person may not be deprived of life, liberty, or property without due process of law or denied equal protection of the laws; provided, that nothing contained herein or elsewhere in this Constitution imposes upon the State of California or any public entity, board, or official any obligations or responsibilities which exceed those imposed by the Equal Protection Clause of the 14th Amendment to the United States Constitution with respect to the use of pupil school assignment or pupil transportation. In enforcing this subdivision or any other provision of this Constitution, no court of this State may impose upon the State of California or any public entity, board, or official any obligation or responsibility with respect to the use of pupil school assignment or pupil transportation,

(1) except to remedy a specific violation by such party that would also constitute a violation of the Equal Protection Clause of the 14th Amendment to the United States Constitution, and

(2) unless a federal court would be permitted under federal decisional law to impose that obligation or responsibility upon such party to remedy the specific violation of the Equal Protection Clause of the 14th Amendment of the United States Constitution.

Except as may be precluded by the Constitution of the United States, every existing judgment, decree, writ, or other order of a court of this State, whenever rendered, which includes provisions regarding pupil school assignment or pupil transportation, or which requires a plan including any such provisions shall, upon application to a court having jurisdiction by any interested person, be modified to conform to the provisions of this subdivision as amended, as applied to the facts which exist at the time of such modification. In all actions or proceedings arising under or seeking application of the amendments to this subdivision proposed by the Legislature at its 1979–80 Regular Session, all courts, wherein such actions or proceedings are or may hereafter be pending, shall give such actions or proceedings first precedence over all other civil actions therein. Nothing herein shall prohibit the governing board of a school district from voluntarily continuing or commencing a school integration plan after the effective date of this subdivision as amended. In amending this subdivision, the Legislature and people of the State of California find and declare that this amendment is necessary to serve compelling public interests, including those of making the most effective use of the limited financial resources now and prospectively available to support public education, maximizing the educational opportunities and protecting the health and safety of all public school pupils, enhancing the ability of parents to participate in the educational process, preserving harmony and tranquility in this State and its public schools, preventing the waste of scarce fuel resources, and protecting the environment.

(b) A citizen or class of citizens may not be granted privileges or immunities not granted on the same terms to all citizens. Privileges or immunities granted by the Legislature may be altered or revoked.

SECTION 8. A person may not be disqualified from entering or pursuing a business, profession, vocation, or employment because of sex, race, creed, color, or national or ethnic origin.

SECTION 9. A bill of attainder, ex post facto law, or law impairing the obligation of contracts may not be passed.

SECTION 10. Witnesses may not be unreasonably detained. A person may not be imprisoned in a civil action for debt or tort, or in peacetime for a militia fine.

SECTION 11. Habeas corpus may not be suspended unless required by public safety in cases of rebellion or invasion.

SECTION 12. A person shall be released on bail by sufficient sureties, except for:

(a) Capital crimes when the facts are evident or the presumption great;

(b) Felony offenses involving acts of violence on another person, or felony sexual assault offenses on another person, when the facts are evident or the presumption great and the court finds based upon clear and convincing evidence that there is a substantial likelihood the person's release would result in great bodily harm to others; or

(c) Felony offenses when the facts are evident or the presumption great and the court finds based on clear and convincing evidence that the person has threatened another with great bodily harm and that there is a substantial likelihood that the person would carry out the threat if released.

Excessive bail may not be required. In fixing the amount of bail, the court shall take into consideration the seriousness of the offense charged, the previous criminal record of the defendant, and the probability of his or her appearing at the trial or hearing of the case. A person may be released on his or her own recognizance in the court's discretion.

SECTION 13. The right of the people to be secure in their persons, houses, papers, and effects against unreasonable seizures and searches may not be violated; and a warrant may not issue except on probable cause, supported by oath or affirmation, particularly describing the place to be searched and the persons and things to be seized.

SECTION 14. Felonies shall be prosecuted as provided by law, either by indictment or, after examination and commitment by a magistrate, by information. A person charged with a felony by complaint subscribed under penalty of perjury and on file in a court in the county where the felony is triable shall be taken without unnecessary delay before a magistrate of that court. The magistrate shall immediately give the defendant a copy of the complaint, inform the defendant of the defendant's right to counsel, allow the defendant a reasonable time to send for counsel, and on the defendant's request read the complaint to the defendant. On the defendant's request the magistrate shall require a peace officer to transmit within the county where the court is located a message to counsel named by defendant. A person unable to understand English who is charged with a crime has a right to an interpreter throughout the proceedings.

SECTION 14.1. If a felony is prosecuted by indictment, there shall be no postin-dictment preliminary hearing.

SECTION 15. The defendant in a criminal cause has the right to a speedy public trial, to compel attendance of witnesses in the defendant's behalf, to have the assis-tance of counsel for the defendant's defense, to be personally present with counsel, and to be confronted with the witnesses against the defendant. The Legislature may provide for the deposition of a witness in the presence of the defendant and the de-fendant's counsel. Persons may not twice be put in jeopardy for the same offense, be compelled in a criminal cause to be a witness against themselves, or be deprived of life, liberty, or property without due process of law.

SECTION 16. Trial by jury is an inviolate right and shall be secured to all, but in a civil cause three-fourths of the jury may render a verdict. A jury may be waived in a criminal cause by the consent of both parties expressed in open court by the de-fendant and the defendant's counsel. In a civil cause a jury may be waived by the consent of the parties expressed as prescribed by statute. In civil causes the jury shall consist of 12 persons or a lesser number agreed on by the parties in open court. In civil causes other than causes within the appellate jurisdiction of the court of appeal the Legislature may provide that the jury shall consist of eight persons or a lesser number agreed on by the parties in open court. In criminal actions in which a felony is charged, the jury shall consist of 12 persons. In criminal actions in which a mis-demeanor is charged, the jury shall consist of 12 persons or a lesser number agreed on by the parties in open court.

SECTION 17. Cruel or unusual punishment may not be inflicted or excessive fines imposed.

SECTION 18. Treason against the State consists only in levying war against it, ad-hering to its enemies, or giving them aid and comfort. A person may not be con-victed of treason except on the evidence of two witnesses to the same overt act or by confession in open court.

SECTION 19. Private property may be taken or damaged for public use only when just compensation, ascertained by a jury unless waived, has first been paid to, or into court for, the owner. The Legislature may provide for possession by the con-demnor following commencement of eminent domain proceedings upon deposit in court and prompt release to the owner of money determined by the court to be the probable amount of just compensation.

SECTION 20. Noncitizens have the same property rights as citizens.

SECTION 21. Property owned before marriage or acquired during marriage by gift, will, or inheritance is separate property.

SECTION 22. The right to vote or hold office may not be conditioned by a prop-erty qualification.

SECTION 23. One or more grand juries shall be drawn and summoned at least once a year in each county.

SECTION 24. Rights guaranteed by this Constitution are not dependent on those guar-anteed by the United States Constitution. In criminal cases the rights of a defendant to equal protection of the laws, to due process of law, to the assistance of counsel, to be personally present with counsel, to a speedy and public trial, to compel the attendance of witnesses, to confront the witnesses against him or her, to be free from unreasonable searches and seizures, to privacy, to not be compelled to be a witness against himself or herself, to not be placed twice in jeopardy for the same offense, and to not suffer the imposition of cruel or unusual punishment, shall be construed by the courts of this State in a manner consistent with the Constitution of the United States. This Constitution shall not be construed by the courts to afford greater rights to criminal defendants than those afforded by the Constitution of the United States, nor shall it be construed to afford greater rights to minors in juvenile proceedings on criminal causes than those afforded by the Constitution of the United States. This declaration of rights may not be construed to impair or deny others retained by the people.

SECTION 25. The people shall have the right to fish upon and from the public lands of the State and in the waters thereof, excepting upon lands set aside for fish hatcheries, and no land owned by the State shall ever be sold or transferred without reserving in the people the absolute right to fish thereupon; and no law shall ever be passed making it a crime for the people to enter upon the public lands within this State for the purpose of fishing in any water containing fish that have been planted therein by the State; provided, that the legislature may by statute, provide for the season when and the conditions under which the different species of fish may be taken.

SECTION 26. The provisions of this Constitution are mandatory and prohibitory, unless by express words they are declared to be otherwise.

SECTION 27. All statutes of this State in effect on February 17, 1972, requiring, authorizing, imposing, or relating to the death penalty are in full force and effect, subject to legislative amendment or repeal by statute, initiative, or referendum. The death penalty provided for under those statutes shall not be deemed to be, or to constitute, the infliction of cruel or unusual punishments within the meaning of Article 1, Section 6, nor shall such punishment for such offenses be deemed to contravene any other provision of this constitution.

SECTION 28.
  (a) The People of the State of California find and declare that the enactment of comprehensive provisions and laws ensuring a bill of rights for victims of crime, including safeguards in the criminal justice system to fully protect those rights, is a matter of grave statewide concern. The rights of victims pervade the criminal justice system, encompassing not only the right to restitution from the wrongdoers for financial losses suffered as a result of criminal acts, but also the more basic expectation that persons who commit felonious acts causing injury to innocent victims will be appropriately detained in custody, tried by the courts, and sufficiently punished so that the public safety is protected and encouraged as a goal of highest importance. Such public safety extends to public primary, elementary, junior high, and senior high school campuses, where students and staff have the right to be safe and secure in their persons. To accomplish these goals, broad reforms in the procedural treatment of accused persons and the disposition and sentencing of convicted persons are necessary and proper as deterrents to criminal behavior and to serious disruption of people's lives.

(b) Restitution. It is the unequivocal intention of the People of the State of California that all persons who suffer losses as a result of criminal activity shall have the right to restitution from the persons convicted of the crimes for losses they suffer. Restitution shall be ordered from the convicted persons in every case, regardless of the sentence or disposition imposed, in which a crime victim suffers a loss, unless compelling and extraordinary reasons exist to the contrary. The Legislature shall adopt provisions to implement this section during the calendar year following adoption of this section.

(c) Right to Safe Schools. All students and staff of public primary, elementary, junior high and senior high schools have the inalienable right to attend campuses which are safe, secure and peaceful.

(d) Right to Truth-in-Evidence. Except as provided by statute hereafter enacted by a two-thirds vote of the membership in each house of the Legislature, relevant evidence shall not be excluded in any criminal proceeding, including pretrial and postconviction motions and hearings, or in any trial or hearing of a juvenile for a criminal offense, whether heard in juvenile or adult court. Nothing in this section shall affect any existing statutory rule of evidence relating to privilege or hearsay, or Evidence Code, Sections 352, 782 or 1103. Nothing in this section shall affect any existing statutory or constitutional right of the press.

(e) Public Safety Bail. A person may be released on bail by sufficient sureties, except for capital crimes when the facts are evident or the presumption great. Excessive bail may not be required. In setting, reducing or denying bail, the judge or magistrate shall take into consideration the protection of the public, the seriousness of the offense charged, the previous criminal record of the defendant, and the probability of his or her appearing at the trial or hearing of the case. Public safety shall be the primary consideration. A person may be released on his or her own recognizance in the court's discretion, subject to the same factors considered in setting bail. However, no person charged with the commission of any serious felony shall be released on his or her own recognizance. Before any person arrested for a serious felony may be released on bail, a hearing may be held before the magistrate or judge, and the prosecuting attorney shall be given notice and reasonable opportunity to be heard on the matter. When a judge or magistrate grants or denies bail or release on a person's own recognizance, the reasons for that decision shall be stated in the record and included in the court's minutes.

(f) Use of Prior Convictions. Any prior felony conviction of any person in any criminal proceeding, whether adult or juvenile, shall subsequently be used without limitation for purposes of impeachment or enhancement of sentence in any criminal proceeding. When a prior felony conviction is an element of any felony offense, it shall be proven to the trier of fact in open court.

(g) As used in this article, the term "serious felony" is any crime defined in Penal Code, Section 1192.7(c).

SECTION 29. In a criminal case, the people of the State of California have the right to due process of law and to a speedy and public trial.

SECTION 30.

  (a) This Constitution shall not be construed by the courts to prohibit the joining of criminal cases as prescribed by the Legislature or by the people through the initiative process.

  (b) In order to protect victims and witnesses in criminal cases, hearsay evidence shall be admissible at preliminary hearings, as prescribed by the Legislature or by the people through the initiative process.

  (c) In order to provide for fair and speedy trials, discovery in criminal cases shall be reciprocal in nature, as prescribed by the Legislature or by the people through the initiative process.

SECTION 31.

  (a) The State shall not discriminate against, or grant preferential treatment to, any individual or group on the basis of race, sex, color, ethnicity, or national origin in the operation of public employment, public education, or public contracting.

  (b) This section shall apply only to action taken after the section's effective date.

  (c) Nothing in this section shall be interpreted as prohibiting bona fide qualifications based on sex which are reasonably necessary to the normal operation of public employment, public education, or public contracting.

  (d) Nothing in this section shall be interpreted as invalidating any court order or consent decree which is in force as of the effective date of this section.

  (e) Nothing in this section shall be interpreted as prohibiting action which must be taken to establish or maintain eligibility for any federal program, where ineligibility would result in a loss of federal funds to the State.

  (f) For the purposes of this section, "State" shall include, but not necessarily be limited to, the State itself, any city, county, city and county, public university system, including the University of California, community college district, school district, special district, or any other political subdivision or governmental instrumentality of or within the State.

  (g) The remedies available for violations of this section shall be the same, regardless of the injured party's race, sex, color, ethnicity, or national origin, as are otherwise available for violations of then-existing California antidiscrimination law.

  (h) This section shall be self-executing. If any part or parts of this section are found to be in conflict with federal law or the United States Constitution, the section shall be implemented to the maximum extent that federal law and the United States Constitution permit. Any provision held invalid shall be severable from the remaining portions of this section.

population—*cont.*
growth of, 2–3, 3*f*
  immigration and, 3–4
  Latino, 3–5, 4*f*
  racial/ethnic distribution of, 5*f*
pork, **69**, 89
poverty, **153–154**
  family levels of, 153*f*
  federal level of, 153–154, 168
  increase of, 6–7
  in San Joaquin Valley, 11
power, **64**, 89
power broker, **44**, 62
precipitation, 179, 179*f*
preliminary hearing, **140**, 148
Preserving Privilege: California Politics, Propositions, and People of Color (Gibbs, Bankhead), 83
president, 18–19, 37
press, freedom of, 128–131
primary elections, **36**. *See also* election(s)
  definition of, 62
  purpose of, 36–37
prison system, 143
privacy, lawmaking and, 85
"private justice," 133
probate, **131**, 148
property taxes, 97–99, 98*f*, 102*f*
  proposition 13 and, 7, 79, 80, 80*f*, 164
proposition(s), **7**
  13, 7, 79, 80, 80*f*, 164
  36, 80*f*, 82
  47, 101
  98, 164
  140, 24
  184, 80*f*, 81–84
  209, 125–126
  215, 80*f*, 82
  definition of, 13
  focus of, 7
prosecution and adjudication, 139–141, 139*f*
prosecutors, 140
public assistance, 156–158, 161
public money, 91–92, 92*f*
public policy, 17
public works, infrastructure of, 8

Quackenbush, Chuck, 72, 76
quid pro quo, **69**, 89

race, voter participation by, 50, 51*f*
racial diversity, 2–3, 3*f*
racial profiling, **137**, 148
Reagan, Ronald, 7
realignment, 120
The Realignment, **102**
  chronology of, 103*f*–104*f*
  overview of, 102, 104

reapportion, 32
reapportion representation, 25
recall elections, 39
recession, 168
redevelopment, 105–106
redistricting
  definition of, **32**
  of legislative branch, 25–26
referendum, 89
reform
  campaign, 47–48
  by Schwarzenegger, 19
  tort, **132**, 132–133
Regents of the University of California v. Bakke, 124–125
regions, **8**, 13
register, 62. *See also* voter registration
regressive tax, 96
regulation, **84**, 89
religion, freedom of, 126–128
Religious Right, 35
representative democracies, 16
representatives, 23
republicans, **34**, 62
republics, **16**, 32
resources
  air, 176–180, 177*f*, 178*f*, 179*f*
  land, 182
  water, 181–182, 181*f*
revenue bonds, **101**, 120
revenue sharing, **101**, 120
Riverside counties, 9
Ross, Andrew, 115
rule making, 90
"rules of the game," 34–35
rural counties, 12

Sacramento
  counties of, 11
  lobbying in, 72
safety net
  income and tax measures of, 155–156
  public assistance, 156–158, 161
  social insurance, 156
sales and use tax (SUT), 96, 97*f*
San Bernardino, 9
San Diego county, 10
San Fernando Valley, 9
San Francisco Bay area, 10
San Joaquin Valley, 10–11
Sanders, Jerry, 29*f*
Schnur, Dan, 112
Schwarzenegger, Arnold
  celebrity politics and, 7
  election of, 19
  endorsements, 19, 21
  executive orders by, 87
  reforms of, 19
seasonal unemployment, 151, 169
The Second Amendment, 86

secretary of state, 22*f*, 23
Senate
  overview of, 23, 24, 24*f*
  standing committees in, 67*f*
  term limits of, 24–25
  Web links to, 31
sentence, 148
sentencing and corrections, 141–144, 142*f*, 147, 148
  death penalty, 141
  drug crimes and, 143
  mental illness and, 143–144
  parole violations and, 143
  spending for, 117–118
service charges, 102
shortfall, **102**, 120
Sierra Nevada Range, 8
Silicon Valley, 10
Simpson, Nicole Brown, 137
Simpson, O.J., 137
"Skelly rights," 133–134
Skilling, Jeffrey, 176
slate mailer, **41**, 62
small claims, **131**, 148
smog, 177*f*, **179**, 184
social insurance, 156
social security, **156**
social security insurance, 168
social services. *See also* public assistance
  Web links, 166–167
sovereign, **17**, 32
Spanos, Alex G., 47
speaker, 23
special districts, **29**, 30, 32
special elections, **38**, 38–39, 62
special funds, 93, 120
speech, freedom of, 128–131
spending
  on corrections, 117–118, 117*f*
  on health and human services, 117, 117*f*
  on higher education, 115*f*, 116
  on K-12 education, 115–116, 116*f*
sprawl, **182**, 185
SSI/SSP. *See* Supplemental Security Income/State Supplementary Payment Program
standing committees, 67*f*
Stanislaus county, 10–11
State Board of Education, 22*f*, 23
state disability insurance tax, 100
state government
  authority of, 17
  jurisdiction of, **17**
  Web links to, 30
state law, federal law and, 28
statutes, 26, 32
Stayner, Cory, 28
"stranded costs," 174
strong-mayor, **29**, 32